PROPHET MARGIN

Also by Sam O'Brien

A Sure Thing

The Mandarin Stakes

The Ruthless Gene

PROPHET MARGIN

SAM O'BRIEN

POOLBEG

Published 2022
by Poolbeg Press Ltd
123 Grange Hill, Baldoyle
Dublin 13, Ireland
E-mail: poolbeg@poolbeg.com
www.poolbeg.com

The moral right of the author has been asserted.
A catalogue record for this book is available from the British Library.

ISBN 978-1-78199-469-6

www.poolbeg.com

About the Author

Sam O'Brien grew up in Ireland surrounded by horses and has spent a working lifetime in thoroughbred racing and breeding.

At nineteen, Sam spent an almost malnourished year attempting to make it as an amateur jockey, before too much height and too little talent put an end to that dream.

Since then, Sam has worked on, or managed stud farms in Ireland, England, Turkey, America and Australia; trained racehorses in China; built a stud farm in Inner Mongolia and broken in wild horses in the sweltering Aussie outback.

Over the years, Sam has written analytical articles for several racing publications and loves nothing better than watching magnificent thoroughbred horses grow up to become tough, successful athletes.

Prophet Margin is Sam's fourth novel.

For Tracy Worcester, who keeps
on fighting the good fight.

Acknowledgements

Once again, Dawn, Caroline and Susan for feedback on early drafts.

Peter for all his help and patience.

Ambrose for insight into the world of private air travel.

Paul and Carl for practical insight into the realities of buying guns.

A duty officer at Newmarket Police Station for kindly answering my logistical questions.

Paula, Gaye, David and everyone at Poolbeg for turning another manuscript into a finished article.

Many thanks to Enda B for pointing me in the right direction, and Todd Ellis and Alice Compton at Sony Music Publishing.

'Born In The U.S.A' Words and Music by Bruce Springsteen © 1984, Reproduced by permission of Eldridge Publishing Company / Sony Music Publishing, London W1T 3LP.

PART 1

Chapter 1

Monday, June 15th

Hundreds of the world's wealthy had turned up to Kensington Palace Orangery to buy racehorses. From Middle-Eastern royalty and tech billionaires to heirs and heiresses.

Claudia Haverford scanned the crowd outside the elegant redbrick-and-white-plaster building. The terrace was packed, as was the marquee erected on the lawn. People milled about in open-necked shirts and glowing tans with easy smiles. They sipped champagne under the evening sun while waiters swooped around with trays of canapés. An oasis in the bustling metropolis.

The horse-sale company and its sponsor, Al Fawala Invaco, had decided this exclusive dining establishment with royal history was the perfect venue for the first sale of

3

racehorses ever held in London, on the eve of Royal Ascot.

Claudia knew that the organisers had to vet applications and actually refuse people access to the sale – supposedly due to limited space, but really it was all about your net worth. Like a high-rollers casino game.

Bloodstock agents like Claudia and her boss Sebastian were here to advise their clients and do business.

Because of limited space, there were no horses present. The thoroughbreds on offer had been viewed by prospective buyers the day before at Kempton Park racecourse. Now images of them parading were being shown on the massive screen erected on the gravel beside the marquee. Only two horses would actually be physically presented for sale. A mare and foal owned by the Emir, which he was reluctant to sell. Claudia glanced at her watch; they should be here any minute.

The auctioneer announced the next lot. Catalogue pages rustled and heads craned towards the screen.

Claudia felt her phone vibrate in her pocket. She was about to fish it out when Sebastian tapped her on the shoulder.

"I'm going to buy this one for the Emir. Where is he?"

She shrugged. "He should be here by now. Typical."

Seb began nodding at the auctioneer. When the bidding climbed swiftly to a million, Claudia nudged him.

"You're way over our estimate," she whispered.

"Who cares?"

"I wish you'd treat other people's money as you do your own."

Seb ignored her.

The gavel went down. "*Sold!* To Sebastian Manton on behalf of Al Fawala Bloodstock."

Seb checked his phone. "Where the hell is he? People expect the sponsor to be here on time."

A pretty girl in a dark suit crunched across the gravel, carrying the buyer's docket. She beamed at Seb and cut a sideways glance at Claudia. People in this business loved to make assumptions about women like Claudia working for men like Seb.

Sometimes Claudia despised girls who thought they could sleep their way to the top, but mostly she wanted to tell them to wake up and respect themselves.

"Who was bidding against us?" asked Seb, squinting through the crowd. "I can't place him, but he bought a couple earlier and now he's being slapped on the back by Adam Greene."

Adam bloody Greene. She'd seen him arrive earlier and work the crowd like he was still in power. Wanker. A memory of Greene's clash with her boyfriend flashed across her mind.

"Claudia? I said, who's he with?"

"Sir John Christian. I think he was at university with Greene. Owns CleanGas, an exploration company. What do they call it … fracking. It's all the rage in America. Apparently they're going to test it out up in Yorkshire."

"*Hmm*. Well, if he's getting into racing, I wouldn't mind having him as a client. Speaking of clients," he tapped at his phone, "where the hell is the Emir?"

Seb's phone rang and Claudia felt hers vibrate again.

She had dipped her thumb and index finger into her back pocket to retrieve it when Seb killed his call and swore under his breath.

"What?" she asked.

"That was Trevor. The lorry's just arrived, they're unloading the mare and foal and the Emir's mooching about in the car park. Come on, Claud."

They weaved through the crowd, marched round the corner of the building and nearly collided with a wiry man in an expensive suit. A bodyguard cut a meaty hand across Seb's chest.

Seb flashed a grin. "Gosh, I'm so sorry."

The man barked at his guard in Russian and nodded at Seb, before continuing towards the sale area.

Seb frowned at Claudia. "Wasn't that –"

"Vasili Komarov? Yes. Acquitted on all charges, apparently."

"So he's looking for horses too? Has he got an advisor?"

"Doubt it."

"Well, he's going to need someone to help him spend his oil money."

Claudia had read articles about how Komarov had got rich, then was locked up, then released. "I think we should stay away from guys like him – far more difficult to handle than the Emir."

"Long as they have the money, Claudia."

All around them, people mingled under oak trees, while up ahead the mare and foal were led towards the Orangery like movie stars working the red carpet.

A plump man in his late thirties with a neatly trimmed

beard walked behind the horses eating an ice cream and trying to look relaxed in a linen jacket and trousers. But the steel in his eyes gave him away. Claudia knew he didn't want to sell this horse but she supposed even billionaire rulers had to make compromises when they sponsored events like this to win political favour with another country. He could look scary when he focused his gaze on someone – Claudia certainly was scared the first time she'd met him, but she'd since learned that it was all for show. Again, something a man in his position had to do.

An entourage of ten men swarmed around him. Neither Claudia nor Seb knew if they were friends, sycophants or security, but the Emir rarely went anywhere alone.

"Typical. He's never where he says he'll be," muttered Seb.

"If he wanted to watch his mare being unloaded, I don't see what the fuss is."

"Whose side are you on?"

Claudia's phone vibrated again. This time she fished it out.

Seven missed calls? Oscar?

Her heart flipped. Then it dawned on her: her brother was this horse's vet. The mare had become pregnant again soon after the birth of the foal, but had miscarried a few weeks ago and Oscar had treated her. He was probably wondering if she'd got to London alright.

She stopped in her tracks as the voicemail played.

Her twin brother was crying. *"Claud, pick up. Please. Call me before it starts. You need to peel yourself away from your job*

7

for a second. Get out of there. You've got to get out of there. I need you. I've – I've – I don't know what to do. I need you, Claud. I've done –"

The message cut abruptly.

"Oscar, how could you?" she mumbled. "You were doing so well." She tapped at the screen, wanting to tell Oscar not to worry, that she'd drop everything and drive straight to Newmarket, but the call went directly to voicemail. Panic rose through her guts, flipped her mind. How could she have been so self-absorbed? Of course an addict could slip at any time. She called again as her eyes filled up.

"Please pick up, Oscar. Please." Still voicemail.

Looking up, she realised the horses had passed her by and Seb and the Emir were standing staring at her.

"What is the matter, Claudia?" asked the Emir in deliberate English, a slight rolling of the R the only verbal clue of his heritage.

"It's my brother, sir. He's in trouble."

"That is terrible. What kind of trouble?"

"He's fallen off the wagon. I'm terribly sorry, sir, but I have to go and help him."

The Emir hesitated a beat. "Would you like to use my car and driver?"

"That's very kind but I'll get myself there."

"Can't it wait?" said Seb. "I mean it's not exactly the first time he's pulled this."

She glared at him. "It's the first time in years."

She turned abruptly and headed for the car park.

*   *   *

Rahim bin Faisal Al Bahar, Emir of Fawala, watched Claudia hurry down the tree-lined avenue, then turned back in time to see his mare and foal disappear round the corner of the building.

"Seb," he said, "it will be a pity to sell those horses."

"That mare losing her pregnancy is a sign of bad luck, if you ask me. Don't worry, I'll find you replacements at the autumn sales." He started towards the sale area.

Rahim stood still and pulled out a pair of phones.

Seb halted. "And anyway," he said, "you've got the reserve set at one-point-five million, so it's not like you'll be giving them away."

Rahim stared at his advisor until one of his devices rang in his hand. He inspected the screen and answered. Listened for a moment, spoke a couple of words, then put the phone to his chest. He put an arm around Seb's shoulders and guided him away from the Orangery towards the trees. "Walk with me, Seb. I need to discuss things with you but I have to take this call first."

"But the mare –"

"I really do not care to see her being sold. Come." He put the phone to his ear and kept his other hand on Seb's arm.

Seb shook it off. "No. I'm going to watch the fireworks, and you really need to take that call later. You're the man who made this day possible. You *have* to watch the bidding."

Rahim put the phone to his chest again and looked Seb up and down as if he were a horse.

Seb fidgeted. "Oh, come *on!*"

Rahim sighed. "Go on then. If that is how you feel, please go."

Seb spun on his heel and marched off towards the building.

The auctioneer's theatrical excitement echoed over the Tannoy.

Raising the phone to his ear, Rahim ambled down the avenue to the nearest tree. He spoke softly through a broad grin. Reaching a large oak tree, he leant back against it, facing away from the Orangery. He watched Claudia's red Audi waiting for a chance to pull into traffic. She was a smart hardworking woman and Rahim had just decided that he'd had enough of Sebastian's arrogance. Maybe Claudia lacked a bit of life experience, but he was sure she would run his horse affairs as well as Seb. Perhaps better.

As he spoke into the phone, he looked up at the canopy of leaves. Such a beautiful evening.

Behind him, the air shattered in a deafening bang.

Rahim's whole body shook. His phones slipped from his hands. He pressed his back to the huge oak. His muscles seemed to freeze while his heart thumped, sending adrenalin coursing and his mind into survival-slow-motion.

Two of his entourage were lying on the ground groaning. One had marks on his back, the other had pulled off his glasses and was rubbing his eyes, howling. "*I can still see the flash!*" he kept repeating in Arabic. The others swarmed around Rahim. One of them barked into a phone.

Rahim picked up his phones. "*Forget calling my car!*" he yelled. "*We are not leaving! Somebody call the police and the ambulance service!*" He pushed past his men.

"*No!*" one of them yelled. "There might be a secondary blast."

Rahim ignored the man and hustled his bulk towards the Orangery, almost jogging. He had to see for himself. His entourage reluctantly followed.

Rahim saw the marquee flapping in tatters even before he turned the corner. Blood spatters and blobs of white flame consumed its canvas. Screaming and moaning cut the air. Bodies were strewn about and people knelt over them wailing.

Rahim forced his breathing to slow, took deep breaths, told his men to fan out and start helping people. But they just stood, staring in shock.

"*Go on!* You've all had first aid training."

They dispersed randomly, as if they didn't know where to begin. The immediate area was peppered with miniature flashes of white flame on every surface. People slapped at themselves and each other.

"*It's sticky!*" screamed one man, having smacked at the fire on his sleeve.

Rahim tripped on something. A horse's leg. Bile rose into his mouth. He coughed and retched.

There was little left of the auctioneer's rostrum and the man's shoes were still on the ground where he had stood.

11

There was so much blood. And chunks of flesh, some charred, some raw-looking. Horse or human, Rahim couldn't be sure.

Then he saw a familiar hand wearing a signet ring and still clutching a smouldering catalogue. There was no sign of the rest of Sebastian Manton.

Rahim staggered towards the marquee, now a mess of overturned tables and chairs. Glass crunched underfoot. A middle-aged woman fell towards him, stumbling over a body. Her blouse was ripped, her arm glazed with burns and blood, her face a mess of fear and tears. "*Help us, help us!*" she wailed.

Rahim righted a chair and sat her on it. Knelt beside her. "Ambulances are on their way."

"I can't find my husband," she sobbed, looking around but seeing nothing.

Rahim patted the back of her hand. He recognised her. A Turkish textiles heiress, she had used her wealth to set up a charitable trust which had given millions to humanitarian causes, including progressive work in Pakistan on human rights and living conditions. Rahim admired and respected what she had done with her money.

"Why? Why?" she muttered.

Why indeed? This woman didn't deserve to be blown up.

He closed his eyes and pursed his lips a moment. Then flicked his lids back open. Forced himself to take in the full carnage. The people on the steps of the Orangery and those in the front rows of the marquee had taken the brunt of it, but it appeared as if shrapnel had penetrated further into the crowd. Every window in the Orangery had imploded from the blast. Rahim imagined people inside shredded by flying glass, like he'd once seen after a car-bombing in a neighbouring emirate.

Not far from where Rahim knelt, the bodies of Sir John Christian and Adam Greene were strewn under part of a table. Little patches of white flame decorated their bodies like votive candles.

The woman gripped Rahim's hand and mumbled a prayer as she sobbed.

Screaming sirens filled the air. Two police cars stopped at the corner of the Orangery building, fire engines and a stream of ambulances behind them. Rahim couldn't even begin to imagine how many would be necessary. He let go of the woman's hand and rubbed his face.

He stood but couldn't make himself walk over to the officers barking orders at each other. Fireman dashed to every flame: dousing, stamping, shouting "*Phosphorus!*". Some of them checked inside the building, glass crunched under heavy boots. Policemen fanned out, directing a swarm of paramedics who began setting up triage, and ferrying stretchers. The whole area was cordoned-off with crime-scene tape and more officers arrived. A policeman asked Rahim's men who they were and they pointed at their Emir. Rahim managed to dip a hand into his inside pocket to retrieve his diplomatic credentials just as one of his phones rang.

The screen said **Claudia Haverford**. What a lucky girl.

13

Chapter 2

The Emir of Fawala's modern training complex in Newmarket was a hive of activity during evening stables.

The slight, craggy-faced man checked his three horses' water buckets. Hanif Ali Mengak closed the bottom latches on each of their stables and told the assistant trainer Ed Tomlinson that he was done for the day.

"Spot on, Hanif," said Ed. "See you tomorrow."

A smile cracked Hanif's tanned face as he made for the car park and his bicycle.

He coasted out of the yard and pedalled up the road. The sun dipped and shadows stretched as a glorious afternoon edged into a long summer evening.

Hanif pulled his flat tweed cap down over his eyes. He liked this very English headgear – it reminded him of the headdress he had worn as a child. He cycled into the town and when he came to a church, he chained his bike to a railing.

Inside, he sat in a pew and tilted his head back, enjoying the tranquillity. He gazed at the ceiling and took deep breaths, letting his thoughts relax from a swirl, to an ebb, to a millpond. Hanif liked churches. He always felt that even the plain ones were so much more serene than gaudily carpeted mosques, which often smelled of feet.

Even if both sets of buildings were as useless as each other.

Hanif heard light steps and became aware of the vicar standing next to him, clearing his throat.

Hanif ignored him.

Another clearing of the throat. Louder.

Hanif turned his head.

The vicar smiled and glanced at Hanif's cap. "We don't wear hats in God's house."

Hanif grinned, bearing his crooked teeth. "In whose house?"

The kindly smile turned to exasperation. "In God's house."

Hanif chuckled, pulled his cap down further and slid past the vicar into the aisle.

*   *   *

Ten minutes later he arrived at the small flat he shared with two English grooms. When he let himself in, the smell

15

hit him immediately. Hanif took off his boots, placing them on a piece of newspaper before padding into the tiny sitting room.

Lee and Des were staring at the television as one cartoon character beat another with a wooden mallet. Thick smoke fountained from a fat joint drooping from Lee's fingers.

"Alright, Hanny," said Des. "How's tricks?"

Hanif nodded and fanned his cap in front of his face.

"Here," said Des. "Does that good two-year-old you do run at Ascot this week?"

Hanif beamed at the mention of the grey filly. "Secular Princess will race on Friday and I believe she will win."

"Nice one," said Lee.

"I am going to make tea, would you like some?" said Hanif.

"Nah, mate," said Des.

"Milk, two sugars," said Lee, grabbing the remote from Des. "I'm sick of this crap. What else is on?"

As he waited for the water to boil, Hanif thought of his childhood and the opium and hashish abuse he'd witnessed. Decent men destroyed by those toxic little plants. Still, he'd found it hard to blame them. It was a way to numb the reality of living in a warzone.

He liked Des and Lee. They were young and silly, but they were hardworking and poorly paid for their graft. Hanif knew they needed a way to brighten their dreary lives, but he could never understand why they didn't simply take up a hobby or a book or something else to occupy their minds instead of chipping away at them with sedative narcotics.

He got out the bottle of single malt that he'd bought as an ice-breaker when he first moved in. Poured a finger of whisky into three glasses and put everything on a tray with the tea.

"Bonus! Nice one, Hanny," said Des, grabbing his glass and downing it.

"You're supposed to fuckin' sip it and enjoy it." Lee rolled his eyes. "Cheers, Hanny!"

They clinked glasses.

Hanif took a long deep smell before he let the whisky touch his lips.

Lee did the same as he surfed the channels.

"Bloody hell," said Des. "Leave that on! What the fuck?"

It took Hanif a minute to realise what he was looking at.

The headline read **London Terror** over images of carnage at the horse sale in Kensington Palace taken from a news helicopter. The picture changed and a grave-faced reporter spoke into camera. Fire crews and ambulances blocked the road behind him. Sirens wailed.

"Details are still sketchy, but police have confirmed that just over half an hour ago a bomb was detonated at Kensington Palace Orangery during a racehorse sale. As yet nobody has claimed responsibility for the attack, but police are not ruling out Al-Qaeda or ISIS militants. Though the attack's intended target – or targets – are still unknown, many influential people were reportedly at the horse sale. Although names have not yet been released, it is believed that former Prime Minister Adam Greene was among those present."

17

"*Oi*, Hanny," Lee smirked. "Reckon that was one o' your Muslim nutters blowing himself up?" He burst into giggles.

Des remained glued to the screen, suddenly focused.

Hanif stared at Lee. "What do you mean – one of *my* nutters?"

Chapter 3

Claudia gripped the steering wheel one-handed, her knuckles white. Her other pressed the phone to her ear, desperate to reach her twin. Eventually she tried his girlfriend. He'd only been with her a few months, so Claudia wasn't even sure if he'd told her about his problem, let alone if he'd have called her for help.

The number rang for an eternity before she picked up.

"Hello?"

"Hello, Sally. This is Oscar's sister, Claudia. We exchanged numbers at the races a few weeks ago?"

A pause. "Yes, I remember. You work for Seb Manton. Aren't you in London at the sale?"

"What? No. I mean, I was. I'm looking for Oscar. Is he with you?"

"No, I haven't seen him since Saturday. Have you seen –"

"Did you speak to him today?"

"No. Look, have you seen the news?"

"No. Why?"

"There was a terrorist attack at the sale. Dozens of people have been killed."

"I'm sorry, could you say that again?"

"A terrorist attack at the sale. A lot of people killed."

Claudia tossed the phone on the seat and turned on the radio. After a few seconds she found it difficult to keep the car straight. She pulled over, took a breath and tried to call Seb.

"The customer you are trying to call is unavailable," said the message. It hadn't even gone through to voicemail.

The radio reporter sounded breathless. *"The area is a chaotic mix of flashing blue lights and police in riot gear. Convoys of ambulances are arriving at the scene. Paramedics are carrying stretchers and placing blankets over bodies."*

Claudia buried her face in her hands. If Oscar hadn't called her ...

She tried Seb again. Nothing. She decided she'd better try the Emir. Her hands trembled as she tapped at the device.

"Hello?" he answered.

"Sir, it's Claudia Haverford. I just heard the news. Are you alright?"

"Some of my people were wounded, but I am unhurt. Fortunately, a large tree shielded me from the blast."

"Thank God! Is Seb with you? Is he OK?"

A pause. "It seems that the bomb was near the auctioneer and the crowd. Seb went to watch the mare sell … My people and I … we ran to the scene afterwards. The area is destroyed … I'm so sorry."

Claudia could no longer speak.

"I have to go now. The police wish to talk to me."

The line went dead.

Claudia sat there, trying to process it all. Her car swayed as traffic flew past. Seb was an arrogant man, but he didn't deserve that. Nobody did. His poor wife Julia … and their children … She tried to pull herself together. Should she call Julia and break it to her gently … if she hadn't seen the news?

But what if Seb *had* survived? The Emir hadn't actually said he was dead. Anyway, it wasn't really her place to make the call to Julia. She started to think about all the other people she knew who had been at the sale.

No, she couldn't let herself get into all that right now. She wiped her eyes, slapped her cheeks and put the car in gear.

She drove on through Newmarket towards Oscar's house. Hoped to find him passed out in front of the TV.

She passed a narrow side road. Flashing lights in the corner of her eye. A police car beside an SUV the same colour as Oscar's.

She hit the brakes. Her hands shook as she manoeuvred and made her way back to the SUV. She checked its licence plate and tried to imagine which drug he had slipped with this time.

21

One of the policemen tied-off crime-scene tape round a tree and came to her window, hand raised.

She opened her door.

"Stay in your vehicle, madam. This is a crime scene. Please move along."

"That's my brother's car. He's a vet. Oscar Haverford."

"Please wait there, madam." He spun on his heel and walked to his partner. The two men spoke for a long minute, glancing at Claudia occasionally.

God, it was overwhelming – first London and now this. She didn't need them to confirm it. Shielding her eyes from the dipping sun, she saw him slumped over the steering wheel. Still, the crime-scene tape seemed a bit dramatic for a comatose addict. She prayed he was just comatose.

She got out.

One of the officers approached her.

"May I see some ID please, madam?"

She reached into the car, pulled her licence out of the sun visor and handed it to him.

He gave it back and produced a clear plastic bag with another driver's licence in it.

"Is this your brother's?"

She nodded. "How bad is he, officer?" She didn't really want to give her worst fear an ounce of thought. But why else would they have cordoned-off the area and put his licence in an evidence bag? It dawned on her. "You found drugs in the car. Is that it?"

The policeman narrowed his eyes.

"Look, it's not the first time. He's been clean for years,

but he's still an addict," she babbled. "I need to get him home and probably admitted for treatment, depending on how bad he is. Surely there's no need to arrest him?"

The policeman motioned for his partner to join him.

"Ms. Haverford, I regret to inform you that the person whose licence this is and who appears to be the owner of the car –"

"Yes?"

"That person is dead. Cause of death currently unknown."

Her heart thumped. "You can't be sure just like that. He can get pretty comatose. No, no. You need an ambulance."

"We are very sorry, madam."

She slumped against her car and covered her face with her hands. Her whole body shook.

She'd always told herself that it would never come to this. That Oscar wasn't *that* bad. And she'd always be there to pick him up after a slip. She wiped her eyes on her sleeve. Streaks of mascara stained the fabric.

"I need to see him."

The officers exchanged glances.

"He's my brother!" she yelled. *"I want to bloody see him!"*

"Madam," said the first one, "I'll allow you to inspect the scene for the purposes of identification and to see if you observe anything out of the ordinary about the vehicle or its occupant, but I have to insist that you refrain from touching anything."

She put one foot in front of the other. Heard slapping sounds as the policemen pulled on latex gloves. One lifted the tape for her as the other opened the driver's door.

Oscar's head was wedged between the steering wheel

and the dashboard, face turned towards her. His straggly blonde hair looked as it always did, but his skin was almost white. His right arm dangled past his thigh, sleeve rolled up to the elbow. Her twin's normally sparkling blue eyes pierced her with a cold grey stare. She reached out to make him peaceful.

A latex glove grabbed her wrist.

"Then can *you* close his eyes?"

"I'm afraid not."

She made herself take deep breaths. Looked over Oscar's body. "I can't see very much from here."

The other officer opened the passenger door. "You'll see more from this side, madam."

She walked round and looked in. Oscar's left arm was draped over the central console and hung down in front of the seat. On the seat, there was a small aluminium tray containing a scattering of white powder.

"I suppose that's cocaine?"

"We believe so, but we are not ruling out ketamine. It's a common veterinary anaesthetic. Dried out, it crystallises and can be inhaled."

Claudia followed Oscar's arm down to his hand and looked at his phone in the footwell. There was something else beside it.

A small syringe lay there on the rubber mat. Two-point-five millilitres with a short, narrow-gauge needle missing its cover.

The officer cleared his throat. "It appears as if he died of an overdose."

She let out a long shuddering breath. "He never injected before," she mumbled. "Always said it was sordid."

The policemen glanced at each other.

Despair and anger boiled inside her. She wasn't sure if she wanted to hug her twin's corpse or smack it on the face.

The policemen led her back to her car and asked for her contact details. She managed to hand them a business card.

"My boss has apparently been killed in that terror attack this evening," she said, almost to herself. "I should have been there too, but Oscar called me. That's why I'm here." She stared past the SUV, down Warren Hill, towards the town. She was vaguely aware of the sound of a pen making notes on a pad. She needed a cigarette. She'd quit years ago in solidarity with Oscar, and then he'd started up again.

"Madam? Madam, what time did he call you exactly?"

"What? Does it matter?"

"It would help us to establish a time of death."

"Oh." She fished out her phone, recited the times and tossed it back into the car.

"Thank you, madam. I would advise you to go home and have a cup of hot sweet tea. We'll be in touch in due course. Are there any other relatives to notify?"

"No. Just me. I'll let his girlfriend know."

"That won't be necessary. If you could just give us her details, we'll notify her immediately along with his place of work."

Claudia told them. "Oh, I suppose you'll want me to let you into his house."

25

"It's not a priority: there's no sign of foul play at the scene. The body will be sent to Cambridge for autopsy. You'll be notified as to when it will be available for removal and burial."

Their lips kept moving but their words became feedback in her brain.

"Madam, I'm asking: will you be staying in the area tonight?"

"What? Oh, I don't know. I really should get back to Berkshire. There'll be so much to take care of, but …"

"Is there someone we can call to drive you?"

She heard herself saying, "My boyfriend doesn't have a car. I'll be OK."

"Are you sure you are OK to drive?"

Her boyfriend? She'd completely forgotten to call Tom. God, if he'd seen the news … Poor thing, it would bring it all back for him. When she got into her car, her phone was vibrating, shuffling across the seat.

"It's all so awful. I feel like I'm watching my own life from a distance," she blurted into the device.

*   *   *

When he heard her voice, Tom Sunderland finally exhaled. He muted the TV.

"I was sure you'd be in the thick of it. A … Well, are you injured?"

"No."

"Thank God. Is it complete carnage there?"

26

"I don't know. I'm in Newmarket."

"You're not at the sale?"

"Oscar called me. He said he didn't know what to do, that he'd slipped, that he needed me. So, I rushed to him."

"Bloody hell! I can't quite believe it."

"Makes two of us."

Silence.

Eventually Tom spoke. "Look, I'm sorry he fell off the wagon … but, well, actually not if he just saved your life."

No reply.

"How is he?"

"He's dead, Tom. Dead. Oscar's dead."

Tom put a hand over his face. He'd always feared Oscar would end up like this. "I'm so sorry, Claud. I'll borrow a car and drive straight up."

"After all these years of me looking out for him, all of a sudden he's … I just saw his body."

She told him about the car and police.

"I never thought he was *that* bad. I mean, he had his work and even a new girlfriend. What the hell pushed him this time? Why now? In the past, there'd always been a catalyst … Oh God. If only I'd picked up the bloody phone."

"Hey, *don't* do *that*."

She didn't answer.

"Seriously. You can't do *that*."

"Can't I?"

"How many times did you pick him up over the years?"

"But I didn't fucking pick him up when he really needed it, did I?" she yelled. "And to top it all off, it turns out he

27

saved *my* life." She took a breath. "I suppose I should feel lucky, but I don't."

"I'll borrow a car, be with you in ninety minutes. I'm not leaving you alone."

"Thanks, but … I just *want* to be alone for a bit. I need some time to process all of this. I'll check his house then I'll go back to Berkshire. See Julia and the stud staff."

"Collect me on the way and I'll come with you: moral support."

"Thanks but I'll manage."

Neither of them spoke for a moment.

"On TV they're saying at least forty dead. I just keep seeing bodies. And horrible burns. It looks like an IED attack, which I suppose it is."

"OK, that's enough. No more details. And Tom?"

"Yes."

"Now you know I'm safe, stop watching TV. It won't do you any good. You'll have nightmares."

"They're saying Adam Greene died too. There's speculation," his voice cracked, "that maybe he was the intended target."

"I saw him there with his buddy John Christian. Made my skin crawl. For God's sake turn off the news."

She was right. He fingered the remote. "OK, done."

"Good." She sighed. "At least my parents aren't alive. They'd never have got over Oscar's death."

Tom wondered what it would have changed. After all, their father had chosen suicide after the big crash had wiped out everything and taken their farm. He was glad

Claudia was more like her mother, although grief had got her in the end.

"Love you," he said.

"Me too."

She hung up.

Tom tossed the phone on his desk and thought back to when he'd first met Oscar. It seemed like a lifetime ago, when they'd both worn uniforms and before everything became so fucked up. He stared out the window onto the bustling streets of Newbury where life went on as normal.

After a few minutes, he switched his gaze to the front cover of a news magazine he'd pinned to the back of the door. It was a close-up of a beaming Adam Greene on his last day as Prime Minister. With two darts stuck right into the man's forehead. Tom cringed. He'd better get rid of that in case the police paid him a visit.

Chapter 4

The Emir of Fawala sat in the back of a police van with three officers and the Commissioner of the Metropolitan Police Service.

"Gentleman," said Rahim. "I have told you everything I know."

"Thank you for your co-operation, sir." Commissioner Trenton looked at his watch. "But I'm afraid you'll have to wait to speak to the lead anti-terror investigator. He, *um*, should be here any minute."

Rahim pulled a tight smile. "You are aware of my diplomatic status?"

Trenton opened his mouth to speak.

Rahim cut him off. "However, I am more than willing to help with this investigation in any way possible. The culprits must be found and I offer you my every resource."

"That's very kind," said Trenton.

Just then the door slid open and a lean man with narrow, restless eyes hopped into the van. He wore a crisp suit but his face looked tired. His skin was nearly translucent and his bony hand gripped an iPad.

The three officers got out, leaving Rahim alone with Trenton and the newcomer.

"Chief Inspector Colin Wallace, Counter Terrorism Command – SO15," he said.

Rahim nodded. "What would you like to know?"

Wallace flipped the cover off his iPad and swiped at the screen. "Everything. From when you arrived, to the time you got into this van."

Wallace's fingers tapped furiously as Rahim spoke.

"Right, thank you," he said, when Rahim had finished. "So, I'll need to see ID's, visas and full personnel files – including family history – on all your employees at the scene."

"I will see that everything is provided for you."

Wallace cocked a finger at him. "That includes those that arrived from your stud farm with your horses."

Rahim closed his eyes and bowed his head for a moment. "You do realise that of the four who journeyed here with my ill-fated horses, only the lorry driver remains alive?"

"I am fully aware of that, sir." Wallace's fingers pecked at his device. "Were they all British nationals?"

Rahim stiffened. "I believe they were."

Commissioner Trenton cleared his throat.

Wallace flicked the iPad closed. "Right then, I'll need you to come to the station in the next day or two and give an official witness statement."

"I will be in residence at the Marriot Hotel on Park Lane or at Al Fawala Stud in Newmarket until the summer is over. I will be glad to dictate and sign anything in privacy but regrettably I cannot visit your police station."

Wallace frowned and opened his mouth. Trenton cleared his throat again. Wallace gave him half a glance, then fixed his gaze on the Emir. "In your opinion, sir, were *you* the intended target of this attack?"

"I seriously doubt it."

"It's just that men – powerful leaders such as yourself, tend to have enemies."

"Really?"

"Usually. Can you think of anyone who would want to see you dead?"

"As your press has reported on several occasions, I intend to change my country with progressive domestic policies and anyone who attempts change usually comes into conflict with those who prefer the status quo." He paused. "You know that some think me blasphemous, godless even?"

Wallace stared.

"Of course, the term is merely a label. I let my people have their beliefs if that's what they desire, but I do not care for religious extremism."

Wallace arched his brow. "Is that a popular point of view in your emirate?"

"It will be." Rahim smirked, shrugged. "Anyway, if my

opponents really wished to get rid of me, they would try it in Fawala. Not in an attack on the soil of one of our trading partners."

"Not even for plausible deniability and to destroy the trade relationship?" suggested Wallace.

Rahim smoothed his beard and looked at his watch.

Trenton cleared his throat yet again.

"If any of your opponents are British passport-holders and are presently in the country," said Wallace, "I would be grateful if you could supply me with their names."

Rahim stared hard. The way his father had taught him. He wasn't sure if Wallace got the hint or simply decided to leave it there for now, but the man thanked him and left, slamming the door.

"If there is any other way I may help with the investigation, please let me know," Rahim said.

"Thank you, sir." Trenton opened the door for him.

Rahim stepped outside and adjusted his jacket as he watched Wallace duck under crime-scene tape and head for the Orangery.

The avenue was lined with paramedics examining shocked survivors wrapped in reflective foil blankets. Closer to the Orangery, forensics teams erected tents while their photographers got to work tagging and shooting. The other end of the avenue was ablaze with camera lights and reporters speaking in dramatic tones to their studios and audiences. The sounds merged and everything became a fuzzy din like a half-tuned radio. At least there was no more screaming or wailing.

A policeman beckoned Rahim. "I'll see you out through the barriers, sir."

He nodded, smiled and allowed the officer to escort him away from the awful scene. There was a throbbing from his jacket pocket. His face darkened as he saw the caller ID.

He answered in rapid-fire Arabic, making the policeman's head twitch in his direction. "I am unharmed. Sorry to disappoint you."

"May Allah the Compassionate be praised: you are safe, my little brother."

"Save your thoughts and prayers, Jabbar. We both know you'd love to see me vacate my position one way or another."

"Sometimes I forget that you picked up the dry British sense of humour during our Eton schooldays. But, seriously, do the British authorities have any idea who is responsible?"

"Not as far as I know."

"I suppose you'll return to Fawala now?"

"I may make a short visit home to see to affairs of state that cannot be settled from here,"

"Yes ... About your social-security programme. As your Prime Minister, it is my duty to inform you that nobody wants to waste money on it."

Rahim chuckled.

Jabbar's voice went cold. "Just let people do their own charity. There is no need for us to make it an obligation of the state."

"I will renegotiate our gas contracts and that will more

than pay for my programme. If your cronies disagree with me, they will keep it to themselves or take their money and leave the country. Understood?"

"Of course, my brother."

"Apart from that, I'll be staying in England to enjoy the racing. I haven't yet decided if I will live on my stud farm or in London."

"You'd do anything to avoid spending summer in the Fawalan heat, wouldn't you?"

"My horses are all in top form. I have a very good two-year-old filly up in Newmarket. I am expecting her to become a champion this year."

"Ah, Secular Princess? I've heard about her. Apparently she is talented but highly strung."

Rahim frowned. "For someone who is far away, you are well informed." He wondered fleetingly if the filly's trainer Michael Craddock had survived today's attack.

"I'll call you later," he said, as his men gathered around him.

Policemen ushered them through the cordons and towards their waiting vehicles. Barriers had been erected at the gates to stop a wave of reporters from advancing up the avenue. TV camera lights shone down on policemen, who ordered the crowd to keep back. An ambulance – sirens blaring, lights flashing – had to stop while the barriers were parted to let it out onto Bayswater Road. Outside the railings, people jostled for space along the footpath, phones held in up front of them.

Rahim took a final look around and was about to slide

into his car when he heard a woman's voice call: "*Sir! Your Highness! How does it feel to have emerged unscathed? What are your reactions to this atrocity? Do you think it was carried out by religious extremists?*"

One hand on the roof of his Bentley, Rahim hesitated a beat, then pulled a polite smile. He searched the crowd straining the barriers. There was a woman in a linen jacket holding a phone towards him. The policeman who was telling her to back up turned his head to Rahim.

Rahim stepped closer to the woman. "Thank you for your concern. I feel incredibly lucky, yet also deeply saddened by the tragic, unnecessary loss of life. As for the perpetrator's motives," he hesitated, "who can say at this stage? Thank you very much." He turned back to his car.

"*Sir, will you be rethinking your sponsorship of horseracing events after this attack?*"

"Not at all. I love Britain. It is my second home. We must not let today's tragedy derail our lives. Thank you very much."

He spun on his heel and ducked into his bulletproof car.

*   *   *

Sir Bernard Trenton stood outside the mobile command van and watched the Emir of Fawala's car ease through the gates onto Bayswater Road.

He pulled out his phone, scrolled and tapped. When the secretary answered, he interrupted her greeting. "This is Commissioner Trenton. My call is expected, please put me through."

"Certainly, sir."

Seconds later a voice boomed out of the device. "Bernard! How did it go?"

"He seems to be taking it quite well. He just told a reporter in public that he won't be pulling out of his sponsorship commitments."

"Really? That's a nice surprise, but you never know with these types. Make sure you keep a personal touch on this."

"Will do, sir."

"I'll still meet with him and his people this Thursday. They'll be able to slip in and out quietly now the press has something horrific to distract them."

"Yes, sir."

"Oh, and do what you can for Greene and Christian's people too. I don't want them throwing their weight about. And, Bernard – was Komarov killed in the blast?"

"I believe so, sir."

Chapter 5

Claudia parked in the driveway of the converted barn that had been Oscar's rented home for the last six years. When he'd got the job in Newmarket's biggest equine practice, Claudia had imagined him here for the rest of his life. Which was, she supposed, exactly how it had turned out.

When they'd been in school, all Oscar could talk about was being an army vet. An army liaison officer had said that if Oscar graduated from RMA Sandhurst, the army could sponsor his veterinary studies in return for a regular commission of service. That had spurred him to work hard and, after he'd aced his A-Levels, he'd taken a three-month holiday in Thailand with friends to celebrate. That was where he'd first tried heroin and the first time he had almost killed himself. Claudia had been working as an intern on a busy stud and she'd had to invent an excuse so as to accompany her mother on the flight to Bangkok. Back in England, they'd put Oscar in home-made rehab so nobody would find out. When he recovered, they'd agreed that he should take the Regular Commissions Board test and go off to Sandhurst as soon as possible.

A fresh start. And that's what it had been.

After Sandhurst, Oscar had studied at the Royal Vet College in London – and had a couple of slip-ups but Claudia had always rescued him and covered up. He'd wanted to specialise in horses and be stationed with the Royal Horse Artillery, but the Army had ordered him to serve time in Afghanistan. Young vets were needed to attend to the Working Military Dogs used in the detection of explosives, IEDs, and suicide bombers. So Oscar did a fourteen-month tour at Camp Bastion.

He'd returned changed somehow. Claudia had found him quieter, as if his enthusiasm and optimism for life had been diminished.

Afghanistan had damaged both the men in her life.

After that, he'd been posted to the RHA in London, but had resigned his commission at the earliest opportunity without explanation. He had another slip off the wagon to celebrate leaving, and that time Claudia had insisted that he attend meetings, threatening that she'd abandon him if he didn't – knowing full well she never would.

He'd then spent a year on an Australian horse farm specialising in reproduction and was subsequently offered the job in the expanding Newmarket practice. He and

Claudia had been delighted and relieved: if the partners had had even a whiff of his addiction struggles, he'd have lost the job and would have been forced to take himself to the Far East, which would have paid him too well and given him access to the things that tempted him.

He'd been doing so well here. In the last six years, the only lapses happened when their parents had died.

What had made him slip this time?

His message meant he must have done something stupid or been in some kind of trouble.

Claudia turned her key in the door and stepped in.

The house smelled of cigarettes: Oscar's one permitted vice. She scanned the small, cosy space, filled with the pieces of their parent's furniture that she and Oscar had divided. She looked at a silver-framed family photo taken back when they'd been happy and comfortable and Claudia had her first big job as office manager to a leading trainer. A few years after that, her father was gone and she'd had to help her mother organise the funeral, sign over the farm and move to a cottage near where she worked. Claudia used to drop by to make sure her mother ate properly, but within a year she too was gone.

In a strange way, Claudia had found her parents' deaths easier to deal with because she'd had Oscar to keep an eye on and her busy job. Now that list had just become shorter. At least she had Tom.

Tom … She couldn't help but wonder if they'd haul him in for questioning. No, surely not, all that business was well in the past.

She blew out a breath and scanned the room. Newspapers were stacked in a corner and the open fireplace was still overflowing with ash and embers from last winter. A thick layer of dust covered the dining table. The carpet was peppered with grit and the odd wisp of dried grass. Oscar had always joked that he'd got so good at keeping himself clean, that the state of his house was irrelevant.

She managed a momentary smile.

The kitchen was tidy, but then Oscar never cooked. She stuck her fingers in the coffee and sugar pots and rummaged for baggies. She checked all the spoons, but none showed signs of having being bent or burnt to use to cook a mixture for injection. If he'd never injected heroin, why would he have decided to do it now with ketamine?

She dropped to her knees and looked behind the sink. Then she started on the clutter in the sitting room and nearly an hour later she checked the bathroom and both bedrooms too.

So, either he'd bought his drugs today, or just raided his practice's ketamine supply. That would certainly have got him fired and disbarred if they found out. Was that why he sounded so desperate?

Oscar had never talked about his time in Afghanistan, but she knew all about Tom's nightmares and depression. Post-traumatic stress disorder? Gulf War Syndrome? Such inane names for such a debilitating condition. Claudia thought it should still be called shellshock. Oscar and Tom had been in the same Sandhurst intake but had gone their separate ways in service.

She knew the next few days would be absolutely unrelenting and intense. There would be so many things to take care of – both for Oscar and Seb. She was used to juggling a million things at once as part of her job, but this was utterly, horribly different. As for the attack at the sales … she should've been there. Was there. Until …

She grabbed a water bottle from the fridge, sat by the fireplace, switched on the TV and immediately changed the channel. For the moment, she really didn't want to know any more about the bombing. She stopped flipping at Fox News, which wasn't showing footage of the Orangery. Senator Daynson from West Virginia was ranting and raving at some rally again, this time about Syrian immigrants being terrorists and Mexicans stealing American jobs. Claudia knew that without Mexicans – and Irish, for that matter – the Kentucky horse business would have a severe labour shortage. Daynson, one State over, obviously hadn't thought that through. The crowd onscreen gave him rapturous applause. What an awful blob of a man with his fake hairline and shiny stretched skin! Last week, a satirical news show had called him *The Plastic Patriot* and the moniker had gone viral.

She rubbed her eyes and let her hands slip from her face to her lap to the cushion. Her left hand brushed off something stuffed down the side of the armchair. She groped and pulled out a leather-bound pocket diary. She hadn't realised Oscar had ever kept a personal diary – at least he'd never mentioned it to her. What else had he never mentioned?

Claudia flicked through it, glancing at occasional entries. Mostly things like dinner reservations, the odd social function with fellow vets and, lately, dates with Sally. He'd also kept a record of any NA meetings he'd attended in Cambridge or Ipswich; he never went in Newmarket or anywhere he could be recognised.

Still, she wondered if anybody else knew about his condition.

Claudia closed the diary. The only person *she'd* told about Oscar was Seb, and only because she'd had to drop everything one morning, not long after their mother's funeral, and dash to help him. Seb had actually been quite understanding and promised that he'd never breathe a word to anyone in Newmarket. As arrogant as he could be – *was*, he was able to keep secrets. Seb had no reason to start a rumour about Oscar anyhow, not when he was such a good vet for the Emir's stud on the other side of town.

She wondered why he had stuffed the diary down the side of the cushion. To hide it, presumably. Perhaps he had been interrupted while writing in it – by a knock on the door for instance – so shoved it out of sight?

She flicked open the diary to this week. On today's date was a big exclamation mark. She went back a page. Yesterday, he'd written: *3am. Mouse. Ha! Monster more like. Sends a shiver up my spine whenever we meet.*

A drug-deal code-name without a doubt. And it looked like it had been an ongoing thing. How could she have missed this? Had Oscar got more furtive or had she just been too engrossed in work?

She went back a week and saw in the notes section: *How the fuck am I going to do it without being seen? Where?*

Underneath that: *I hate myself.*

What the hell, she mouthed. She hadn't heard him say stuff like that since he left the army.

She wondered, if she asked around, would she be able to locate a local drug dealer called "Mouse?" Perhaps she should let the police do that? She'd discuss it with Tom. She pocketed the diary and found herself drawn to the small red-and-white box on the mantelpiece, a lighter perched beside it.

She stared. Hesitated. Snaked out an arm, grabbed the box, stuffed a cigarette into her mouth and fumbled with the lighter. Her hands shook as she lit up, inhaling deeply, savouring the rush. It had been so long. Her vision went speckled and she wobbled with headspin. She flopped back in to his chair and smoked right down to the filter, nearly burning her fingers. She was exhausted.

She climbed into bed in the room where she always stayed and sank into oblivion, dreaming that her phone was ringing.

Chapter 6

When she woke, the phone was still ringing and the sheets were damp with perspiration. She wished she'd got more than a few minutes' sleep.

She fumbled for the device. "Hi, Tom. Can I call you back? I've only just got to bed."

"Oh. Were you with the police all night?"

"What? I'm in Oscar's house." She checked her watch: 8.30am. "Holy shit! Is that the time?"

"I'm not surprised you passed out. You'll have needed that." He paused. "But I was worried: I'd tried you several times. How are you feeling?"

"Awful. But I suppose I'm rested."

"I couldn't help but watch the early news. Nobody's claimed responsibility yet, but the police have confirmed the death toll at forty-six, plus the two horses. Greene, Sir John Christian and Vasili Komarov are amongst the dead. Plenty of racing names that I'm sure you'll recognise. Dozens more injured. You should turn on a TV."

"Later, perhaps."

"There's also plenty of hysterical speculation from the Prime Minister about ISIS, Syrian refugees and anyone else he can think of. Makes me sick: he's as bad as Greene was. Oh, and I've had Julia Manton on the phone – she's been trying to get you too. She says she needs you back at Crangate, that there's so much to organise. I did tell her about Oscar, but I don't think it registered."

"I suppose that's understandable."

"I can go there this morning, if you want?"

"No. It's OK. Can you just call Julia and tell her I'll be there later? I'll go to Newmarket police station and see if they've got any news. Find out when they'll release his body. Then I suppose I'll have to call the undertaker –" Her voice cracked. She started coughing.

"Claud?"

She took a gulp of water. "Look, I found some stuff written in his diary. I'll tell you about it this evening. I'll have to go over to the Emir's stud after the police station, offer my condolences and see if there's anything I can do to help."

"Haven't you got enough on your plate?"

"Yeah, well. Oscar was their vet and they had three members of staff who probably perished with the mare and foal yesterday. Seb and I handled a lot of their stallion bookings and bought most of their horses. I have to take care of business too. I have to keep going, I owe it to Oscar *and* Seb."

She hung up, got up, had another cigarette and showered. Made a mental note to turn off the water heater and contact Oscar's landlord.

*　　*　　*

Chief Inspector Wallace hustled his lanky frame up the steps and onto the bustling pavement outside St. James's tube station.

After his examination of the scene and interviews, he'd returned to the office to write reports, estimate then confirm the death toll and supervise the processing of evidence. Forensics had worked through the night, trying to establish identities. Where possible, Wallace's team had informed next-of-kin and set up visits for formal identification of remains. Then, he'd had to deal with the private security detail of Adam Greene. They'd appeared at three in the morning, armed with two solicitors, and whisked Greene's remains away from the morgue. Wallace had protested, but had been told to shut up by Trenton. Wallace had never cared for commissioners or politicians.

He'd finally stolen home at 6am for a shower, change of clothes and a gallon of coffee.

He stuffed a cigarette into his mouth and marched the short walk to the steel-and-glass 1960s tower block that every filmgoer knew from its rotating sign. He liked the New Scotland Yard building and, like most of his colleagues, he was appalled by the Mayor's decision to sell it. The fact that it had been bought for 120 million *over* the asking price didn't mean a thing to the average copper. Everyone knew that the funds would make little difference to their daily lives and, to top it all off, rumours were flying that their new HQ over on Victoria Embankment wouldn't even be big enough to house everyone. The move was going to be chaos. As if terrorism hadn't made their lives difficult enough.

Wallace stopped short of the security barriers to finish his smoke. He ran his eyes over the building.

"Take a long look, Chief Inspector. It'll be torn down as soon as we move," said a voice behind him.

"We're sellin' off half the city," muttered Wallace.

"I heard a Middle-Eastern investment group bought it," said Detective Sergeant Gibson.

"Yeah. What's new?"

"Imagine if we had a loony politician like that American – whatsisname – oh yeah, Daynson – talking about banning Muslims from the country. I bet they own plenty of real estate over there too."

"No doubt they do, Gibson. So, did your guys get all that camera footage last night?"

Gibson nodded like a dashboard ornament, a nervous tick that drove Wallace mad.

"A simple *yes* will suffice, Gibson." He dropped his cigarette butt and rubbed it into the pavement with his shoe.

"They've been going through it all night."

"Come on then. Let's look at the highlights."

Wallace led the way past the barriers, through security and up to the slightly shabby open-plan space on the ninth floor. Officers took phone calls, hustled from cubicle to cubicle and marked charts stuck onto portable whiteboards.

Wallace made his way down to his glass-walled corner office and dialled the lab.

"It's Wallace. You processing the debris and fragments?"

"Yeah. Be a few days before I can give you definite results," said the officer, yawning into the phone.

"And in the meantime, what's your opinion?"

"Oh, professional and expensive. A dirty little mixture detonated by radio or phone signal: white phosphorus, thermite, C4, and shrapnel."

"Jesus Christ. Thermite?"

"Well, that and the phosphorus would explain all the burning, gluey blobs all over the place. The C4 would ignite the whole lot from an electrical current."

"Homemade?"

"*Mmm.* By a professional. This device was designed to pack a huge punch for its physical size. Thing is, though, judging from what we picked up, they didn't use ball-bearings or nails – the usual shrapnel for this kind of thing."

"What then?"

"Well, I could be barking up the wrong tree so I don't want to say just yet. I'll know later today, but if I'm right it'll cause a shitstorm and the injured survivors could be in for some long-term suffering."

Wallace knew better than to push him to speculate. "Call me when you know for sure."

He stared at the map of the scene on the wall behind his desk. Red pins denoting dead bodies littered the area in front of the Orangery.

Gibson appeared at the door. "Tech's ready for you."

Wallace sprang up and followed him down to a soundproofed room containing banks of screens, computers and recording equipment. Three technical-support officers sat at terminals.

"Whatcha got then?" asked Wallace.

"Not much apart from a bunch of rich fuckers swanning around guzzling champagne and buying horses that weren't even there," said a stocky young man sipping on a Coke.

Wallace growled.

"Until," the young man cocked a finger in the air, "two actual horses turn up with their handlers and a couple of other escorts. Now, I've been over this a dozen times and I still can't quite get my head around it. See what you think." He tapped the mouse and the image on a large screen began to play. "This is from the camera above the Orangery doorway, behind the auctioneer's rostrum. Image quality's great – but no sound, before you ask."

Wallace watched the mare and foal being led into shot by uniformed grooms. An older man led the mare. Wallace could see he looked proud: head up, back straight. The foal followed its mother, led by a young woman with her head down and what looked like a large *Greenpeace* badge pinned to her shirt. A young man brought up the rear, constantly looking about. He waved his hands when the foal hesitated in front of the crowd.

"It was hot yesterday," said Wallace. "Why's he wearing a zipped-up jacket?"

The animals were led about in circles.

Wallace's eye stayed on the third groom. "He looks nervous. What's he doing with his hands?"

"Wait for it," said the tech.

"Can't you zoo–"

Onscreen there was a blinding flash, then nothing.

Wallace gaped. "I don't sodding believe it! That can't be right."

"Told you," said the tech.

"What now?" asked Gibson.

"Rewind the bloody thing, for starters," said Wallace.

He watched it another seven times before thanking the tech. "Keep a lid on this for the moment, right?"

The tech nodded.

"And keep up the good work."

The tech grinned.

Wallace marched back to his office, Gibson on his heels. "Get me the employment list from that Emir's stud farm. I'd better let *on high* know about this. MI5 too," he said, picking up the phone. "Then, get the car ready. We're going to Newmarket."

Chapter 7

Claudia thanked the police sergeant and left Newmarket station. They'd told her it was probable that the death would be considered misadventure involving narcotics. In which case Oscar's body would be released by the end of the week.

"Blood results will likely confirm intravenous overdose," the sergeant had said. "From what we've been able to establish, your brother was well-liked and respected as a vet. His colleagues are in shock."

So is his sister, she'd wanted to say.

In the car park, she pulled the last cigarette out of Oscar's pack and called Sally. Neither of them could hold back the tears. Claudia said she'd arrange cremation and let the vet practice know.

*   *   *

The guard buzzed the ornate wrought-iron gates open and Claudia drove into the Al Fawala Stud and up its tree-lined avenue. The Emir had bought the 1,000 acre property four years ago from a threadbare baronet and spent millions refurbishing. The renovation had been completed with the same urgency as all aspects of the Emir's investment in racing and breeding. He had entered the sport with a passion so fierce that Claudia sometimes wondered if it would burn out as quickly.

She shouldered the office door and entered the over-lit and over-carpeted reception area.

When the young secretary saw her, she stood. "Oh Claudia, I'm so sorry. I heard about your brother and Mr. Manton, and then there's Roy and Kim and Danny and the poor mare and foal –" She started to sob and Claudia hugged her, struggling to keep her own tears at bay once more.

"It's all just so awful, Louise, but we," she paused, "we have to soldier on – no matter what. Or else the terrorists have won."

Louise nodded and dabbed the corners of her eyes with a tissue. "I suppose you're here to see Mr. Gilford? He's in his office, composing letters of condolence to the families. I didn't really know Danny, but Roy had been here since Sir Phillip's time and Kim was such a nice girl. A bit heavy on the environment and organics, but she loved horses."

Claudia hugged her again.

53

"I'll be OK," she sniffed. "Like you say, I'd rather be busy, and someone has to answer the phones."

"That's the spirit!"

Claudia let herself into Mark Gilford's office.

Al Fawala Stud's general manager was slumped over his desk. Head cradled in his hands. Staring at a blank sheet of paper. He had dark shadows under his eyes and looked a decade older than forty-three. Claudia had known Mark for years; she and Seb had been instrumental in getting him this job.

"Mark, I'm so sorry. How're you holding up?"

His eyes looked vacant, far away. He sighed. "Running a stud, you don't ever think you'll have to deal with members of staff being blown up or going missing. I've always found it tough to deal with the death of a *horse*, but this," he ran a hand through his greying hair, "this is … I mean, how do I write letters to their families? What do … Oh God, I'm sorry, Claudia … I heard about Oscar."

"Thanks, Mark. I suppose the whole town's talking about it by now?"

"You know what Newmarket's like."

Air hissed out between her teeth and she sat down heavily. "Yes. Look, I also came to reassure you that, business-wise, you don't have to worry. I have a feeling that Julia Manton will want me to take over from Seb and I fully intend to keep the Emir's equine affairs running smoothly. If you need any staff from Crangate to help out, just say the word."

"Thanks, but I'll manage until I can replace Kim and Danny. Old Roy, on the other hand, was one of a kind. You just don't find guys like that anymore. Oscar too, he was the best reproductive vet I've ever seen and so good with the student workers, always eager to share his knowledge." He paused. "I'm going to erect a memorial on the farm for all of them. Oscar included. Seems the least we could do."

Claudia's eyes lit up for the first time since she'd left the sale. "That's a lovely idea."

They sat in silence, trying to hold themselves together.

The desk phone let out a shrill ring and they both flinched. Mark picked up the receiver.

"Yes, Louise … What? Bloody hell! Well, you'd better show them in." He hung up, mumbling, "The police have arrived. Anti-terror squad from London." He got to his feet but stayed behind his desk.

Claudia picked up her handbag. "Well, I'd better leave you to it."

Louise led two men in. One, tall and gaunt with a grave look and a tailored suit. The other just as thin, in a drab jacket and slacks.

"Chief Inspector Wallace, Counter Terrorism Command," said the former with a flourish of ID. "And this is DS Gibson."

"Mark Gilford. How can I help you? Please, take a seat."

They sat and Wallace flipped open the cover of his iPad.

"I'm in charge of the investigation into yesterday evening's bombing and I need to ask you some questions about members of your staff."

Claudia hovered, caught between wanting to get away and wanting to ask about the attack. Wallace glanced at her.

"Claudia Haverford," she said, offering her hand. "I was wondering whether you had any leads?"

"Don't worry, madam, you can rest assured that the full power of the police and security services are at work on this." His voice droned like a recorded message.

Claudia blinked. "It's just … I was there yesterday, I know many of the people who were there, and –"

"Hang on – you were *there*?" Wallace examined her. "You said your name was Haverford?" He tapped a file on his iPad.

"Claudia Haverford."

He scrolled down some more and flicked a glance at Gibson.

"We interviewed everyone apart from the seriously injured before they were allowed to leave the scene. How did you slip the net?"

She told him everything: from Oscar's call to finding his body.

Wallace tapped notes. Mark leaned on his desk, horrified and enthralled.

The retelling of events gnawed at Claudia's emotions. Fear, anger, grief – all frayed and vying for dominance in her head. She rummaged in her bag for a tissue but what she really wanted was a cigarette.

Wallace eyed her intently and stopped taking notes. "So, you're telling me that your brother called you away from the sale moments before the attack and now he's dead?"

She nodded and blew her nose.

"What did your brother do *exactly*?"

"He was a vet."

"Yeah, you told me that."

Mark cut in, trying to be helpful. "He worked for the big practice in town, but spent most mornings here. He was our number-one reproductive vet."

Wallace turned his full attention to Mark.

"You know, examining mares and such like," Mark's voice wavered. "Making sure they get pregnant."

Wallace glanced at Gibson, then back to Mark. "Could you give me the details of your employees who were sent to London with the horses yesterday? I asked your boss for them, but I still haven't received anything."

"Certainly. Kim Lowther, Roy Ferguson and Danny Marsh were the three killed, and the lorry was driven by Trevor Rafter, but he's not at work today."

"We interviewed him yesterday."

"I'll get Louise to get you all their particulars."

"Right," said Wallace. "Did any of those employees have a … particular relationship with Oscar Haverford?" His eyes flicked from Mark to Claudia.

Claudia looked blank.

Mark shrugged. "No, not as such. I mean, Oscar was always so helpful to the young workers. Answering their questions and getting them to think about veterinary stuff. I suppose Kim would've been the one who talked to Oscar most – her and Murad." Mark glanced at Claudia. "I think Kim fancied Oscar."

"Sorry – *Murad*?" asked Wallace.

"Yes, Murad. He's been here a year or so. Young guy,

great little worker. Very shy, but he seemed to get on with Danny and Kim. And Oscar for that matter. I guess Danny's death has hit him hard – he's taken off, gone missing. If he's not back by tonight, I'm going to have to alert the local police."

Wallace stared right into Mark. "You've got a missing worker?"

"Yes."

"You said he spent time with Oscar Haverford?"

"Well, he worked in the barn with the Emir's best mares. Actually, he looked after the mare we sent to the sale. He was upset when she lost her pregnancy a few weeks ago. He was such a quiet mousey little fellow at the best of times but, after that happened, you couldn't get a word out of him at all. In fact, Oscar, Danny and Kim were the only ones he ever really spoke to. He lived alone in a flat on the farm. Rarely went out or socialised. Was kind of embarrassed by his accent, I think."

"Accent?" asked Wallace.

"Yes. He spoke English like a cartoon Indian. He's from Pakistan originally, but the Emir brought him over here last year with a bunch of racehorses that had wintered in Fawala."

Wallace chewed his lip and tapped notes.

Mark's words echoed in Claudia's brain: *quiet mousey little fellow*. It was just a figure of speech, but she recalled the note in Oscar's diary. *5am. Mouse*. She went to say something, then stopped herself. But not before Wallace had registered her hesitation. Claudia ignored his searching look. Murad was probably just a low-level dealer. She knew there were plenty of young guys like that in Newmarket. But maybe Murad knew something? What if he'd killed Oscar over a drug deal gone wrong? Her head spun. She looked out the window to a mare and foal in a paddock.

"Something wrong, Ms. Haverford?" asked Wallace.

She half-looked at him. "Just thinking about my brother."

Wallace turned back to Mark. "Any radical tendencies amongst the deceased, or missing workers?"

Mark's eyes widened. "Gosh. Well, Roy was a bit of a UKIP supporter – if you could call *that* radical. Kim was one of those militant-environmentalist types, not that you'd know it to look at her. Lately, she'd also got very upset about the wars in the Middle East. I heard her arguing about it once with Roy. Come to think of it, one morning during examinations a few months ago, I remember her and Murad asking Oscar about his time in the Army, but he just shook his head and told them *'You don't want to go there'*. But, I mean, none of them'd harm a fly. They're – were – decent people."

"I'm going to need to look through this Murad's flat. Same for Roy, Danny and Kim's accommodation."

Mark sighed. "Roy and his family didn't live on the farm, but Kim and Danny shared a cottage in Yard Five and Murad lived alone in a tiny flat above one of our quarantine units."

"Quarantine units on a horse farm?" asked Wallace.

"Well, of course. We use them for all sorts of reasons.

We had our mare and foal in there before we sent them to the sale."

Wallace tapped at his iPad, snapped the cover shut and sprang to his feet.

"Let's show you those flats then," said Mark.

"I'd better be off too," said Claudia.

Wallace offered her his card. "I'll also need *your* contact details, Ms. Haverford."

Claudia gave him a card from her bag and turned to leave.

"One more thing, Ms. Haverford."

"Yes?"

"You saw your brother at the scene of his death?"

She nodded.

"In your opinion, was there anything that would indicate foul play?"

She hesitated a beat. "Look, I know it sounds silly, but there's just no way he'd have injected himself. This is going to sound strange, but he thought it was sordid, beneath him. He … preferred to ingest his drugs by smoking or snorting."

They scrutinised each other for a moment.

Wallace nodded. "OK, thank you. I'll be in touch."

Claudia hurried out of the office as her phone began to chime. She told Julia Manton that she was on the way.

Chapter 8

Mark drove slowly through the stud with the policemen in tow. He pulled up at a redbrick yard of twenty-four stables and opened the back door of the adjoining cottage. The staff never locked their accommodation. With a secure perimeter and security guards screening everyone at the stud's main gate, there was no need.

Inside, the kitchen was tidy, except for a pair of cups and cereal bowls left in the sink: Kim and Danny's last meal. Mark felt like he was walking on someone's grave. The policemen pulled on latex gloves, went through to check the sparse sitting room and split up down the corridor to take a bedroom each.

"Mr Gilford, can you come here, please?" Wallace called out.

Mark entered the small bedroom and squinted in the gloom: a messed-up bed, an open wardrobe spilling clothes onto the carpet. Wallace flung the curtains open and light poured in. Mark's eyes settled on a framed photo of a young man in uniform.

Wallace cleared his throat and gestured with a finger. "What do you make of this?"

The room's walls were completely covered with posters. Pinned up edge to edge, they formed a collage of horses and … Mark followed Wallace's finger to a poster of last year's Derby winner. It was surrounded by pictures of balaclava-clad people picketing at fences, chained to trees, blocking the entrance to a nuclear-power plant. Mark filtered out the horses on Kim's wall and focused on several other images of so-called eco-warriors. There were posters for films about everything from industrial agriculture to GMO crops to fracking for shale gas.

"You mentioned she was a bit of a tree-hugger."

"She's – was – a passionate girl."

Gibson appeared in the doorway and let out a small whistle. "A tad obsessed, was she?" he said to nobody in particular. "The other room looks almost unused."

"Danny and Kim were an item the last couple of months," said Mark.

Wallace nodded as if he'd already worked this out. He poked about, rummaging through a stack of bank statements, wage slips and nightclub flyers on a chest of drawers. He swung around abruptly. "Right, that's enough for me."

Mark followed the men out of the house.

"Make the call," said Wallace.

Gibson swiped at his phone.

"You must lock this house immediately," ordered Wallace. "It is out of bounds until our forensic team conducts a complete investigation."

Mark almost smirked.

"Something amusing?"

"No. Sorry, but that sounded like something from a TV crime show."

"We are conducting an investigation into the nation's worst terror attack since 7/7, Mr. Gilford. No stone will be left unturned."

Mark nodded, chastised. But part of him still couldn't quite believe that the stud was involved in a terrorist attack.

"Now show us Murad's flat."

Mark drove to the farthest corner of the property. He passed a copse of trees which hid a large concrete pit for composting dirty straw bedding and pulled up at a set of double gates separating the quarantine unit from the rest of the farm.

As Mark opened the gates, he heard the familiar snapping of latex gloves, reminding him of the sounds before most veterinary examinations.

"We have a small five-stable unit here with five little paddocks behind it," he said. "Murad lived alone up in the flat."

The policemen fell in beside him, scanning the surroundings. The stables were empty, yard swept clean and tidy.

"Where does that lead to?" asked Gibson, pointing to a wide set of iron-framed gates lined with thick wooden boards.

"Directly onto the road. We have it set up like that so if we're receiving horses from a sale or another country, the truck can deliver them straight in here. They're always locked."

"Did Murad have a key?"

"No. I mean, yes. They're electric – he had a remote control. He used it as a shortcut into town on his bicycle."

Mark walked between the stable block and the small hay shed, rounded the corner and went up the steps. That door was also unlocked. It opened directly onto a tiny kitchen/living area.

Mark pressed himself to the wall to let the policemen past him.

Wallace ran his eyes over the kitchen, two-seat sofa and bare coffee table. The place was immaculate. The pungent smell of bleach cut the air. He walked to the old TV and wiped his finger along the top. Inspected his glove. "Bit of a tidiness freak, was he?"

"He was an excellent worker. Always did everything to the highest standard."

"*Mm.* Not a speck of dust."

Gibson made for a door beside the TV.

"There's only one bedroom and bathroom," said Mark.

"He always live here then?"

"Ever since he arrived. He usually worked elsewhere on the farm but when that poor mare lost her pregnancy, we kept Murad here looking after her and her foal."

"And Murad was alone here all the time, was he?"

"Yes, apart from when the vet visited to treat the mare. When that happened, Kim would sometimes accompany him, to assist."

"Would this be the same vet who's now dead?"

Mark pressed his lips together, nodded gravely.

Wallace balanced his iPad on an open palm. Tapped furiously with the other hand.

Gibson reappeared. "Bed and bath are spotless, too."

"The team'll have to go through this place as well," said Wallace, tapping away. "But I'll bet they won't find a single print."

*   *   *

Wallace leaned on the duty desk of Newmarket police station while the constable busily scribbled notes.

Another undermanned station, he thought. Sometimes he wondered if the geniuses in Whitehall thought the country could do without a police force. Or maybe they just wanted to privatise law enforcement.

"Alright," he jabbed a finger at the constable's notepad, "read the name back to me."

"*Er*, Murad Kazemi. K, A, Z, E, M, I."

"Spot on. I want him found ASAP. Number-one priority, understand? If you need extra bodies give me a bell and I'll swing it for you." He slid his card onto the counter.

"Yes, Chief Inspector."

"Now, about this dead vet: call your sergeant at Cambridge

morgue and tell him to get hands and clothes swabbed for explosive residue, if they haven't already washed and scrubbed all the evidence away."

"What?"

"You heard me. Where's the vet's car?"

"Parked in the yard, why?"

"Keep it there. Locked. I'm sending a forensics team to Al Fawala Stud. When they're done there, they'll go through that car and anything in it."

"Last time we did a forensic sweep up here the lab took weeks to process everything." His brow shot up. "Does this mean you suspect the stud farm and this vet of the London bombing?"

Wallace plastered on a tight smile. "I'm afraid I can't divulge. I'll call you back first thing in the morning. I'll expect you to have a lead on Murad Kazemi by then."

He pushed the door open and hurried out to his car. His phone rang as he got in.

"No, I'm not in front of a TV," he growled. "What? Come again? Who claimed responsibility? I don't fucking believe …" His throat went dry.

Chapter 9

Claudia stubbed her cigarette in the ashtray as she drove into Crangate Stud. Three hundred acres of rolling Berkshire that Sebastian Manton had inherited. In the seven years Claudia had worked for Seb, he'd transformed Crangate from a quiet, old-fashioned cattle farm into a busy stud and bloodstock agency. A transformation significantly aided during the last four years by salary, fees and commissions flowing into Seb's pockets from the Emir's vast wealth. She parked by the office and crunched across the gravel to the back door of the Georgian farmhouse. She paused with her fingers on the handle and took a breath.

Julia Manton was sitting at the kitchen table, staring at an iPad. She looked thinner than usual and her normally flowing dark hair was limp and dull. She tore her cobalt eyes from the device and looked right through Claudia.

"Oh, you've finally arrived." She stood. "Coffee?"

Claudia was ready to give Julia a hug but decided against it. "I know you wanted me here last night, but I just had too much to deal with. I –"

"Yes, Tom told me about your brother. I suppose we've both had our worlds upended, along with many others. The Prime Minister has declared next Sunday a day of national mourning and you've heard Ascot is cancelled today as a mark of respect to all the racing people who died?"

Claudia shook her head.

"Not like you to miss the news. They're also saying that the Queen will wear black at the races for the rest of the week …" Her babbling ran out of steam.

Claudia seized her chance. "I'm so sorry about Seb. I feel like I should have been killed too. I still can't get my head around it."

"You're a lucky girl," Julia said, offering Claudia a steaming espresso.

Claudia took the cup and put a hand on Julia's shoulder. "Whatever I can do to help you pick up the pieces, just let me know."

"Pick up the pieces? How apt." Julia stared at the floor. "Apparently that's all they could find of Seb: his left hand still clutching his bloody catalogue. Oh, and they found his face."

Claudia wobbled, sank into a chair and plonked her cup on the table, spilling coffee.

Julia crossed her arms and leaned back, resting her bum

on the counter. "I don't mean his head, you know," she continued, her voice winter-cold. "Just his face. According to our solicitor, whom I sent to deal with the police, the skin was torn clean off his skull. Like you'd tear a strip of wax off those long legs of yours. So, I won't be having a burial. Waste of a coffin, really. I'll scatter his ashes here. Well, that's the plan, but our solicitor also says it might be months before the police release the bits: criminal investigation and all that. But Adam Greene'll be having a state funeral according to the BBC. *Huh!* They'll pull out all the stops for him." She tapped her heel off the floor. "There'll be plenty of racing funerals to attend as well."

Claudia screwed up her face. She hadn't thought of that.

"Don't worry," said Julia. "I'll go to those on behalf of both of us. It's what Seb would've wanted me to do. We must carry on, mustn't we?"

"That's what I told Mark Gilford this morning."

"Right. I want you to take over the business. Run it for the children and me. We've got to keep the show on the road."

"You're sure?"

"Of course I'm sure, I don't want to sell this place." She flapped a hand around the room. "We've got to keep it all running. It's what Seb would've wanted."

Claudia managed a smile. "I agree."

"He liked you. Respected you. He'd have wanted you to take over."

"I'm flattered. And don't worry, I'll keep things going."

69

"I respect you too. You know the business well and," she paused, "and you refused to sleep with him. Well done, you."

Claudia gaped at her.

"Oh, I know he had his dalliances and I know he'd have liked having you on a string too, but I never wanted anything like that so close to home. So, thank you, Claudia."

Claudia's mouth was still open.

Julia clapped her hands together. "Right, we'd better address the staff."

Up to today, Claudia had only ever seen Julia in social-butterfly mode. A charm weapon Seb would turn out for tactical luncheons and dinners with clients or prospective clients. Now, she saw her for what she imagined she'd always been: a tough, smart woman who knew little about horses, but had probably always been in charge of the marriage.

"It would help if you didn't dwell on your brother either. After all, it was bound to happen sooner or later."

"What was?"

"Once an addict, always an addict. No matter if he'd been clean for years – they always relapse."

Claudia's face hardened.

"I know it's not what you want to hear, but Seb *did* worry about Oscar. He was concerned that he'd snap and make a fool out of himself. Last time we had dinner with the Emir in London, we had quite a discussion about it."

"Hang on, you mean you discussed my brother's past with *the Emir*? When was this?"

"Oh, a year or so ago. You were in Newmarket, as I recall."

"I can't believe the Emir knew about it."

"Well, of course. Although, to be honest, I think Seb just wanted to lay the cards on the table and let the Emir and Mark Gilford make their own minds up about Oscar. Fortunately, everybody agreed that as long as his work wasn't affected, then it wasn't an issue."

"You mean Mark Gilford knew back then as well?"

"The worst-kept secret in Newmarket, as it turns out. One of the senior partners at his practice found out too. Seb said the man was willing to turn a blind eye because it meant the practice was getting all the Emir's work, but you know what Newmarket's like. They were probably just waiting for Oscar to publicly relapse so they'd have an excuse to fire him."

"I didn't have a clue it was an open secret. I'm sure Oscar didn't either."

"People are seldom aware of the gossip that circulates about themselves."

Suddenly, Claudia wondered if someone in Newmarket hadn't given Oscar a helping hand to slip up this time.

They crossed the yard to the office and ten minutes later Bill, the Stud Groom, brought the staff into the reception area. Everyone shook hands with Julia, offering stuttered condolences. Bodies shifted from foot to foot.

Claudia sat on the corner of the desk, smiled as warmly as she could and announced that things would go on as before to honour Seb's memory. That was it.

When the staff exited, Bill shut the door and cleared his throat.

"What is it, Bill?" asked Claudia.

"We'll still start yearling prep next week as planned?"

"Absolutely."

"Then we'll need extra staff ASAP."

"Yes, Seb told me he'd hired three students. She turned to her desk. "Their details must be here somewhere. Oh, and he said that the Emir's sending a guy down from Newmarket. Wants him to learn the ropes on a stud farm."

"Learn the ropes? I want experienced people for yearling prep."

"Don't worry. I'm sure he'll be fine. Anyway, we're not in a position to say no to the Emir."

"I suppose not." Bill left.

Julia jumped up. "Well, I'll leave you to it, Claudia. I need to call the solicitor again. Oh, and we'll have to put in an appearance at Ascot on Friday."

Claudia's eyes flickered.

"That good two-year-old filly you and Seb bought for the Emir is running. What was her name again?"

"Oh, right. *Um*, Secular Princess. I can go alone if you like."

"We'll discuss it tomorrow."

Claudia crossed the hall to Seb's office. It felt strange sitting at his desk, but she'd better get used to it.

She flicked through Seb's desk diary, then found the CVs of the three new workers under a glass paperweight. A Post-it note was stuck to the top of the pile: *Hanif Ali*

Mengak. Fawalan passport. Visa OK. Good rider and horseman. Yearling prep. With Craddock. Here after Ascot. This must be the guy the Emir was sending down here, she thought. No doubt he was another Pakistani groom the Emir had brought to Fawala to work at their racetrack on the edge of the desert. Claudia had attended the big racing festival in Fawala every January for the last four years. The first year she'd been amazed that virtually all the grooms had been immigrants from countries at the other side of the Persian Gulf. The Emir had told her that he offered the trip to England to only the very best workers.

She decided to call Michael Craddock to find out more. Perhaps Hanif knew the young guy who'd gone missing from Al Fawala Stud? The guy who'd probably sold drugs to Oscar.

She rolled her hips to one side, fished her phone out of her back pocket and dialled.

As the number rang, she suddenly remembered that Michael had been at the sale yesterday. God, was it only yesterday? At least the number was ringing. That was a good sign surely?

The tone rang out and broke for a second, as it does when the call is being forwarded. Claudia winced and chewed her lip.

A solemn voice answered. "Craddock racing stables, Ed Tomlinson speaking."

"Ed, hi. It's Claudia. Is Michael OK?"

"No ... I'm afraid he didn't make it."

"Oh my God, I'm so sorry."

73

"We're all in shock here. This morning in the yard, I just kept looking at my watch and wondering where he'd got to."

"Oh Ed, it's all just so horrific."

"He was like a father to me," he sighed. "With no wife or kids to take over from him, it looks like I'll end up holding the fort, unless the Emir wants to get in someone else. I've tried calling him, but I can't get through."

"I'll give him a call," she paused. "I might as well tell you now – Julia wants me to take over the business, so in essence nothing will change. Picking up from Seb, I'll be your direct point of contact to the Emir on all racing matters."

"That's great, but do you think he'll like having a woman running his bloodstock affairs? Guys like him aren't known for women's rights."

"I've always got on perfectly well with him. He's an absolute gentleman. Anyway, I'm really calling to check about a groom." She glanced at the note. "Hanif Ali Mengak."

Ed sighed again. "Don't want to lose him. You know he's looking after Secular Princess?"

"I didn't. And she's a tricky filly, isn't she?"

"She is."

"Do you want me to have a word with the Emir about it?"

"Michael tried that last week through Seb. No joy."

As open and reasonable as the Emir was, Claudia knew that when he didn't care to listen, you were wasting your time trying to communicate. "OK then, when can I expect him?"

"He's supposed to stay with me until the filly runs on Friday, then he'll hand over his horses and I'll put him on a train. He'll have to change stations in London."

"Can he manage that?"

"I suppose so. Oh, and you'll have to get him a bicycle. He likes to cycle everywhere."

She chuckled. "Just like Tom. I'll put him in a flat over the main yard. Is he sociable?"

"Quiet. Very shy."

"OK. Oh, and how's Secular Princess?"

"Top form. She should win."

"OK, Ed, hang in there and see you Friday."

"Thanks … We could do with a nice win after all the tragedy."

Claudia hung up.

She clicked through the *Racing Post* website. It listed all the people dead and injured in the attack.

Chapter 10

His Highness Rahim bin Faisal Al Bahar sat in an armchair in his suite. Whenever he came to London, he took a whole floor of the Park Lane Marriot for his advisors and staff, effectively allowing him to deal with many affairs of state remotely.

The four men sitting around the coffee table competed desperately for his attention. Rahim enjoyed the spectacle and he always felt it kept them sharp.

Sheikh Abdullah, Rahim's cousin, and close friend of his brother Jabbar, slammed a hand on the table.

"You are not listening to me!" he shouted in Arabic. "Fawala is a tiny emirate, and we must keep an edge over our larger competitors in the Gulf area. Luxurious modern infrastructure and easy banking conditions are the keys to

that. Then all the Russian, Chinese and African billionaires will come to us with their illicit money. We can copy the British model and become world bankers."

The others nodded politely, while trying to read Rahim.

He scratched his short beard. "I agree that we have to build infrastructure: schools, universities and social facilities. We must educate *everyone* who calls Fawala home – prepare them for the future. We must assume our gas fields will one day run dry." He paused a beat, pondered whether to tell them about the latest surveys. Decided against it. "Just like our oil wells did."

Abdullah flapped a hand. "Our fathers benefitted from the oil as we shall benefit from the gas."

"Not everyone benefitted. Anyway … our fathers squandered their oil money on weapons, trinkets and religion."

The room went still. Rahim looked at the open mouths. "Those days are over and I do not wish to see history repeat itself. We have to renew our contracts, sell all the gas futures we can for the highest possible prices and use the revenue to take care of the forgotten, invisible people in our desert kingdom."

Silence.

"It is time, and it is the right thing to do."

Abdullah spoke with a sly grin. "Well, from a purely business perspective, we are in a much better position since the bombing at the horse sale."

"That is true," another joined in. "The Russians have already blotted their copybooks with the British – poisonings et cetera. And remember that Vasili Komarov was the Kremlin's secret mediator here in London. They say that's how he got out of a Moscow jail with his head intact."

"Only to lose it in a London bomb!" said another with a snigger.

Abdullah cut in again. "Allah be praised! Komarov's father slaughtered countless Muslim brothers and sisters in Chechnya."

Rahim glared. "Now you're praising Allah for death?"

Abdullah averted his gaze but Rahim could see anger ripple across his face.

Further discussion was pointless. Rahim turned on the TV and watched a British news channel. There was coverage of the political life of Adam Greene. An image of Sir John Christian flashed onto the screen. Suddenly, the picture went blank a moment, then the studio reporter appeared, his face solemn yet afraid. Rahim knew the look from American TV networks: tone-setting to hype up a new drama.

"And this just in," said the anchor. *"We have received information that a previously unknown environmental extremist group calling themselves Nature's Wrath has claimed responsibility for Monday's appalling atrocity: the deadliest terror attack on British soil since the 7/7 attacks of 2005. Police are following leads to apprehend the members of this despicable organisation, which announced that Sir John Christian, owner of natural-gas drilling company CleanGas, along with Adam Greene, were the primary targets of the attack. However, the group also stated that striking at a gathering of rich irresponsible*

horse owners was a logical choice as many of their number make money from exploiting the Earth's natural resources to catastrophic effect."

Rahim stood and went to the window, leaving his men glued to the TV laughing about the deaths of Komarov, Greene and Christian. Revelling in a pleasant side-effect to such a terrible event.

He was about to tell them all to get out when a phone rang in his pocket. He pulled out the device, smiled at the screen and answered.

"Good afternoon, sir," said Claudia. "I'm just calling to say that I've spoken to Michael Craddock's assistant, Ed Tomlinson." She told him about Craddock's death.

"That is very tragic. Please tell Ed that if there is anything I can do, he only has to inform you."

"Certainly, sir."

"I hope Ed will want to take over the licence and train my horses?"

"I'm sure he will."

"Good. How is Secular Princess?"

"She's in top form, sir. But, I'm really calling you to say that Julia Manton has asked me to take over the running of Seb's business. So, if you're happy that I will be overseeing all your equine affairs, then for you, sir, nothing will change."

Rahim remembered that he'd decided to promote her anyway. Claudia would be the first female to serve him in an important position. She deserved it, especially after all that had happened to her. She'd lost enough and might yet have to go through more in the coming days.

"Of that I have no doubt, Claudia. I am delighted you will be in charge. I'll see you at Ascot on Friday."

"Certainly, sir. Goodbye."

He looked across the room at his advisors bickering like spoiled children. One day, he would put a couple of women in government positions in Fawala. Women were trustworthy and hard workers. Men of such value were so difficult to find in Fawala. But, to promote women as leaders he would need to change social attitudes.

Rahim sank into a chair. Once he completed negotiations to ensure continued desire for Fawalan gas, he would unveil his social reform programme and show his people that *he* had changed their lives, not an entity they wasted their time praying to. Then he would go after the power of the religious leaders. A new dawn for Fawala would be at hand. Not a moment too soon.

His phone buzzed in his hand and broke his reverie. Mark Gilford's name was on the screen. Rahim rejected the call. The man would just have to learn to deal with Claudia.

Behind him, Abdullah raised his voice. "Shouldn't we be worried that climate-change politics and," he gestured to the TV, "environmental lunatics will pressure the British government to seek other means of energy supply?"

"Don't worry," said Rahim. "I suspect that these environmental extremists will have helped neither their cause nor image with that attack."

"Perhaps that is true, but the British are looking into alternative power sources. They are buying nuclear-

80

generated electricity from the French and soon the Irish will be supplying them with wind-generated power, all of it imported using subsea interconnectors."

Rahim waved a hand. "Those measures are merely stopgaps or political gestures. They need huge amounts of energy. Don't forget, they are currently importing over thirty-percent of their needs and our gas is still perceived as being cleaner than oil or coal. Relax, Abdullah, I have every confidence that we will secure the new deal before their parliament goes on its summer holiday. Although," he paused, "we may have to buy some more London property and make a gesture of some investment money for their bankers to play with."

Abdullah smiled. "We can buy weapons. It is always fun to make a shopping list at an arms fair."

Rahim stared.

A junior aide appeared in the suite, holding a sheet of stiff paper.

At Rahim's gesture to proceed, he read the letter aloud. *"The Prime Minister wishes to express deep shock that His Highness the Emir of Fawala was present at the site of the terrorist attack and to express his delight that His Highness was uninjured. The Prime Minister assures His Highness that their scheduled meeting will go ahead as planned this Thursday. The Prime Minister would like to extend an invitation to luncheon before the meeting."* He continued in Arabic. "That is all it says, but they have requested the names of our delegates to issue security passes."

"See to it that they have everything they ask for."

81

The young man nodded and left.

Rahim smiled broadly at Abdullah. "Now, we get lunch," he said in English. "You may be right about there being advantageous side-effects to my presence at that horse sale."

Abdullah knitted his brow and replied in English. "Your presence? I don't follow."

"Did you not notice the wording of that letter? They assume I am deeply offended by my proximity to the bombing and disgusted at their ineptitude in preventing the attack. It looks like they will want to please me at this meeting."

Abdullah rubbed his hands together.

In the background, the TV blared with news of candidates jostling for their parties' nominations in the early run-up to the American Presidential primaries.

Rahim turned up the sound when there was a clip of an obese, coiffed politician drumming up fear of Syrian immigrants bringing terrorism to America. Rahim instantly recognised Senator Rick Daynson. The man launched into a rant about the current president's "*scaredy-cat*" policies towards ISIS.

Rahim rolled his eyes.

Abdullah swore at the screen in English. "Do you think he really believes what he says?"

"Like most politicians he is a businessman. He will say whatever he needs to in order to close the deal and right now the deal is getting to the White House."

"*Pah!* The man is an idiot."

"Well, you'd better find something to like about him. I'm sending you to Washington in September to lobby for a meeting with him."

Abdullah stared deadpan at the TV. "His eldest son was at Yale with me. I think I met him once at a fraternity party."

Chapter 11

Claudia stared at the TV in her office and thought of Tom. She pulled the last cigarette out of the pack, cracked the window and exhaled her smoke outside.

Her desk phone rang.

"Hello, Crangate Stud."

"Claudia? How're y'all holding up?" drawled the baritone voice of Case Felsom, manager of Al Fawala Stud USA.

"We're trying to soldier on. Thank you, Case."

"I'm so sorry to hear about Seb."

"Thank you. I'll pass that on to Julia. Oh, and while I've got you on the line I should let you know that I'm taking over the business, so you'll be dealing with me from now on."

"Really? That's great an' all, but I usually communicate

directly with the Emir. It's the way he likes it. Way he wants it, or so he said. Hell, I thought you knew that?"

"I always assumed you called Seb."

"Only as a courtesy to keep him in the loop. Don't worry, I'll do the same with you."

"OK, thanks. How are things on your end?"

"Horses're all good, but I got staffing issues."

"Anything serious?"

"Could be. I tell ya, I got some pissed-off guys here. They work their asses off and have to listen to fat guys in suits talking trash about 'em. Got a couple senators and some businessmen making anti-immigration noises, trying to get headlines now the presidential race is starting up."

"That's the last thing you need."

"Tell me about it. Couple of my guys are veterans too. Hell, if it wasn't for Mexicans – and the Irish, for that matter – the horse industry in Kentucky'd be in deep shit!"

"Funny, I thought the same thing when I saw that Daynson ranting and raving on TV."

He snorted. "That man speaks before he thinks. Anyway, I gotta go. Keep safe, Claudia."

"I will. Thank you, Case."

A minute later, her mobile rang.

"Are you watching the news?" said Mark Gilford.

She nodded, then remembered he couldn't see her. "It's on in the background."

"I've tried to call the Emir, but he won't pick up. I –"

"He wants all communication to go through me," she cut in.

"*Um*, right." He paused. "It's just that I had to show the cops where Kim, Danny and Murad lived. Kim's room was full of militant environmentalist stuff. They're sending up a forensic team. Murad's still missing and on top of it all I've a feeling the police think that Oscar was involved somehow."

"What? That's ridiculous! Why? How?"

"They got rather excited when I mentioned that he'd been treating the mare in the quarantine unit where Murad worked."

Claudia stubbed her cigarette on the windowsill and binned the butt. She pulled Wallace's card out of her bag. "OK, thanks, Mark. I've got to go. I'll be in touch."

She cradled the receiver and stared at the business card. She should tell him of her suspicions about Oscar's death. Something weird was going on if they were trying to link Oscar to the bombing.

Chapter 12

Wallace shifted in the chair and scowled at his watch. Trenton's secretary sat across the foyer. Her fingers rattled her keyboard. Wallace wished he could type with the same agility.

"Can you buzz him, please, Martha? I've got an investigation to run."

Martha looked over her glasses at him and started to shake her head when the office door opened. Two men in expensive suits emerged. Trenton thanked them – smiley jovial remarks.

They glanced at Wallace as they made for the elevator.

He got up, muttering "At long last."

Entering the office, he closed the double doors behind him.

"You wanted to see me, sir?" He threw an obvious glance at the wall clock.

Stony-faced, Bernard Trenton smoothed his thinning grey hair and sat behind his large mahogany desk, incongruous amongst the steel-and-glass table, chairs and bookshelves. Two full sides of the room were windows giving a view over the city commensurate with the status of Trenton's position.

"Those men were from the offices of the late Adam Greene," he said. "Here on behalf of his widow. They want to help with the investigation."

"Oh yes?" said Wallace, supressing the urge to roll his eyes. "Did they return Greene's remains to the morgue?"

Trenton tapped his fingers on a manila file. "They gave me this. Thought it pertinent to the investigation. You are to arrest the subject of this dossier."

Wallace looked incredulous.

"Links to environmental terrorists and a personal vendetta against Greene and probably Sir John Christian." He pushed the file across the desk.

Wallace flipped it open, looked at the photograph. "I'll go through it and see what it says."

Trenton looked addled. "Just bring him in under the Terrorism Act and grill him for a month. See if he cracks."

Wallace gave him a deadpan look.

Trenton raised a hand. "I'm getting political heat from all angles on this thing. Between Downing Street wanting to keep the Emir of Fawala happy and Greene and Christian's people baying for heads on sticks." He blew out his cheeks.

"Not to mention the Russian ambassador; although to be quite honest I think *he's* just going through official motions – I'm not sure he really cares that Vasili Komarov was killed. Anyway, it's all a bloody disaster. And then I find out that you've sent forensic teams up to the Emir's stud farm and have Suffolk constabulary looking for a missing non-British-national. Please tell me you're just being thorough?"

"I told Tech to send you a copy of the blast footage. Have you watched it yet?"

Trenton grimaced, nodded.

"There's something about this environmental thing, though." Wallace shook his head. "I don't know. And if this guy," he nodded at the folder on his lap, "really is linked to it in some way. Well …" he trailed off.

"Just keep any mention of Al Fawala Stud and its owner out of the news. There are delicate matters of state involved here." He swore. "Why do they have to name their properties after themselves or their countries?"

"What matters of state?"

"Never mind."

"What d'you mean 'never mind'?"

Trenton looked out the window.

"*Huh.* Politicians," said Wallace. "Look, I told Newmarket to find this missing stud worker, Murad Kazemi, at all costs. He's the key to it all, I know it. Oh, and I've just had confirmation that traces of depleted uranium were found at the scene. Most probably used as shrapnel in the explosive device."

"Jesus Christ. So now *that's* being traded on the black market?"

"Apparently there's quite a bit of it lying about in recent warzones. I suppose it's being scavenged and sold off."

Trenton cradled his head in his hands. "So, anyone that was injured with shrapnel …"

"Studies show that there's no risk from proximal exposure … but …" Wallace hesitated.

"But?"

"I've been told that people hit by such toxic shrapnel could face organ failure and/or increased risk of cancer," Wallace finished.

"Christ. What about radioactivity?"

"It's only weakly radioactive. It's the toxicity of the metal that's the main concern. We've informed the hospitals treating the seriously wounded and I'll have people get in touch with everyone else at the scene: tell them to get checked out. That includes emergency service responders."

He sighed. "OK. Keep me informed."

Wallace turned to the door.

"I'm being summoned to Number Ten tomorrow morning," Trenton called after him, "for a joint press conference with the PM. He's pushing the environmental angle. We'll say we're looking for those still at large and appeal to people to contact the hotline. Now we'll have to alert the public that the terrorists have radioactive materials. Furthermore, I plan to mention the stud worker by name *and* say he's a non-national."

Wallace spun on his heel. "But that'll cause panic. Have people scared of half their neighbours. There'll probably be a rush on Geiger counters and Hazmat suits too, so I suppose someone'll profit, like always."

"You just arrest the guy in that file."

Wallace blew out a breath as he shut the doors.

*   *   *

Claudia left Crangate and drove home. She slid her car into the garage beside Tom's bicycle. The front door opened as she put her key up to the lock. Tom stood there with his arms out and black rings around his grey eyes. She dropped her bag and fell into him as if they'd both just returned from war.

He whispered in her ear. "I'll run you a bath and bring you a glass of wine."

"Oh, that would be divine."

While she sipped and soaked, she could hear him cooking dinner with the TV news on in the background. She wished he wouldn't do it to himself, but perhaps he really was getting over it. She couldn't remember the last time he'd woken up with a nightmare.

After dinner she rummaged in her bag and pulled out a fresh pack of cigarettes. Tom stared at her.

"I know, I know, but I had one last night to calm me down and now I just want them."

"It's OK, I get it."

"I'll quit again when all this," she waved a hand at the TV, "is over." She took a long drag and chewed her nails. "Apparently the police seem to think that Oscar and some workers in Al Fawala Stud had something to do with the bombing."

"Oscar? That's ridiculous. Who told you that?"

"Mark Gilford."

"What the hell has he got to do with it?"

"I was with him this morning when the lead investigator came to see him," she took another drag. "A man called Wallace. Anyway, I told Wallace what happened to me – why I left the sale. Then Mark mentioned that Oscar was their vet and Wallace seemed interested."

"What, just because he called you away to help him? I wish they'd stop adding one and one and getting three." He shook his head. "Then again, I suppose they've got to be clutching at straws over this thing. I'm surprised they haven't blamed it on the usual suspects."

Claudia knitted her brow.

Tom threw his hands wide. "Al-Q, ISIS … You know, this whole Nature's Wrath thing sounds like cover-up bullshit to me. I mean, there's no way. There's just no way."

"It rings fairly true to me. John Christian was killed and he's – was – the man pushing to start fracking for shale gas in Yorkshire. There were huge demonstrations up there last month. Christian stood to make billions if the government passed the bill. With him out of the picture, his company'll be in disarray, at least in the short term." She cocked a finger at him. "Don't forget, Greene was lobbying for Christian, here *and* in Europe. If you knock them off together, I suppose you kill two birds with one stone?"

"But an act of terror would set the green movement back years."

"That hasn't stopped them pulling stunts in the past."

"And what's that supposed to mean?" snapped Tom.

"Oh, I didn't mean your thing with Lady Alex. Give me a break, Tom." She rubbed her temples.

"Sorry, it's just the whole dirty episode came back to me today."

"I know, I know."

"Stunts or pranks are one thing, Claud, but blowing up a crowd of innocents just to get to two of them –"

"I see your point, but Komarov and the Emir were at that sale too – they could've been bonus targets. Komarov's father '*bought*' an electricity company after he left the army when the Soviet Union fell and Fawala has made money from oil and gas for decades." She threw a hand around the room. "Hell, it's pretty much paying for our lives."

They sat in silence a while until Tom put his arm around her and drew her close. "I just don't see it being enviro-terrorists," he said. "I mean, Lady Alex is about as militant-enviro as they get, but she was horrified by the bombing *and* the claim of responsibility."

Claudia nodded, not wanting to discuss it anymore. She yawned and dropped her head onto his chest.

He carried her up to bed, but she just couldn't fall asleep. Tom lay beside her in the dark, twitching. She stroked his forehead, hoping they'd both drop off. His eyes flicked around the ceiling and walls, checking shadows for ghosts. Sweat beaded on his forehead. Eventually, he closed his eyes and Claudia fell into a fitful sleep.

Chapter 13

Rotor blades thumped through the air as the helicopters descended on the village. Dust clouds rippled up around them. The gunships hovered at rooftop level like angry wasps. Multi-barrelled weapons roved as their controllers scanned the area through darkened visors, heads robotically arcing side-to-side.

Behind them, a fat-bellied troop carrier hovered low and dropped its rear open, spewing out soldiers like insects.

Women's burkhas billowed as they scrambled for doorways, dragging children with them. Some men scrambled, others stood, covered their faces from the whipping dust and stared at the invaders. Why should they run scared in their own village?

Troops fanned out. Taught. Itchy-trigger-fingers. They kicked in doors and barked demands over the rotor wash. Their interpreter was as terrified as the villagers. He could barely get his words out. They went house-to-house, room-to-room. They opened goat pens and shooed the animals out, which pissed off their owners. A stone flew out of nowhere and hit a soldier's leg.

Dust swirled. Soldiers shouted. Despite their training, they too were a hair's breadth from blind panic.

An old man shouted back and advanced on a soldier. There was a shot.

For a second everything seemed to freeze. The whole scene looked paralysed. Until the old man dropped to his knees.

Then someone else threw a stone and everything became a storm of lead, screams and dust.

He awoke sweating. He almost always woke when the bullets rained. Getting back to sleep would be impossible so he filled his mind with plans.

Chapter 14

The following morning the sun was edging over the horizon on the Newmarket heath as Ed Tomlinson rode at the head of the first lot like a cavalry officer leading his troops back to camp. Twenty-eight horses walked in a rough line behind him as their riders talked about the bombing. Everybody wore the blue-and-gold jackets of the Emir's racing colours with black armbands as a mark of respect for Michael Craddock's death. Though the general mood was subdued, the grooms were all glad Ed would take up the reins for the Emir and guarantee their jobs.

The horses reached the road crossing. Ed waited for traffic to stop, then let the string file past him over the road. Last of the lot was Secular Princess under Hanif Ali Mengak. Ed fell in beside the filly and watched her ears flick as she took in her surroundings without any nerves showing in her comportment.

"Well done, Hanif, you kept her beautifully settled this morning. She'll be spot on for Friday."

Hanif bowed from the neck. "It will give me a great thrill to lead her into the winner's enclosure."

"We could all do with a boost. I'm sure the guvnor'll be up there," he pointed his whip skyward, "giving her all the help he can."

Hanif looked at him strangely, his brow furrowed more than usual. "The horse will win if she is the best, fittest and most prepared in the race. Luck and energy may play a part, but there are no other factors involved."

Ed made a face.

Hanif's eyes flickered. "I am sure she will win for you, the stable, and the memory of Mr. Craddock."

Ed's face brightened.

They rode on down the horse-walk. Hooves clacked on the hard surface.

"Hanif, I'd really like you to stay here with this filly for the remainder of the season. You're good for her and I don't mind telling you that it was always the Emir's plan to send her over to Kentucky for the Breeder's Cup at the end of October. He's sponsoring a race there, so he wants to have a runner. You'd get a nice trip out of it."

Hanif's eyes sparkled. "Thank you, but I must experience yearling sale preparation at Crangate Stud. You see, I would like to see an English Thoroughbred auction sale. But I would also very much like to go with this horse to the

Breeder's Cup." He rubbed the grey filly's neck.

"*Mmm*. I think it's more important you stay here with her. Besides, if you want the trip, you'll have to put in the work."

Hanif shot Ed a hard glance. "I *have* put in the work." Then he looked away, as if remembering himself. "She was a nervous wreck when I arrived here. She can be handled by anyone now."

Ed blinked, surprised at Hanif's tone and command of English. He'd never heard the man speak more than a few words before today. All the other grooms gossiped about how shy he was.

"Well, I'll going to have another chat to Claudia Haverford and the Emir about it. I want you to remain with Secular Princess."

Chapter 15

Claudia looked at her watch through bleary eyes: nearly eight. She dragged herself out of bed and into the shower. Tom was already up and making breakfast. Usually they rose together, did stretches and yoga together for half an hour, but not today.

She'd just finished drying her hair when she noticed two cars pull up outside, blocking the short driveway.

She threw on her clothes, hurried downstairs and opened the door a crack. Two serious-looking men, in black anoraks over what appeared to be bulletproof vests, stood on the doorstep. She saw two more men disappear behind the garage and could've sworn they were carrying guns.

"Good morning, madam. Detectives Jenson and Steele, SO15." They flashed IDs.

She squinted at them. "Is this about my brother?"

Jenson's eyes narrowed. "Is Thomas Sunderland your brother?"

The bottom fell out of her stomach. "No, he's my partner. What's this about?"

"May we come in, please?"

"Oh yes, of course. Sorry."

Tom appeared in the hallway carrying two mugs. He froze. Looked for a second like he was going to throw the coffee at the police and run. Instead he put the mugs on the sideboard and rubbed his face with his hands.

"Thomas Sunderland," said Jenson, like he'd already recognised him.

Tom nodded and looked at Claudia. He opened his mouth, but no words came out.

The cops advanced on him, steel cuffs appearing in their hands. "We are arresting you under the Terrorism Act of 2006 …"

The policeman's words faded into background noise as Claudia struggled to stay on her feet. As she watched cuffs being snapped on and Tom being marched out of their house, she felt like a crutch had been kicked from under her. In the past 48 hours her organised, busy life had been blown to smithereens almost as surely as if she'd been caught in the blast.

She groped for her cigarettes. *Need to call that Wallace man, need to tell him a few things.*

Chapter 16

A sound technician fiddled with the microphone cluster on the lectern, making sure her channel's logo was prominent. She scurried away as the iconic black door opened and the policemen stood aside to let the Prime Minister and Metropolitan Police Commissioner onto the private street outside the seat of British government.

The whirr-snap of cameras drowned the city noise while flashbulbs strobed the scene. Reporters murmured into headphones, readying studio feed.

The Prime Minister stood at the lectern and grabbed its edges. Shoulders square, jaw cocked, trying to look like the nation's saviour. He waited for silence.

"I stand here this morning in the aftermath of the worst terror attack we have seen in over a decade. Our thoughts and prayers are with the victims, their families and loved ones. This was a callous, horrific act carried out against people who were enjoying a summer's evening at a horse sale. My predecessor was among the victims, as were several captains of industry and individuals whose charitable and philanthropic endeavours were in stark contrast to the barbarity which claimed their lives. The perpetrators of this atrocity clearly seek to disrupt modern society and strike at the traditions and pastimes which make Britain great. Neither us, nor our allies around the globe will ever be cowed by terrorism. The so-called Nature's Wrath group claim to be environmental activists, but don't let a name fool you: they are nothing more than murderous terrorists. Unfortunately, we have seen an increase in militant behaviour from environmental groups in recent months, but this atrocity takes their depravity – supposedly in the name of the planet –" he stopped abruptly and almost appeared to be stifling a smirk, which he turned into a clearing of his throat, "to new depths. I have been informed that some members of this terror group died in the attack, but I want to stress to every citizen of Britain: the organisers of this despicable act will be brought to justice swiftly and without mercy."

He paused for effect and wore a look that was trying to shout strength, but seemed to whisper arrogance.

"Furthermore, we are stepping up our security measures and increasing our defence budget as part of a new initiative in the global war against terrorism. The Defence Secretary will issue details of these measures as soon as they are devised. The British people can rest assured: my government and I will take any and all measures to keep this country safe and eradicate violent extremists, no matter what their ideology. To that end, I would encourage everyone to conduct their daily lives with vigilance against the all-engulfing threat of terrorism. I will now hand over to Commissioner Trenton. Good morning and God bless."

Trenton straightened his uniform, tugged at the peak of his hat and stepped up to the lectern, clasping his hands in front of him.

"Sadly, Monday evening's bomb attack is further evidence of the enduring, real, and very complex face of modern terrorist threats. We can no longer pigeon-hole certain groups and say 'they are terrorists'. We have to consider that a violent threat can come from anywhere at any time and be directed at anybody. As the Prime Minister said, we believe that the orchestrators of this atrocity are still at large and may be planning further attacks. Although we do have a suspect in custody, I would urge members of the public to contact the hotline if they believe they possess any information at all about the so-called Nature's Wrath movement, or about any suspicious activity in their vicinity. Television news bulletins have shown a photograph of a suspect still at large: twenty-four-year-old Murad Kazemi, a foreign national residing in Suffolk on a work visa. Counter-Terrorism Command are looking closely at Mr. Kazemi's movements prior to the attack and any known associates but, again, if anybody out there has any information at all about this man, please contact the hotline or your nearest police station. Members of the public and emergency services also need to be aware that the perpetrators of this crime may be in possession of toxic, radioactive materials." He nodded gravely. "Thank you very much and may God bless you all."

*   *   *

Claudia silenced the TV and paced the room, disgusted at the fear-laden speeches. And a nice little mention that more money would be spent on weapons and surveillance. What about simply stopping wars in other people's countries? She'd seen what conflict could do to people who were sent to fight. She knew bits about Tom's experiences, but Oscar had never spoken to her about Afghanistan although he'd confided in Tom a few times over the last couple of years. Tom had told her that most soldiers can only talk about war with other soldiers. If indeed they ever talked about it at all. She could only imagine how the natives of war-devastated countries would feel and how their trauma might turn into extremism.

So, of course, frustrated and demoralised environmentalists could reach the same conclusion: that their only option was violence in the face of global climate catastrophe.

When the police had driven off with Tom she'd called Wallace several times, but he hadn't answered. Then she'd called Julia and Bill to tell them she wouldn't be in until she knew what had happened to Tom.

She checked her phone again: nothing. She paced. And smoked.

Two hours later, the device hummed.

"Ms. Haverford, this is Chief Inspector Colin Wallace."

"Why have you guys taken Tom? When are you going to let him go?"

"Tom?"

"Thomas Sunderland. My boyfriend. Why have you taken him?"

"Your … Bloody hell, what the … He's waiting to be interviewed."

"Why? All that Adam Greene stuff is in the past."

She could hear a tapping sound on the line. Fingers on a tablet. She wondered if she'd somehow just made things worse.

"And while we're at it, I just can't believe my brother was involved in the bombing somehow," she blurted. "There's just no way."

Wallace took a long breath. "Why no way?"

"He once wore this country's uniform and did his bit to help prevent deaths from bombs. He was a vet for military dogs in Afghanistan, you know?"

Another sigh. "Look, I'm sorry, I know it can't be easy. But soldiers do crack. Just last year an American suffering from depression went on a shooting spree in his own base. And, well, let's not forget a certain Lee Harvey Oswald was a former Marine."

She opened her mouth, but no words would come. After a few sharp breaths, she managed, "And I can't see him injecting himself with drugs either."

Wallace grunted.

"He thought it was something only out-of-control

addicts did. So – so that means that somebody injected him to intentionally overdose him." Was that doubt dulling her words?

"Ms. Haverford –"

"Please, call me Claudia."

"Alright, Claudia. You told me your brother sounded bad on the phone and, in light of the bombing, I'm inclined to think that it's entirely possible he injected himself to commit suicide."

Claudia opened her mouth but couldn't utter a word.

"He served in Afghanistan, didn't he?"

"What's that got to do with anything?"

"Did he enjoy his time in the army?"

"Enjoy?" What a strange question. She wanted to tell him that it changed Oscar – and not for the better – but, after the speech she'd just heard on TV, she decided not to. "Yes, he did. He was doing what he loved: vet work."

"Really? So why would he resign his commission at the earliest opportunity, even after he got the posting he really wanted with the RHA in London?"

God, how did they know all this? "I don't see how that's relevant. Tom was right – you lot really are clutching at straws."

*   *   *

Bernard Trenton followed the Prime Minister into his private office.

There was a striking middle-aged woman with hawkish

eyes and salt-and-pepper blonde hair sitting on the sofa by the wall.

The Prime Minister slid behind his desk and Trenton forced a smile at the head of MI5. "Good morning, ma'am."

"Good morning." No smile.

Trenton didn't think Lauren Condicote would eat her young, but her husband *had* passed away suddenly last year. Lauren had never been a fan of Greene. Trenton wondered if she'd warmed to his successor. He sat opposite the Prime Minister.

"Sir, your plans for Adam Greene's state funeral can go ahead," he said. "But it is a pity that we have not been allowed to keep his remains in custody, along with all the other victims."

The Prime Minister narrowed his eyes. "Sometimes exceptions have to be made, Bernard." He pursed his lips. "However, on a more delicate note, this Kazemi you're looking for worked at Emir Rahim's Al Fawala Stud up in Newmarket."

"That is correct."

The Prime Minister glanced at Lauren. "Well, Bernard, make sure the connection to that man's stud farm stays quiet until after I meet with him. I don't want him all over the news with the implication that he's involved."

"They can't imply that."

"Oh, come on, Bernard. You know what the press are like. Keep a lid on it. I almost wish you hadn't put Kazemi's name out there, but I suppose in the interests of public safety … Anyway, thank you so much for coming in. Keep in touch."

Trenton had no choice but to leave.

*   *   *

When the door closed, the Prime Minister turned to the head of MI5. "Thank you for seeing me directly, Lauren. I know you usually report to the Home Secretary."

She nodded, expressionless.

"Any intelligence on this Nature's Wrath group?" he asked.

"Suspiciously little, I'm afraid."

"What does that mean?"

"It means they're too invisible. Active terror groups almost always leave a footprint on the Deep Web. If they use the surface Internet, they favour YouTube, chat rooms or social media. As far as GCHQ and our own sources have been able to ascertain, Nature's Wrath doesn't appear to exist. Either that, or they're operating with military standards of discipline and secrecy. Which would be unusual for a bunch of climate-change lunatics."

"Meaning what? That they've got ex-soldiers on the payroll? Bernard told me this morning that traces of depleted uranium were found at the scene. I mean, how the bloody hell does that happen?"

Lauren just about masked her surprise and anger. "Prime Minister, if this information had been shared directly with me as it was discovered, I would have answers for you by now."

He drummed his fingers on the desk.

Lauren stood. "I'll liaise with Wallace at SO15 about the DU."

"Thank you, Lauren."

She spun on her elegant heels.

"Oh, and Lauren?"

"Yes, Prime Minister?"

"If it wasn't Nature's Wrath, are we looking at misdirection by the usual suspects: ISIS, Al-Qaeda or other home-grown Islamic lunatics?"

"It's possible, sir. However, those groups usually jump up and down with glee after a successful operation. Added to which, none of our undercover agents reported any chatter or planning prior to this attack. Either it really is a highly secretive, disciplined, enviro-looney group or it's a false-flag operation."

"Oh come off it, Lauren. I want real answers. Don't tell me a woman in your position resorts to *conspiracy theories*."

Lauren's jaw clenched. "I thought conspiracies were a part of my job, Prime Minister?"

The door opened and a tall, moon-faced man entered. He smiled at Lauren as she left and closed the door behind her.

George Barnett, the Energy Secretary, sat opposite his PM. "John Christian's company's having a meeting to see who takes over but his sons are pushing to sell-up to an American."

"Really? Whatever happens, tell them to make sure it never comes out that Adam Greene had shares in it."

Barnett nodded. "The board of directors do want to know if we're going to push on with streamlining the application process for their experimental drilling despite the attack and last week's demonstrations?"

The Prime Minister pondered this for a moment. "Tell them we don't anticipate a change of policy, but that their choice of CEO will be an important factor in the government's decisions on energy production."

"I'll pass that on. On a separate note," he picked fluff off his trousers, "now that Komarov's dead, we'll have no choice but to deal with the Russians head-on."

"That'll get messy. I don't want to be seen conducting cosy, over-the-table business with them."

"I'll throw out a few discreet feelers, see if we can find another back-channel intermediary. Russian billionaires are almost ten-a-penny in London."

"Indeed they are, but most of them are camped here to *avoid* their president. No, let's keep the Russians at arm's length. What about the nuclear plant? Any progress?"

Barnett shook his head. "We're still waiting for the final go-ahead from the French, but now they're saying that even if they *can* build it for us with Chinese financing, it won't be ready for a decade."

"I imagine they're just stalling so they can sell us power from one of their north-coast plants. Anyway, with all the *hoo-ha* over John Christian's bloody fracking proposal and these enviro-lunatics blowing people up, I'm quite happy to delay construction of a nuclear power plant." The Prime Minister wagged a finger. "You know, when it happens, fracking won't be an instant miracle either."

"I agree, Prime Minister. I think we should stick with the devil we know. Which brings me to Fawala. We've never had any trouble with the Fawalans. They're easy to deal with and with only Emir Rahim and his brother in charge, the country is more stable than many of their neighbours. Less family infighting."

"Their father was a smart man having only two sons. Very unusual for that part of the world, but I suppose he learned from having seven elder brothers rule Fawala before him with all the bickering and mistakes that brought about." The Prime Minister looked at the painting of Margaret Thatcher on the wall. "And, in a stroke of luck, despite getting caught in the attack, Emir Rahim hasn't thrown all his toys out of his pram. We dodged a bullet there, I tell you." He drummed his fingers on the desk. "However, I'm concerned that Rahim's a bit of a law unto himself."

"Really?"

"Well, as you know, he's pushing prices up which goes against market trends. Furthermore, our ambassador tells me he's planning to make radical changes on the domestic front."

"Maybe we'd be better off if his brother seized power?" Barnett chuckled.

"Let's see how the meeting goes tomorrow."

*　　*　　*

During the local news bulletin, there was an appeal for information on a missing young man who worked in the Newmarket area. Des and Lee perked up at the mention of their town. A photo of Murad Kazemi was put up onscreen.

Des took a long pull of his joint and frowned. "Didn't we see him around in the pub or something?"

Lee shrugged. "Dunno, mate."

Des was muddled, but something nagged him about the photo of the youth. He just couldn't put his finger on it. Anyway, he wasn't about to call the hotline in his state.

Chapter 17

"What's your problem with Adam Greene anyway?" asked Gibson.

"I should have thought that was well documented at this stage," said Tom, leaning his elbows on the plastic table.

"Why don't you humour me?"

Tom rolled his eyes. "He sent us out to fight a bullshit war. Friends and comrades of mine got blown to bits. I got captured. And for what?" He grunted. "War on terror, my arse."

Gibson was tired of hearing this. "You were sent out there to defend your country. To keep us all safe from terrorists."

"Oh yeah? How's that working out then? Reckon we're safer?"

"Look, that's –"

"And how do you rationalise blowing the shit out of somewhere halfway around the world as *'defending our country'*?"

*   *   *

Gibson hit pause and stared at himself on screen. He regretted his outburst, but he was just so sick of bleeding hearts like Sunderland. Usually he could remain impartial, but he'd slipped up during that interview.

He fast-forwarded a few seconds then continued watching the footage. Wallace stepped out to smoke while he made a call.

Every now and then, Gibson glanced at the suspect through the two-way mirror.

Wallace returned, looking pensive.

"Alright, stop the tape. Let's go over it again."

"Captain Thomas Sunderland," Gibson jabbed a pen at the file as he spoke, "career soldier, served in Afghanistan as aide to Major-General Shaw. Their helicopter was shot down, the general was killed – highest-ranking soldier killed in action since World War II. Sunderland survived the crash and was held captive in Afghanistan for nearly two years before his rescue by special forces. Decorated, discharged, and spent another year in therapy for post-traumatic stress disorder. Subsequently arrested for throwing a condom full of shit at then PM Adam Greene at a remembrance service he had been invited to attend."

Wallace tapped at his iPad. "That was when he came out of the closet as an anti-war activist."

"You have to admit, he planned the prank pretty well, using his position as a war hero to get close to Greene at the service."

Wallace nearly smiled. "I'd love to have seen that tosspot Greene covered in shit. How come Sunderland didn't get jail?"

"Well, he probably should've. But his employer – that old enviro-looney-bird – what's her name?" He clicked his fingers.

"Lady Alexandra Telson."

"That's it. She hired a hot-shot lawyer who argued that torture in captivity and Afghan War Syndrome were contributing factors to Sunderland's state of mind. Greene decided a restraining order was sufficient punishment. Political compassion, I'd call it."

"You what?" Wallace rolled his eyes. "You don't think Greene actually gave a shit, do you? He just wanted to look magnanimous."

Gibson grunted.

Wallace cut him a sideways glance. "You voted for him, didn't you?"

Gibson looked at his notes. "So, fast-forward a few years. Shortly after Greene left office, Lady Telson accosted him and his wife at a charity fundraiser and swore that one day Greene would pay for his crimes."

Wallace sighed and turned to look at Tom through the two-way mirror: eyes flickering as he stared at the wall, head cradled in his hands.

"I just got off the phone with that dead vet's sister," said Wallace.

"Oh yeah?"

"She's having trouble accepting her brother's involvement."

"Understandable, I suppose."

"And you'll never guess who her boyfriend is." He flicked a glance at the glass.

It took Gibson a second, then he cocked his jaw at the file. "How did Greene's people miss that?"

"They couldn't have known it'd be relevant. Anyway, I checked: their house is in his name."

Gibson chewed his pen. "Don't you find it a bit of a coincidence that he's with the dead vet's sister?"

"You reckon they blew up a horse sale just to get Greene?" Wallace looked incredulous. "It's a far cry from a condom full of shit."

"Yeah, but the MO's the same. See, between his state-entitlements and private contractors, Greene's security was always water-tight. Social occasions however, have inherent difficulties for bodyguards because their presence needs to be invisible and, therefore, somewhat distant. So the sale was probably the best opportunity for someone to get close to Greene." Gibson looked at Sunderland through the glass. "He might've helped the vet get the DU? Helped him put the bomb together?"

Wallace looked unconvinced, uneasy. Something nagged at him. He made a call.

"Yeah, it's me. Any explosive residue on the vet's hands or car? Well, find out! Oh, and see if Thomas Sunderland and

Oscar Haverford served together in Afghanistan. And call GCHQ, ask them to hurry up on the location for the phone that rang in the detonation." He hung up. "Where the fuck do you get depleted uranium from anyway? I mean, I know they use it in certain types of ammunition, but soldiers – or ex-soldiers – can't just pocket bullets and stroll off a base with 'em. Anyway, Tech said the DU was shrapnel, like junk pieces or tips of already-fired rounds or shells."

Wallace's iPad pinged. He swiped, let out a whistle and showed the screen to Gibson.

"Holy shit," said Gibson.

"To be honest, I was just keeping *on high* happy and crossing my Ts hauling him in here. Only now we know he went to Sandhurst with his girlfriend's brother – our chief suspect."

"What now?"

"We've got twenty-eight days under the Terrorism Act, so there's no hurry to charge him with anything. We should have the residue results from the vet soon." He nodded at the glass. "Tell you what, bring *him* down to the machines and get every inch of him swabbed. Clothes, shoes, skin, under his nails, the lot."

Chapter 18

The following afternoon, Trevor Rafter reversed the tractor and trailer up to the piles of horse manure. He pulled the hydraulic lever and watched the trailer tip up, emptying its load onto the concrete at the foot of the last pile.

Steam rose from the mountains of manure. The muck heap wasn't due to be mixed with the composting machine for another two weeks but, with the sunny weather of the last few days, it was heating up. Trevor would get a severe bollocking from Mr. Gilford if the mass of rotting straw and horse dung caught fire again.

The composter was a like a cross between a combine harvester and a giant lawn mower. Trevor climbed into its cab, flicked switches and the hulking beast roared into life. Its wheels passed either side of a pile while the blades churned up the straw and dung, releasing heat, gas and speeding up the decomposition process. He looked down at the machine's hungry mouth and eased the throttle. The process couldn't be rushed.

Amongst the straw and dung getting sucked into the composter, he thought he saw a flash of blue and gold. It wasn't beyond a student to fling someone's work jacket into a trailer as a prank. Trevor certainly wasn't going to stop the machine just to fish it out. He'd ask about though: find out who was missing a jacket, try and discover the culprit. If poor old Roy was still alive, he'd know exactly whose jacket it was. He wiped a tear with his knuckle. Three days ago Roy was still alive.

As the garment disappeared underneath, he glimpsed something that definitely wasn't a jacket. There was a forced grinding from the motor.

"Bloody 'ell."

Trevor slapped his palm onto the emergency stop and jumped from the cab. He bent down and checked the intake. And promptly vomited. But not from the smell.

*   *   *

Mark Gilford floored his SUV, forgetting his golden rule forbidding anyone driving fast on the stud. He got to the muck heap, found Trevor in tears and shed a few himself when he looked under the composter. Then he called the local police and straight after that he called Chief Inspector Wallace.

Chapter 19

The gates of Downing Street swung open to let Rahim's motorcade slip into the Whitehall traffic. A pair of blacked-out Mercedes minivans carrying advisors and security sandwiched Rahim's silver Bentley.

He loosened his tie and undid his cufflinks. He always donned western dress when travelling, even for State events. He allowed himself a smile and picked up a phone.

"How did it go?" said the voice on the line.

"The British were easy. They agreed to the price rise and to the seven-year terms. We no longer have to worry about volatilities on the financial markets. And for the next phase, I already have somebody suitable in mind. I will make the visit in November. And don't worry, I will provide everything."

*　　*　　*

When Wallace and Gibson got to the scene, forensics had already cordoned off the muck heap and erected a large tent over the front of the composter.

Mark Gilford stood by the tape barrier, visibly shaking.

Wallace clapped a hand on his shoulder. The man jumped.

"Best thing you can do is go back to your office, have a cup of tea and calm down," said Wallace.

Mark nodded blankly and ambled towards his SUV.

The policemen ducked under the tape. The Scenes of Crimes Officer glanced at them as he snapped photos. "Alright, Chief Inspector?"

"I've been better. That's a hell of a contraption."

"Industrial composter."

"Who knew horse farms were this high-tech?"

"According to the manager, there's a few hundred horses here. So that's a lot of shit."

"Who found him?"

He nodded towards a sobbing man wrapped in a blanket sitting in the back of a police van. "Name's Trevor Rafter. In charge of the composter and spreading the shit back on the land when he's not driving horses around in a lorry."

Gibson ducked back under the tape and went to interview the man.

Wallace stepped closer to the body, wrinkled his nose.

The pathologist was in disposable white coveralls, face

mask and goggles, and crouched on hands and knees at the mouth of the composter. He glanced at Wallace. "It's fairly well rotten."

Wallace cocked his jaw at the body and hugged his iPad with both arms. "Watcha got, Sid?"

"Male victim. Early twenties, dark skin, black hair, wearing a blue-and-gold Al Fawala Stud uniform jacket. No head trauma. Legs are mangled to the knees by the machine. I'll start to remove him once you've checked the scene."

"Must be our guy Murad. Time of death?"

"Off the top of my head: couple of days, maybe more. All this steaming rotting shit's confusing me. I can't decide if it's preserved him or cooked him."

"Isn't that supposed to be your job?"

He rolled his eyes. "I'll have to check the Body Farm textbooks back in the office. It's not every day you get one dumped in a compost heap."

"Is it possible he died the same day as the vet and the bombing?"

Sid looked directly at Wallace. "More than likely, but I'll know more when I get him on a slab and PM him."

"You checked his pockets?"

He shook his head. "Was waiting for you."

"Go on, then."

Sid pulled four plastic bags from a dispenser box, opened them and sat them on the straw. He turned on a voice-recorder clipped to his suit and spoke as he worked.

"Outside pockets of victim's jacket empty. Opening zip. Two inside pockets. One containing a mobile telephone."

He fished it out, dropped it in a bag and sealed it. "Other pocket." He withdrew his hand. "Fawalan passport." He flicked through the document. "In the name of Murad A. Kazemi. Work visa on page seven." Dropped it in a bag. "Along with a twenty-pound note and a small remote-control device."

"Must be his zapper for the back gate," said Wallace.

"Hang on, something else here." Sid turned on his head-torch, picked up a forceps and held the pocket wide with his other hand. He inserted the forceps, grabbed the object and carefully withdrew. A small syringe with a tiny, uncovered needle was clamped in the forceps.

Wallace narrowed his eyes.

Sid dropped it in a bag and probed again with the forceps. "No needle cover in there … Jeans' pockets empty …" he felt under the body, "back ones too."

Wallace put his iPad under one arm and snapped on a glove. "Right, give me the bags. I'll get that phone down to Tech. Cheers, mate. Oh, and –"

"Let me guess: you want the post-mortem done an hour ago?"

"You know me too well, Sid."

He arrived at the van as Gibson was finishing his interview.

"You'll be summoned to Newmarket station later today to make a formal statement. Once again, thank you for your co-operation, Mr. Rafter," said Gibson in a soothing voice, placing a card on the man's lap. "If you should think of anything else …"

Trevor just stared at it. "Twice this week I've been interviewed after the death of someone I knew. What else is there to say?"

They left him and made for the car. Wallace put the evidence bags on the central console.

Gibson eyed them. "Don't tell me Kazemi was a junkie?"

"Who carries their passport at work?" asked Wallace.

"It was probably his only form of ID."

"Yeah, but his visa's in it, so if he lost it or it got nicked, then he'd be in the shit." Wallace grimaced.

Gibson stared at the bags for a beat, then looked at the composter. "You reckon he was dumped there to let the body rot for a few weeks before it got run through that thing?"

Wallace put the window down and lit up. "If you're the vet and you've got this poor sap to help you with the bomb and you need to get rid of him afterwards, this is your ready-made disposal unit. You'd expect that his passport would get mangled too."

"So why hide the body at all if you're going to do yourself in?"

"Fuck knows. Maybe the vet wasn't planning to off himself initially. Maybe he was just high – probably needed to be to get it done. Or maybe he got high with the vic to celebrate then …" Something nagged at Wallace for an instant, then it was gone. "Anyway, I'm damn sure that's the phone used to activate the bomb."

"Chalk it down it is. I'll give it to Tech when we get back."

"Get it printed and," Wallace tapped the syringe, "we need that checked ASAP. We'll swing by the locals on our way through the town. Collect the syringe they found in the vet's car. Compare analysis."

Gibson started the engine.

Wallace's iPad pinged as they drove past paddocks of mares and foals playing in the glorious summer sun. He tapped at it, opened the attachment and screwed up his mouth as he read.

"Oscar Haverford's hands were negative for explosive. So was his car, but there were traces of DU residual radioactivity. Very weak, as you'd expect, but there all the same. Oh, and turns out he died of a massive ketamine overdose after all. Would've made him pass out and then stop his heart peacefully. We'd better have a look at his house. Fuck, I can't believe I didn't send a team there before now."

"If Oscar did Murad in, cleaned his flat and offed himself after rescuing his sister," said Gibson, "and Kim and Danny were killed in the blast, then who called in the claim of responsibility?"

"Good question," hissed Wallace. "Phone a friend or ask the audience?"

Wallace dialled Trenton: let *him* figure out what to release to the press. After all, he was the one having to deal with the fucking politicians.

Gibson used GPS to find Oscar's house while Wallace relayed everything to Trenton. They parked up behind a red Audi.

"Nice bachelor pad," said Gibson, crunching across the

gravel. "Must be good money in getting thoroughbreds pregnant."

The door to the converted barn was ajar. Wallace pushed it open with his iPad. "Hello? Anyone at home?"

Claudia appeared from the kitchen, carrying a cardboard box. "What are you doing here? I thought you were busy interrogating Tom?"

"Interviewing, Claudia. Interviewing."

"Does that mean you've let him go?"

"I'm afraid not. And I have to ask you not to touch anything else in this house either. It is now considered a crime scene."

The box slipped from her hands, its contents clattered on the floor. "Come again?"

Gibson snapped on gloves and walked into the kitchen.

Wallace hesitated a beat. "At present, the evidence points to your brother being a major player in the conspiracy to bomb the horse sale."

"*You can't be serious! What evidence?*"

"Normally, we can't discuss details, but it'll probably end up with the press soon anyway, so …" He screwed up his face.

Claudia stared.

"Video footage of the Orangery revealed that the mare literally exploded."

"*Meaning?*"

"That the bomb was inside her." Wallace arched a brow.

Claudia wobbled. The room spun. She ended up pressed against the wall, blinking, open-mouthed.

"We also found evidence that the device had been in his car."

"And what about that syringe?" she said, her mind whirring, grasping. "There's something else going on here. It can't be as straightforward as that. It just can't."

Wallace sighed.

Claudia stuffed a cigarette in her mouth and offered him the box.

He took one. "Thanks. Look, I just got the full results from your brother's body. He did die of a ketamine overdose. By all accounts it would've been a very peaceful death."

She took a long drag and closed her eyes for a moment. "I can imagine. I'd seen him high on the stuff a long time ago. He just fell into a kind of happy stupor. But he dried it out and snorted it back then."

"And he did have a mark on his right arm that could be consistent with an injection, but his nasal membranes were coated with crystal residue too, so there's no way to determine how the fatal dose was administered."

"Oh, Oscar!" Tears welled up. She flicked the butt in the fireplace and rummaged for a tissue.

Wallace inspected her.

"You might as well know," he said. "We found Murad Kazemi, this morning."

"Oh, good!" She'd go and ask him if he was the dealer *Mouse*. "Did he give you any new information?"

"He was found dead in the muck pit on Al Fawala stud."

"*What?*" Another death. Her mind spun. "Poor kid. How did he die?"

127

"He was murdered. It'll be announced within the –"

"So whoever murdered him could've killed Oscar too?"

Wallace took a long drag and shook his head. "The evidence leads us to believe that your brother was working with Kazemi and a couple of other members of staff at the stud and that they carried out the attack in coordination with another individual currently in custody."

"When you say 'another individual' you mean Tom? My boyfriend?"

Wallace nodded. "It is thought that the motive for the attack was extreme anti-war protest as much as it was environmentalist."

Claudia tried to process it all. Both men close to her gone, in one way or another. Supposedly terrorists. She shook her head. Oscar's voicemail replayed in her mind. *"Claud, pick up. Please. Call me before it starts. You need to peel yourself away from your job for a second. Get out of there. You've got to get out of there. I need you. I've – I've – I don't know what to do. I need you, Claud. I've done –"* She covered her face with her hands.

After she recovered, she looked at Wallace.

"Over the years, I tried to get him to talk to me about the war. Told him it was better than keeping it all bottled up. He talked to Tom once or twice, but ... but ..." her voice trailed off. "Look, he was only over there for a year or so, and he was only supposed to be looking after dogs, but ..." Again, she trailed off, sobbing. "Tom always said that we were only there because of our politicians and an oil pipeline: no just reason."

Wallace looked tetchy. "And is there a just reason for a bomb at a horse sale?"

"Of course not … I lost friends too, you know." She reached for another smoke.

Her phone rang. It was Mark.

"Mark, I've just heard. I'm with the police now. It's so terribly sad. How are you holding up?" She looked at Wallace as she spoke. "Yes, of course. I'll call him straight away." She hung up.

Wallace arched his brow.

"I have to call the Emir. All information from his stud or racing stables has to go through me."

"Even when there's a dead body found?"

"He's a busy man, he can't have dozens of people calling him when one will do."

Wallace shook his head. "The rich really are on another planet."

Claudia walked outside to make the call.

She broke the awful news to Rahim.

"That is very tragic. I don't really know what else to say. Please tell Mark that I will see to it that the young man's family in Fawala are informed and lavishly compensated."

"Yes, sir."

"And how are you managing, Claudia? Will I still see you at the races tomorrow?"

"I took today off from Crangate to start packing my brother's things, but now the police want to process his house because they suspect *him* of planting the bomb. *Inside your mare.*"

"What did you say?"

She told him what Wallace had said.

Silence on the line.

"Are you still there, sir?" said Claudia.

"Yes, I just cannot quite believe it."

"Neither can I. My boyfriend's been taken in for questioning too." She chewed her lip. "Look, if you want to change your mind and terminate our agreement to avoid a scandal, I'll understand."

"Don't be ridiculous, Claudia. Why on earth would I do that? You are an intelligent, dedicated woman. I like having people such as you around me. If there is anything I can do for you, please know that you only have to ask."

"Thank you, sir." A long breath leaked out of her. "With everything that's happened this week, work's all I have left."

"Then I will see you tomorrow at Ascot. We will have a winner to boost everybody's morale."

Claudia turned and looked at the house. She might as well just leave it to the police, go home and try to sleep.

Chapter 20

The following morning, Claudia woke on her sofa with a headache, an empty bottle of wine and an overflowing ashtray.

She scrolled through her phone and scanned the morning news. Headlines blared Murad's murder, her brother's photograph, mention of a suspect in custody. Radical tendencies, environmental extremists; brain-damaged war veterans and *blah, blah, blah*. She closed the app.

A few hours later, showered and dressed in black, with make-up hiding dark rings around her eyes, she was as ready as she'd ever feel.

Usually she loved big race meetings, but today felt like her first day back in the saddle after a fall. She held the car keys and hovered in the doorway. She supposed she wasn't the only one who felt like this in the racing world. Not this week.

She went to Crangate and collected Julia, who looked a radiant widow. All black dress and tanned limbs.

"Seb wouldn't want me to look dowdy at Ascot. Not ever," she said, apparently reading Claudia's thoughts. "I wish I had your legs though."

Claudia half-smiled.

As they drove, she told Julia about Tom, Murad's body, the police conclusions about Oscar and her call to the Emir.

"Whatever your brother did, it's nothing to do with you." Julia looked at her, watched her knuckles grip the wheel. "And it sounds as if the Emir can see that too. If you get any shit from anyone in racing, let me know and I'll give them an earful. So, chin up and on we go."

Claudia smiled tightly.

"I tell you one thing though," said Julia. "We deserve a bloody glass of bubbly when we get there."

Upon arrival, Claudia's car was given the once-over by police with sniffer dogs patrolling the car parks. Special response units and more dog handlers funnelled all racegoers towards the metal detectors and X-ray units installed at the entrances. More squads marched down and back on every floor of the Grandstand. Weapons rustled against Kevlar vests. Even the Royal Procession was flanked by police outriders with a helicopter overhead as it arrived from Windsor Castle.

Claudia stood on the balcony of the Emir's box, sipped her second glass of Dutch courage and looked at the lawn below, barely visible under the throngs of racegoers and roving police patrols. The day lacked the usual atmosphere. People were calm, serious. Sombre. The press would probably call it "*dignified British defiance*". It was unlike anything she'd ever experienced on a racecourse.

Down on the turf, the runners for the Albany Stakes cantered down to the starting stalls.

The Emir, Ed Tomlinson and Julia joined her on the balcony.

"Sorry, sir. I just couldn't face the parade-ring preliminaries," said Claudia.

"You have nothing to apologise for. However, if the filly wins, I must insist that you and Julia accept the trophy." Rahim's smile dazzled under his dark eyes.

Claudia brightened. "I think I could manage that." She pulled a cigarette out of her bag.

Rahim stepped back inside to watch the race on TV.

Ed sidled up to Claudia. "I'd love one of those for my nerves."

She offered the pack.

"Thanks. Afterwards, I'll introduce you to Hanif – Secular Princess's groom."

"Oh, right. I'd almost forgotten about him."

"Look, I *really* don't want to lose him." He darted a glance through the doorway at Rahim. "Do you think you could ask the Emir, one more time, if he can stay?"

"I'll see what I can do, but you know what he's like when his mind's made up."

Ed nodded. "Thanks."

Down on the track, the starting gates clattered open and the crowd roared as fifteen two-year-old fillies erupted onto the track. Secular Princess was settled against the rail, her jockey's hands dropped, encouraging her to relax.

"Good," said Ed, his binoculars glued to the action.

Claudia's heart thumped. She hardly ever got nervous watching a horse that she'd selected with Seb, but today emotions seemed heightened, exaggerated. She heard herself shout, "*Come on, come on!*" She put down her glass and slapped her rolled-up race card off the balcony railing.

The runner to Secular Princess's outside faltered and edged towards the centre of track. The filly shot through the gap and darted two lengths ahead of the pack in a matter of strides, ears pricked, enjoying herself. She flashed across the line alone. The stands shook with applause.

A tear fell down Claudia's jaw and dripped off her chin. She looked in her bag for sunglasses.

Ed went slightly floppy as the tension left his body. When the Emir appeared and slapped him on the back, he nearly fell over.

"Congratulations, my new team! Out of the ashes of tragedy rise new beginnings!"

Claudia smiled below her large shades. "I'm sure Oscar and Seb were up there kicking her on for the line."

"Michael too," said Ed.

Rahim narrowed his eyes. "Up where, exactly?"

Claudia and Ed both stared.

"Perhaps their energy was simply redispersed in our favour?" said Rahim.

Claudia smiled. "I'd like to think so."

They hurried out to the corridor and into an elevator under the watchful eyes and guns of a special-response team.

When the lift opened at ground level, Rahim's entourage formed a perimeter around him, while Claudia, Julia and Ed followed. People parted to let them cross the tarmac. Policemen fixed them with stares. Claudia flicked furtive glances into the crowd. Thought she caught a few stares and whispers.

A bowler-hatted official opened the gate to the parade ring. They walked across to the area reserved for the winning horse. The large oval parade ring was slightly sunken into the ground and surrounded by viewing areas which were now full to capacity, giving it the feel of a small stadium. Claudia and Ed stood near the presentation podium, which was flanked by two policemen. Everyone waited for the victorious athlete to arrive.

Claudia had attended Ascot before, but had never been in the winner's enclosure. That was something Seb had always kept for himself and Julia. She felt a bit like she was walking on his grave. She'd have loved Tom and Oscar to be somewhere in the stands. Watching, waiting to celebrate.

The Ascot Chairman appeared and offered congratulations to Rahim.

"Thank you," said Rahim. "Which member of the Royal Family will be presenting the prize?"

"Ah. The Prince of Wales *was* scheduled but, in light of Monday's tragedy, Mrs. Greene is in the royal box today."

He glanced over Rahim's shoulder. "Oh, here she is now. Let me introduce you."

Claudia spun on her heel and involuntarily backed away from the tiny woman. Amelia Greene wafted through the gateway, steely eyes darting on her pinched face. She was surrounded by sharp-looking men with earpieces who scanned the crowd like robots.

Claudia wondered if the taxpayer still had to shell out for Mrs. Greene's protection.

"She looks bigger on TV," said Ed.

Her guards fanned out as she gave Rahim a hint of a curtsey.

Then she shook Julia's hand, patted it with her other. Greene wore the same penetrating, concerned look that her late husband had perfected during his time in office.

She moved on to Ed, who kept beaming. Even his eyes lit up.

Claudia shook the woman's hand. Detached, looking through her. Not hearing the polished smiley words. She watched the woman mount the podium and inspect the silver trophy.

Would another condom full of shit be worth Claudia's career, if she had it in her handbag? Would they lock her up without charge like Tom?

"The filly should be here by now," said Ed, watching the tunnel entrance.

A second later, two more policemen emerged from the darkness just ahead of the heaving, sweating grey thoroughbred. Her jockey pumped his fist at the crowd, which responded with polite applause. The filly was led across the lawn by a diminutive leather-faced man wearing a flat tweed cap and an open-necked shirt under a half-zipped-up bomber jacket. Crooked teeth escaped through a huge grin as his dark eyes darted over the scene.

Amelia Greene's guards stared like they'd never seen a horse or a groom before.

Ed bounded over to his charge, high-fived the jockey and slapped the groom on the back. He patted the filly's slick sweaty neck as she sucked lungfuls of air.

The jockey slid off and unsaddled, giving a breathless report to Ed before jogging off to weigh-in.

Greene's guards twitched, stared. Claudia imagined men like this would consider an incident-free day an anti-climax.

The swarthy groom walked the horse in small circles. Ed glanced at her heaving flanks and flaring nostrils then tapped the guy's shoulder.

"Hanif, this is Claudia Haverford – you'll be working for her from Monday."

"Congratulations, Hanif," she said. "You've done a super job with this filly."

Hanif looked blankly at Claudia, his craggy mahogany features expressionless. The filly whinnied and tossed her head. Hanif turned her in another small circle. He began murmuring, almost as if in prayer.

"OK, Hanif," said Ed. "Take her away."

As Hanif turned her away, he took a hand off the lead rope and slipped it inside his jacket. His eyes darted about.

One of Greene's guards raised his hand to his chin. Moved his lips. In a blur of movement, two others whipped their heads to Hanif while three more bee-lined for the podium. Rahim's men reacted to the rush of Greene's guards and swarmed around the Emir, brushing Claudia aside. She stumbled and nearly fell over.

The filly's ears pricked. She snorted loudly. The men grabbed Hanif's arms, pulling his hand into view. He clung to the lead rein, but the filly panicked and reared, tugging the leather lead through his fist. She spun and kicked out with her hind legs. One of Greene's men got both barrels in the chest, sending him backwards with a loud crack, as if he'd been shot.

Rahim's men rushed him away, knocking Claudia and Julia over like skittles. Amelia Greene was swiped from the podium and carried across the lawn like a rugby ball.

The crowd stood in shocked silence until someone screamed. Then they ducked, dived, fell, shouted, scrambled. Policemen scattered, trying to harness the panic. Special response officers fanned out at the top of the viewing area, weapons trained on parade ring below.

Amidst all this, Secular Princess pranced across the grass, eyes bulging, tail in the air.

Claudia picked herself up and saw a guard holding Hanif down, while another carefully unzipped his jacket and opened his shirt.

Hanif didn't struggle, nor did he appear angry. His muscles relaxed and he looked resignedly at Claudia. Claudia gave him a concerned look and he blinked slowly in acknowledgement. Almost as if he'd been through this kind of thing before.

The kicked guard lay prone but his colleagues ignored him.

The guards accosting Hanif seemed relieved and disappointed all at once. Four policemen marched up to them and words were exchanged.

The policemen helped Hanif up, patted him down and spoke into their radios. The Ascot Chairman reappeared, looking about to either explode or burst into tears. A policeman reached into Hanif's inside pocket and produced a passport and what looked like a folded handkerchief. More talk into his radio.

Most spectators had dashed away but those fallen or remaining now began to realise the panic was over. Men got up, helped women and brushed themselves off. Special-response teams relaxed a notch and chattered into radios.

Claudia's attention switched to Secular Princess prancing around the parade ring, dodging the efforts of the stewards to grab her reins.

The more the filly kept prancing, the more sweat dampened Ed's hairline.

Keeping an eye on the armed cops in the viewing areas, Claudia slowly approached the police with her palms up. They were now demanding IDs from Greene's guards.

"Excuse me, officer," said Claudia, butting in. "Are you finished with this man?"

Heads whipped towards her. A cop with a sergeant's

pips on his epaulettes eyed her up and down. "And you are?"

"I represent this man's employer, His Highness the Emir of Fawala. This man is needed to catch that loose horse before it or anyone else gets hurt."

The coppers exchanged looks. One spoke again into his radio and pocketed Hanif's passport. "Alright, catch your horse. But two officers will stay with you, and bring you to the mobile command unit afterwards to answer a few questions."

Hanif nodded and dashed a few steps. Then he slowed abruptly, hunched his back, turned sideways to the filly and lowered his head. He spoke in what Claudia presumed was his native tongue and whistled in a calming rhythm as he sidled towards the filly. The horse flicked her ears, slowed and arched her neck sideways, inspecting Hanif. He grinned and kept making soothing sounds. Everyone in the vicinity stopped and stared at the sight of this tiny man subtly calming half-a-ton of nerves.

Secular Princess kept walking, but now she circled Hanif, snorting and sniffing the ground. He pivoted on his heel so she never got a front view of him. After a couple of circles, she stopped near his shoulder. He calmly reached for the lead rope and closed his hand around it. The filly blew a breath on his sleeve and he slowly put a palm to her forehead and rubbed. She leaned into his caress and visibly relaxed.

There was a collective sigh of relief. Someone started clapping and after a few moments, everyone watching joined in.

The Ascot Chairman shouted: *"Bravo, that man! Bravo!"*

Hanif led the horse away, accompanied by two policemen.

Everyone wondered what would happen next.

The Ascot Chairman was given a microphone and his plummy tones announced it had been a false alarm and that the presentation would now proceed as normal. As would the rest of the afternoon. People returned to the viewing areas and applause echoed around the whole place.

Julia muttered obscenities and Rahim reappeared with his entourage. Claudia and Julia stepped onto the podium. A moment later, a clearly fuming Amelia Greene arrived with her guards a few extra steps behind. She mounted the podium, switched on a beaming smile and hoisted the elegant silver cup. Julia accepted it with a warm smile and uncharacteristically teary cheeks. Amelia Greene glanced at Claudia and her smile slipped. She mouthed a few words to Julia. Claudia couldn't make out the words and she didn't want to get closer to the Greene woman. Julia held the cup aloft for the cameras and Claudia stretched a hand to its plinth, mustering a smile.

Then Ed accepted the winning trainer's memento and they all left the podium.

On to the next race.

Rahim's men opened their perimeter and Julia offered him the cup.

"Please, keep it in the office at Crangate."

"That's very kind."

Ed shot a look at Claudia.

141

She took the cue. "Sir, I wonder if I might persuade you to allow Hanif to stay with Secular Princess for the remainder of the season? It could only help her to have the same groom for the rest of the year."

Rahim looked at Ed.

"Sir," said Ed, "Hanif has done a wonderful job with her and I'd like that to continue right up to, and including, the Breeders' Cup in Kentucky. As you'll have seen just now, he really has a way with her."

Rahim squinted. "I'm afraid that it is his express wish to work with yearlings. And I have an obligation to my late father to look after Hanif."

Claudia was wrong-footed by his reply. She waited for an elaboration. None came.

"Can't he prepare yearlings next year?" said Ed.

The Emir stared hard.

Claudia and Ed nodded in unison.

"But," said Rahim, "in the interest of the horse, I will compromise. Hanif will prepare the yearlings at Crangate, then he will resume work with you in time to travel with the filly to Kentucky."

"Well," said Ed, "it's not ideal."

Rahim stared again.

"As you wish, sir."

"Oh, and more thing."

"Yes, sir?"

"I think you should make arrangements to fly her to Kentucky at least two weeks ahead of the race, instead of the usual four or five days. It will give her more time to settle in."

"That's a very good idea, sir."

"Furthermore, I feel it would be better for her to be stabled at my farm. There is a training track there and a swimming pool. It would be quieter and nicer for her, don't you agree?"

Ed pondered it for a second. "Well, if she could be trained as normal, I don't see why not. The press and the work watchers won't like it though. They love to see the runners working on the track in the days before the races. *Breakfast with the Stars*, they call it."

"I care about my horse, not the media. Anyway, I do not want her stabled in one of those filthy, depressing old trackside barns."

Ed chuckled. "I couldn't agree more."

"Well, I'm glad that's settled," said Claudia.

Ed ran off to catch up with Hanif and his horse. Rahim's men escorted everyone else to the elevator. Claudia checked her watch and glanced at Julia as the doors slid open.

"Sir, I'd like to get back to Crangate," she said. "That winner's enclosure ordeal has drained me."

Rahim laughed. "It was what you would call a storm in a teacup. I will stay to watch the remaining races and hopefully no more over-eager security guards will molest us. Thank you both for coming. Oh, and by the way, perhaps Case has let you know that I will be sponsoring a race at the Breeders' Cup?"

"He did mention something. Which one?"

"The one Secular Princess will run in."

"That'll be fun if you can win it."

"That is the idea."

Rahim stepped into the elevator. "Claudia, I almost forgot. I will go back to Fawala tomorrow to attend to a matter of state. You may reach me on my mobile as usual."

The doors slid shut.

*   *   *

On the way home Claudia exhaled smoke out the cracked window. She could feel Julia's icy gaze.

"You know," Julia said eventually, "Mrs. Greene had a little word with me on the podium. Bloody inappropriate, but what else would you expect?"

"And?"

"She said: *'Whoever killed my husband was obviously targeting His Highness as well. Do tell him to be careful. That Haverford girl's lunatic enviro-extremist boyfriend is capable of anything.'*"

Claudia felt her hands shudder and the car veered slightly. "I fucking wish they'd leave Tom alone. There's no way he had anything to do with it, regardless of what the police think."

"Has he been released yet?"

"*Huh!* He's in a black hole wearing an orange jumpsuit, for all I know."

"Have they charged him?"

She shook her head. "Not as far as I know."

"And what about your brother? Do you think he could have had a part in it?"

"According to the police, there's not much doubt." Her shoulders slumped. "He usually kept things bottled up until some kind of trigger made him explode. That was how his addiction worked anyway."

*   *   *

An hour later, Ed paced outside the police mobile command unit. He already had to send the lorry on its way so the filly didn't start pawing the ground and worrying. Eventually, the door opened and an officer preceded Hanif down the steps.

"You responsible for him?" said the officer, looking Ed up and down.

"Well, I'm his employer, but he's a grown man responsible for himself."

The policeman gave Ed a look that was almost a snarl. He held Hanif's passport and for a split second looked like he was going to give it to Ed, before nearly tossing it at Hanif. "Thank you for your cooperation," he muttered, like the words were making him sick.

Hanif bowed from the neck.

Ed checked his watch. "Right, let's hit the road."

Pulling into traffic, Ed asked, "Did they give you much shit?"

"They catalogued, photographed and printed me. They checked everything against my visa, entry scans and prints." He shrugged. "They were just doing their jobs."

Later, when they'd escaped onto open road, Ed asked

Hanif what he thought of Royal Ascot races. When there was no reply, he glanced at him. Hanif was sound asleep, head against the window. Tweed cap pulled over his eyes.

Chapter 21

Wallace was hunched over his desk, scrolling through documents on his iPad. He rubbed his eyes, stood and paced. The bomb had definitely been in the vet's car, but he couldn't have assembled it in the vehicle and his house had turned up clean like his body and clothes. So, Murad must've done all that – or they did it together and then scrubbed and disinfected his flat.

Something wasn't quite right. Wallace stared out at a sunny London evening. He actually preferred it when the city was cold and grey. When it was warm, it was like a stinking pressure cooker.

Gibson appeared with tea, biscuits and a breezy smile. "Weather's supposed to hold for a week or so. Be nice to have a decent summer. Think I'll take the kids to the park at the weekend."

"What fucking weekend? Be lucky if we get Sunday off at this rate."

"Cheer up. I've got a good one for you. Just got off the phone with a mate of mine on duty at that Royal racing conflab at Ascot. You know, the one everyone's been shitting themselves about cos the Queen won't hear of it being called off."

An exasperated sigh. "Get to the point, Gibson."

"Yeah. Well, anyway, Amelia Greene was there presenting a cup – to the Emir of Fawala, by the way."

"Fuck me, that man's everywhere this week."

Gibson cocked his head to one side. "Yeah, I thought that. Funny coincidence, but there you are."

"For the love of God, get fucking on with it, Gibson."

Gibson recounted a version of the parade-ring drama.

Wallace let out a wheeze of a laugh. "Private security twats! And to think, some people'd like to make *that* the future of law enforcement."

"Anyway, our boys calmed it all down and checked the groom. My mate interviewed the groom afterwards. Clean as a whistle. Fawalan passport, current visa, been in the country several months. Articulate, very good English. Earning a regular wage, bank-account savings, the lot."

"So why did the dickheads jump on him?"

"Wearing a bulky jacket on a hot day. Reached into it, apparently."

"Bunch of wankers."

"That Haverford bird was there too."

"Really?"

"Yeah, she spoke to my mate. Basically demanded he let the groom go and catch his horse."

"Did she now?"

"Do you reckon she knew about her boyfriend's involvement?" asked Gibson.

"Probably still thinks someone did her brother in." Wallace glanced at his pinging iPad, tapped and read the mail. "*Fuck*. Right, Murad Kazemi's body was supposedly negative for explosives too, unless all the rotting shit disrupted the swab analyser. Anyway, whatever, it means *he* can't have assembled the fucking thing either."

"What about whatshisname?" Gibson scanned the mesh of photos and information pinned to the board behind Wallace's head. "Yeah – Danny."

"Nah. If it was him, why put it in the horse? Why not just strap it on yourself and Bob's your uncle? No. Far as I can see, Kim and Danny knew nothing about it. They were just cannon fodder."

"*Hmm*." Gibson looked at the photo of Tom on the wall. "I know Greene's people are a bunch of arseholes, but …"

Wallace arched his brow. "They might just have thrown us a bone giving us him?"

Gibson launched into his nodding.

Wallace screwed up his face. "You know, this whole thing might not be about the environment at all." He spun his chair to face the board. "At least not in the way we think."

Chapter 22

The first rays of morning sun reflected off the Emirate of Fawala's official state Boeing Business Jet as it made its final approach.

Rahim scanned the décor in his private cabin. His father had bought this plane in the first year of his short reign. At the time, young Rahim had considered it an incredible extravagance, but by today's standards it was small and almost low-key. The last time Jabbar used it, he had complained that an upgrade was long overdue.

The wheels thudded onto the tarmac at Fawala's international airport and the plane taxied into its private hangar.

Rahim disembarked into a plain grey Mercedes people-carrier with blacked-out windows. His entourage filled another just like it and the vehicles slipped out the cargo entrance of the airport.

The asphalt shimmered as the sun rose. The road sliced through the desert, towards the coast and Daralaam, the Emirate's only city. After ten kilometres, arid sand and rock gave way to the lush turf of a 36-hole golf complex looking as green and clipped as Augusta during the Masters. Willow trees swayed in the breeze as irrigation sprinklers soaked the grass.

Directly after that came the racecourse. A 2000-metre turf track encircled another of a state-of-the-art synthetic surface. Beside it were low-slung stable complexes shaded by hundreds of towering palms. The track's enormous grandstand glowed in the sunlight. Beside that was a six-star hotel, looking like a gargantuan cruise ship that had been dropped into the sand.

Next came a sprawling development of shiny villas with tiled roofs and more tall palms poking over the sandstone perimeter wall. Rahim knew the wall was less about security and more about concealing the opulence and indolence inside. They passed the community's bunker-like guardhouse as heavy gates slid open to let a Rolls Royce glide onto the road.

His tiny country had several such developments, including one constructed on an artificial island and populated almost exclusively by wealthy foreigners. Purchasers received a special discount on their villas for every million they sent to Fawalan banks and asset-management services. That had been one of Jabbar's better ideas, but Rahim had been unable to impose a sufficient processing tax which would have helped to finance his social-security programme and education fund. The moment he'd suggested it, Jabbar told him investors would simply take their money to a neighbouring emirate.

Rocks and sand reclaimed the area for a few kilometres until the road merged with the almost deserted triple-lane highway which skirted Daralaam and connected to the gas refinery up the coast. The skyscrapers of the city centre were barely visible through the haze.

After two junctions, Rahim's driver prepared to pull off the highway.

Rahim pressed the intercom. "No. Take me to Kaabahaa."

At the following junction they pulled off the gleaming asphalt and onto a road which became more sand-strewn and pitted with every metre. The driver slowed as he dodged a series of potholes and a couple of dead dogs.

Rahim propped his elbow on the armrest, put his chin on his palm and stared through the tinted window at the dirty bricks of the flat-roofed structures. Most men were already at work but, in the shade of flapping tarpaulins and the occasional tree, old men sat while women served them tea. Houses were huddled together in an effort to keep the sun's rays out of the alleys between. A breath of wind blew dust over the van as the driver stopped to let a cluster of construction workers cross the road to catch their service bus. The men were thin, wearing dirty western-type work clothes and sombre faces under tatty taqiya head caps.

Nobody gave a second look at the vans. Just another

convoy of rich people cutting through the neighbourhood.

The intercom crackled. "Where do you wish to go from here, Your Highness?"

"Drive around the area for a few minutes."

They took a left turn on to a littered street lined with shops selling cheap plastic household goods and a few market stalls offering locally grown dates, and vegetables cultivated in massive greenhouses on the coastline.

The market vendors all wore dishdashas with blue-and-white checked keffiyehs wound and knotted around their heads. Women lugged sacks of food, their black abaya robes flapping in the breeze. Although they all wore hijab headscarves, Rahim was pleased that the more complete facial covering of the niqab was nowhere to be seen. Five years ago, in his first speech as Emir, he had announced that women were no longer required to wear it. He'd backed up his wish with a carefully-phrased medical opinion that the niqab restricted free breathing of God's air and prevented women from fully expressing their God-given voices. The religious leaders had not dared to question him personally though many had approached Jabbar to voice their concerns for a loosening of modesty standards. Rahim had then instructed a trusted employee to gather evidence on a certain religious leader with questionable moral habits. Opposition to the niqab question soon died down.

However, Rahim knew that to further open society he needed free, secular schooling and social facilities in these districts. Then disadvantaged children would have a better start and poor women would feel stronger. Women in

Fawala were now just over 30% of the population. Rahim knew his country needed foreign women to come and live happily here but, in order to achieve that, Fawalans would have to move on from their particular interpretation of Sharia Law and find a more liberating compromise.

They turned into a side street which degraded into a glorified shantytown underneath a spider's web of electricity cables. Satellite dishes adorned every rooftop. Rahim grinned. Next year he planned to set up a new TV channel, devoid of advertising and religious sermons.

On the left a group of old men sat cross-legged on empty grain sacks, shouting and gesticulating. A young woman spilled tea as she poured and received a clip round the ear. Rahim resisted the urge to have his car stop so he could give the old bastard a pummelling.

He'd long ago accepted that he couldn't change the older generation. Their outdated ways were too ingrained – they stifled and rotted them as equally as shiny toys and unsustainable lifestyles rotted the new Fawalan rich.

A secular, educated middle class would take his country into a new era. Rahim was glad his father had sent him to England to the famous Eton College, even if that school was more like a club for its predominantly upper-class pupils. Preparing and enabling them to perpetuate the system they lived in as they went through their lives.

Rahim wanted Fawalans to question their lives, question the contents of that book they could so often recite. Even to question their leaders.

He laughed.

There was plenty they could question him and his brother about. Plenty of answers they might not like, even if Rahim's plans would help them more than their faith.

They reached the end of the street. A gleaming white Range Rover pumped up on golden alloys cut across them, sounding its horn and throwing up dust. Through the glass division, Rahim saw his driver mouth obscenities.

"Stop the car," Rahim said into the intercom.

He turned and watched the gaudy SUV cruise down the street and grind to a halt by the old men. A man got out of the passenger seat, opened a rear door and let a much younger man step onto the street. This man opened the trunk, hauled out a freshly slaughtered goat wrapped in cellophane and tossed it at the feet of the old men. They darted to the carcass while offering their hands to the sky. One attempted to kiss the hand of the young man. He jerked it away and heaved a bag of rice from the vehicle, dropping it by the goat.

Ignoring the old men, the young man cleaned his hands with a moist wipe, depositing both the wipe and its wrapping on the ground before shutting the trunk and sliding back into the vehicle. The servant closed his door, got in and the SUV sped off.

Rahim shook his head slowly. This was not charity, not concern for others, merely relief of guilt. After all, Rahim knew a little bit about the concept as well.

People always assumed Rahim was an absolute ruler like some of his neighbours. But that system never really worked unless one was willing to go down a darker road.

He'd long ago given up trying to change the class system or the taxation percentages and his current plans to cut salaries and slash perks for his advisors and ministers were hitting the same wall. That's why he wanted to renew the gas deals: so he could siphon money into social-security programmes, schools and universities for those Fawalans who had slipped under the radar and for the thousands of immigrants who worked in the refinery, on construction sites, hotels and in the houses of the wealthy. Everybody who called Fawala home deserved a proper chance in life and access to a share of the energy wealth. But everyone else in his government simply wanted more luxury developments to encourage foreign investment. Hell, there was even talk of a ski complex. All these things, his advisors and Jabbar told him, would secure the future of Fawala long after the gas and oil had either run out or simply gone out of fashion due to climate change. Not that any of them really cared about climate change.

Rahim told his driver to continue. They took the highway around the city to the coast, passing the massive desalination plant which provided Fawala's businesses and three million people with nearly 100 million litres of drinking water a day at a financial cost of nearly ten dollars per 100 litres. Although that was merely a financial way of measuring the electricity consumed to quench the country's thirst.

They arrived at the ambitious shipping port where the derricks stood underused. The port had been part of Jabbar's plan to make Fawala a major hub, but he had been unable to poach business from a neighbouring Emirate which could do things on a greater scale, with cheaper labour and juicier tax breaks.

Rahim still hoped that he could put the place to proper use one day. Perhaps as a shipbuilding yard? That would provide employment. He'd have to think of a way to entice a manufacturer here.

Next to the port was a marina packed with yachts. The silver vans headed past the luxury boats to a checkpoint. Uniformed guards stood aside. The private jetty was supposed to contain an official state yacht, but Rahim had never been a fan of boats, so Jabbar kept his own ship moored here.

The convoy slid to a halt in the shadow of the yacht. Donning sunglasses, Rahim got out and ran his eyes over the behemoth. He had to admit it was impressive, even if its extravagance made him cringe to the extent that he'd only ever been on board a handful of times. 195 metres long, it had a crew of 70 and was the largest in the world. Jabbar liked to joke that at least Fawala was Number One at something. In private, Rahim sometimes teased Jabbar that it was merely a penis extension, which always drove him into a rage. Rahim stepped into a dockside elevator tower, which took him up to the stateroom level gangway.

On board, a liveried servant greeted him. Rahim strode down the portside decking to the main reception room. A blast of cool air hit him as he walked through the cavernous room. Gold leaf, crystal chandeliers and mirrors. White carpeting with matching leather sofas and chairs. Jabbar had shown the designers photographs of *Galerie des Glaces* in Versailles Palace along with a long list of demands. Rahim preferred the original.

The room opened out onto a rear observation deck. Shielded from the sun by a side-less Bedouin tent, the deck was covered in woven carpets and cushions. Rahim thought he could still see a bloodstain from the last sheep Jabbar had sacrificed and cooked on the open firepit at the stern. At least, he hoped it was sheep's blood.

He joined his brother at the railing, gazing out at their city. The docks seemed so far below it was almost as if they were in one of the city's skyscrapers.

"Good morning, little brother," said Jabbar, a porcelain smile on his angular, clean-shaven face. "How was your flight on that old bucket of bolts?"

"Perfectly adequate."

"You know we are the only Emirate that still needs to refuel after a trans-Atlantic flight? Everyone else has new 787s or big Airbuses."

"I suppose you'd like a plane to match the size of this thing?"

"You don't complain about my boat when you need to used it to impress a foreign dignitary or have a secret meeting, do you?"

Rahim rubbed his forehead.

"I am surprised you did not take a helicopter from the airport," said Jabbar.

"What? Oh, I wanted to drive through the city to take things in."

"*Hmm*. Strange, then, that you only visited Kaabahaa. A little slumming?"

Rahim cut him a sideways glance. "I don't see why we couldn't have met at home," he said.

"The palace has too many ears. Here we can speak in English and my servants will not understand us. Besides, I imagined you would like to relax a little after your terrorist ordeal and your meeting with the British.

The horn sounded and a servant pattered along the outer deck to inform them the captain was casting off.

"So, it went well with the British government?"

Rahim chuckled. "They were quite concerned that I would throw all my toys out of my pram after I was caught up in that attack."

"It's like I have always said: the British are desperate to keep doing business with us."

"No, not desperate. They just want our gas and they are almost insistent that we send their own money back to them in the form of payment for expensive war toys, overpriced property or financial products and services. They would be happiest if we squandered it all on things like this ..." He rapped a knuckle on the guard rail. "However, I want something different: quite simply money in exchange for gas." He shrugged. "What I do with it should not be their concern, but I don't think they see it that way. That is why I, we, must tread carefully."

"But you are raising prices – how will you keep them happy?"

"We, that is, Al Fawala Invaco, paid them 120 million

pounds over the asking price for that shabby London police building. That will suffice. If they expect more, I will simply stall, bluff, and change my mind." He shrugged. "They tend to expect petulant behaviour from people like us. Our neighbours are the regional champions at it."

"You love to play with fire, don't you, Rahim?"

"I have always been good at it. That is the difference between us. You would burn everything except your own fortress to serve your short-term interests. I prefer to consider the final objective *before* starting the game."

Jabbar crossed his legs and lowered himself onto a cushion. He fingered an elaborate remote control and a servant appeared with tea.

"The Americans will be easier to deal with," said Rahim, reclining onto a cushion.

"As long as we deal with the right man ... Preferably someone who has a chance of ending up in the White House."

"It is largely irrelevant who ends up in the White House. We'll be able to deal with all but a few of them. But I will still be careful with regard to the price I ask. I don't want them to think we are overstepping the mark." He cocked his chin at the horizon. "Or we might end up like the late Saddam at the other side of the gulf."

Jabbar glanced at the throbbing jugular on his brother's neck.

As the boat turned for the open Gulf seas, the brothers looked back at their domain. Sun reflected off towering buildings. A twinkling, modern oasis powered by gas and sea water. Several miles down the coast, the stacks of the refinery and its super-tanker docking facility were just visible through the haze.

Jabbar pulled a satisfied grin. "We have a wonderful country."

Rahim only saw so many things that needed to change.

"You know we have to find a balance between the construction of meaningless concrete-steel-glass monstrosities and building of a well-educated populace."

Jabbar threw his arms up. "You and your socialism! You're like a dog with a bone. Do you think we would have all this," he waved a hand, "if Father had been a socialist?"

"Do you even know what democratic socialism is?" Rahim narrowed his eyes. "Anyway, do you think we would ever get anything achieved at all, if Father had had a dozen children, like *his* father had? Or like you are on your way to having with your three wives ... and how many pregnant mistresses over the years?"

"And why no wife yet for you, my brother?"

Rahim ignored the dig. "Father realised that things must change, adapt."

"Relax, Rahim. Father is only dead five years. You must slow down and let change come at a pace that people can understand."

Rahim fixed his dark eyes on his brother. "No. The time is now. If I do not push then nothing will ever happen. You know this."

"You think you can change everything, don't you? But you can't. You can't challenge God's will."

Rahim burst out laughing.

Jabbar bristled. "Did I challenge Father's wish to make you Emir?"

Rahim searched his brother's face. "Not then, you didn't. No."

"What is that supposed to mean?"

Rahim sighed. Changed the subject. "We also have to find better ways of living and invest in environmental technologies – we simply can't keep desalinising sea water with the existing technology."

"The environmentalists really did get to you in that attack."

"No. I have just been thinking seriously about our future."

"Oh, the non-religious prophet! *Ha!*" he bellowed. "The Great and Holy Prophet Mohammed would not be pleased with you."

Again, Rahim ignored the dig. "If I don't do it, nobody else will."

Darkness flickered across Jabbar's eyes.

Rahim finished his tea and refilled both glasses. "Quarrelling will serve us nothing."

Jabbar shrugged. "I have to admit you are right."

"Oh, and speaking of environmental technologies, how is the solar farm construction coming on?"

Jabbar made a slapping gesture at the air. "Behind schedule, as expected. I feel obliged to point out that it is a waste of money. For all its size, it will never provide all our power."

"Of course not. No *one thing* will replace the gas, but it will help enormously. It might even become the sole power source for the desalination plant. If it works well, then we can construct another one in the hills near the border and sell power to our neighbours."

Jabbar paused, glass at his lips. "You know, *that's* not a bad idea at all. We'll charge them a fortune."

Rahim clapped his hands together. "Wonderful! Agreement over something. Let's leave it there," he stood. "I will have a swim and take out a jet ski."

He could feel Jabbar's eyes following him as he went inside.

*   *   *

Jabbar watched him leave, then pulled a phone from his shorts pocket. His first call was made to a device *currently unavailable*. A string of Arabic obscenities ensued as he swiped and found another number. The tone rang for nearly a minute before the call was answered breathlessly.

"Abdullah, don't tell me you ran to answer this?"

"*Erm*, no cousin. I was –"

"Never mind," Jabbar cut in.

"How did it go?"

"He's not going to budge."

"I will be going to America in September. It is official."

"How interesting."

Chapter 23

Hanif sat alone on a bench at London's Paddington Station waiting for the Sunday afternoon train to Newbury. People bustled by, chatting on phones. He watched their urgency with a sense of wonder. A woman walked past him with two small children. Despite the warm weather, she wore a long coat and had a headscarf wrapped tight around her brow and cheeks. She looked young, not yet thirty.

He thought of his own mother, her niqab, and the way she'd always looked at the ground when she walked the village. One day he'd asked her not to wear it, to let her hair flow and to look up at the mountains and sky. She had explained to him that it was an important part of her faith that she remain covered. Hanif had kissed her on the cheek and never mentioned it to her again. He'd assumed it was his mother's choice to wear whatever she wanted, but later on he'd wondered if she might have been an unwitting accomplice in her own oppression. So he'd asked his father why her veil was necessary. *Why God would want such a happy face concealed?* He'd received a barked order not to question things that were written.

That hadn't stopped him though, much to the disgust of the religious men who insisted that his father straighten him out before he became as godless as the invaders. But Hanif had never stopped questioning.

A sleek train arrived. People poured out of it and trotted up the platform, staring at their phones or pressing them to their ears.

As he got up, Hanif's gaze fell on a bronze statue of a bear wearing a floppy hat and sitting on a suitcase. A month or two ago, he'd gone with Lee and Des to see a children's film about the bear. Hanif felt a bit like this small bear. Uprooted. Searching. Lonely. And, like the bear, he'd found a surrogate family followed by a purpose in life. But not quite fulfilment.

He boarded his train and found a seat opposite two teenage boys wearing headphones and swiping at tablets. Nobody took the seat beside him so he turned his back to the window, removed his polished shoes and put his feet up. The teenagers regarded him strangely, but he knew his feet didn't smell so he smiled, slowed his breathing and tried to meditate.

Hanif watched the boys giggle at the flashing screens. After a while, one of the lads complained when his battery

165

ran flat. The ticket inspector informed them there was a power outlet at the end of the carriage. The boy grinned and went to charge up.

So easy, free with a train ticket.

Hanif closed his eyes. If only they realised what energy really cost.

Chapter 24

The following morning, Rahim donned the traditional white dishdasha and dark-blue keffiyeh of the Fawalan royal family. He was met on the jetty by his blue-and-gold Maybach. Like the Bentley he used in England, it was both bulletproof cocoon and official state vehicle. Two motorbike outriders preceded him and the usual van with his team followed.

The domed white government building had been built by his father and adjoined the Royal Palace compound so the aged Emir could govern without the need to leave his home.

Rahim arrived at a small entrance shrouded by an awning. Double doors were opened onto an elevator which took him directly to a concealed entrance to the suite which adjoined his private office.

Rahim found his morning meeting set up and ready. He greeted Sheik Ahmed bin Khaled Al Bahar, the Chief Operating Officer of FawGas, with an embrace and a kiss to both cheeks.

"How are you, my cousin?" asked Rahim with genuine warmth.

"Allah be praised, I am fighting fit and delighted to report that the first offshore wells have at last been completed."

"How long does this buy us?"

Ahmed flicked prayer beads between his fingers. "Previous estimates were rather optimistic. At present rates of extraction, we're going to need to start deep-sea drilling in two years. We'll need American consultants. In my opinion, they are better at it than the British."

Rahim stared at his desk. "Ahmed, as you know, the first graduates from my foreign studies scholarship programme will be returning to Fawala after the summer."

"Ah yes. I intend to interview the engineering graduates and offer the best one a job."

"Good. Good." He stroked his beard. "As you know, there are twenty women in the programme."

A slow nod: hesitant.

"You will see to it that you employ them."

Ahmed opened his mouth.

Rahim raised a hand. "I am not talking about *positive discrimination*, nor do I expect you to hire someone you do not need."

"So, what then?"

"I will be talking to my cabinet and other business leaders about the matter. I will require that all of these women be treated as experts in their respective fields."

"Even if there is a man better suited to the job?"

"Not if he *really is* better qualified. But if the best candidate is a woman, you will give her the job. Is that clear?"

Ahmed looked at the floor as he nodded.

Chapter 25

Claudia pulled up outside Newbury train station. Hanif stood at the kerb wearing his tweed cap, with a small beaten-up old backpack on his back and a holdall at his feet. He flashed his crooked teeth at Claudia.

"Sorry I'm late, Hanif. I tried the mobile number Ed gave me for you but it's turned off. Everything's been in a heap lately." She opened the car boot.

With a silent nod, he swung his daypack off, stuffed his holdall in beside it, pulled a phone from his pocket and turned it on.

"Supermarket's shut," Claudia said as they moved off. "But I've stocked your flat with a few things to get you started."

"Thank you very much," he said in gravelly tones.

"We found you a bicycle, too. Not new, I'm afraid. It's an old one belonging to my boyfriend."

"Ms. Haverford, I –"

"Claudia, please," she said, darting into the ring-road traffic.

He cleared his throat and spoke deliberately. "Claudia, I understand that Mr. Manton was a good horseman. It is a great tragedy that so many human lives are lost to acts of violence in the world."

Claudia slowed the car a bit. Unsure how to respond, she just nodded.

"Violence is a terrible cycle," Hanif continued. "Once it is started, it is so difficult to break as every successive act creates the will to further violence."

It took Claudia a moment to process his words. "How right you are. That's like something my boyfriend would say." She half-smiled. "You should have a chat with him." She sighed. "If the bloody police ever let him go."

They swung into Crangate and Hanif sat up in his seat and took in the paddocks, trees and horses grazing. "A beautiful place."

The car crunched to a halt outside the office. "Right, I need you to sign a couple of forms – routine employment stuff."

She unlocked the office while Hanif grabbed his holdall and backpack from the car boot and produced his passport. "I assume you will want to photocopy this."

"Oh, right. Yes, well done."

He followed her in, wiping his feet carefully on the

doormat. Claudia led him through reception into her office.

Hanif sat and stared at the bookshelves full of old sales catalogues, pedigree-analysis tomes and history books of thoroughbred racing and breeding.

She pushed a pen and three sheets of paper across the desk. "They faxed us all your details from Craddock's, *um*, that is, Tomlinson's. So all you need to do is sign here and here."

Hanif signed his name with an elegant looping flourish.

"You have a bank account?"

He nodded, handing her his passport, while his other hand rummaged in his bag.

She took it, rounded the desk and went out to reception to turn on the photo copier. The machine seemed to take an age to warm up. Claudia drummed her nails on it as it hummed and whirred. She glanced back into her office and saw that Hanif's chair was empty. The machine purred into life and spat out a copy. She grabbed it and returned to the office.

Hanif was standing at the window. He spun around and pointed to the silver cup on the windowsill. "That is what Secular Princess won, is it not?"

Claudia beamed. "It certainly is. Thank you again for your part in that."

"Do you mind if I look at it?"

"Be my guest."

Hanif carefully picked the ornately worked cup off its plinth and admired the hunting scene carved into its side.

"A beautiful prize for a beautiful horse," he said, putting it down and returning to his chair. "Horses are so pure."

Claudia looked up from the file as she arranged papers. "Yes, they're so honest with their feelings."

"When I am with a horse, it is the only time I can really relax and forget about the horrors of the world."

Claudia saw something flicker in his eyes. She sensed that this man had indeed had a hard life, just like the Emir had said. What kind of hardship she couldn't imagine, but she'd once seen a similar look in Tom's eyes after he'd woken with a nightmare. And in Oscar's once or twice, come to think of it.

She cleared her throat and flipped the file closed. "Right, I'll show you to your flat and let you get settled in."

She took Hanif out to the main yard. The redbrick quadrangle had originally been built for dairy cows and carriage horses, but Seb had converted it into modern stabling. The hayloft over the stables had been turned into a series of one-bedroomed flats for seasonal workers.

They climbed the staircase to Flat 1. Showing him in, she took a key off her ring. The sparsely furnished, open-plan kitchen-sitting room led to a small bedroom with a tiny bathroom. Hanif nodded his approval.

"Don't lose the key," said Claudia. "Or we'll dock you ten pounds."

Hanif closed his hand around it as if it were a precious stone and Claudia just knew that Hanif, unlike some of the younger students who came to get experience preparing yearlings at Crangate each year, would be utterly careful and responsible with his key *and* the flat.

"You start at seven-thirty in the morning. Walk across the yard to the tack room and ask for Bill. He'll show you the ropes and assign you four horses to groom and walk. OK?"

"Thank you."

She smiled as she closed the door.

*   *   *

Hanif moved to the window, watched her cross the yard and disappear under the archway.

Chapter 26

"That's confirmed then. Murad Kazemi's phone was the one that rang in the detonation," said Gibson.

Wallace raised a hand. "Correction: the phone we found *in his possession* was used to trigger the bomb. Technically, that's all we know about the device."

"*Hmm.* Yeah."

A young constable stood in the doorway and knocked on the glass partition.

"Yes?" said Wallace.

He handed Wallace an envelope. "This was just delivered to the duty desk by a legal assistant from some firm in the City."

Wallace thanked the constable. When the young man had gone, he muttered, "Not fucking Greene again," ripping open the thick white envelope. His eyes bulged as he read the short solicitor's letter.

"Well, fuck me, if it isn't from Lady Alexandra Telson – the old bird who employs Tom Sunderland. Well, her lawyer anyway."

Gibson knitted his brow.

"Says she's given a sworn statement in Newbury police station in the company of her solicitor saying that Tom was with her in her office in Newbury the day of the bombing and that he hasn't been to Newmarket for several months." He tossed the letter across the desk. "Says Thames Valley Police'll be sending it up to me ASAP."

"You want me to call Newbury, chase it up?"

"No. It'll get here when it gets here." Wallace frowned. "Pull Tom Sunderland's phone out of his possessions bag, give it to Tech and call CGHQ. Tell them to check locations of every call and text on it." He blew out a breath. "Should've done it when we took him in, but I didn't see the point."

"I'll get right on it." Gibson stood.

Wallace's phone rang: Trenton.

"Chief Inspector. Have you seen the news?"

Chapter 27

Claudia sat cross-legged on the sofa in her pyjamas. She'd come home early from work and gone straight for a bottle of wine and a tub of ice cream. And at least twenty cigarettes.

She'd failed to lift her mood by watching a comedy, so like a rubbernecker passing an accident, she turned on a trashy news channel.

Her phone rang. When she saw Lady Alex's number, her heart jumped.

"Any news?" she blurted.

"I'm afraid not, but I can confirm that my statement was delivered to that Wallace man. Hopefully it'll grease a few wheels and get Tom released."

"Thank you so much."

"You're more than welcome. Oh, and for what it's worth,

I don't believe that this attack had anything to do with environmental activists."

"Nothing at all?"

"No. If this Nature's Wrath group really existed, I'd have heard of them."

"Are you sure about that?"

"Indeed I am. Look, I don't usually talk about this, and I suppose they're probably listening to my phone, but I do get approached by all types, you know."

"What do you mean?"

"Loonies and extremists. They'd all like me to write them cheques, preferably with no questions asked. Some of them even tell me their barmy ideas."

"Seriously?"

"Yes. Oh, I don't mean that I've heard about anything like that bomb – they mostly go in for corporate sabotage or publicity stunts but, ever since our prank on Greene backfired on Tom, I've gone off that sort of thing. So I send them packing and ask my lawyer for advice. However, I do know a few youngsters who are very definitely *out there* on the limits of activism and they've told me that this Nature's Wrath claim is, to use their word, *bullshit*."

"So why don't they tell the press?"

"Their public image is, sadly, the stereotypical grungy-crusty-hippy thing which the press love to mock. Their views, however, do tend to be well thought-out and researched."

"Surely you can get one of them to shave, dress up and get interviewed?"

"They'd never agree to change just to get on TV. By the way, I know it's of little consolation to you but, tragic as it is, Greene and Christian's deaths might actually have thrown a lifeline to the anti-fracking campaign in Yorkshire."

"Does that make it worth it?"

"No. It does not. However, despite rumours that an American is interested in buying it, CleanGas appears to be rudderless, giving everyone in Yorkshire breathing space, time and impetus to keep up the political pressure."

Claudia grunted. "You're right, it is of little consolation to me."

The hourly news came on TV.

"Thanks so much for calling, Lady Alex, but I'll have to let you go. I want to take in all the gory news details."

"Don't wallow in it, Claudia. You never let Tom watch too much war news, do you?"

Claudia hung up. Her hand hovered over the remote. She knew Lady Alex was right, but she couldn't help herself. She just had to watch. Just for a few seconds to get the gist.

Then a photo of Oscar in uniform was plastered on the screen and she was transfixed.

"Police now believe that the target was Adam Greene. In a particularly macabre turn of events, it transpires that the bomb was placed inside the uterus of a horse presented for sale. A bizarre, macabre procedure made physically possible due to the horse's recent miscarriage, according to a spokesperson for the Royal College of Veterinary Surgeons whom this news channel has spoken to. The main culprit, Oscar Haverford, was a deeply

troubled veterinarian who had served in Afghanistan. Haverford was, by all accounts, a diligent and hardworking vet beset by personal problems including drug abuse and alcoholism, possibly resulting from post-traumatic stress disorder. It is understood that he either recruited, or coerced Murad Kazemi, a young man of Middle-Eastern origin working in Newmarket, to help him insert the device into the horse whose stretched, post-miscarriage cervix and uterus allowed a device of sufficient size to be inserted, ironically without harming the horse until the moment of detonation. The bomb was made from white phosphorus, thermite plasma and depleted uranium fragments purchased on the black market and detonated remotely. Haverford and Kazemi are both dead in an apparent murder-suicide pact – a bizarre twist indeed on the concept of suicide bombing. Their bodies were found in Newmarket and a phone in Kazemi's pocket was confirmed as the device which rang in the detonation. Two young people who escorted the horse to the sale and died in the blast may well have been accomplices. The main motive for the attack is thought to be protest over the wars in Afghanistan and Iraq, which commenced under Mr. Greene's tenure as Prime Minister. In a further twist, police have discovered that Haverford attended the Royal Military Academy Sandhurst with disgraced war hero Thomas Sunderland, currently in custody, who infamously threw a condom full of excrement at Mr. Greene some years ago. It is believed that these individuals may well have been the founder members of so-called Nature's Wrath."

There it was, neatly packaged. Both men in her life portrayed as terrorists.

There followed several minutes of studio discussion. Well, it was presented as discussion but Claudia realised that they weren't actually saying anything, merely drilling in the central message of fear and the ever-present spectre of terrorism.

Then the leader of the opposition was interviewed live. He looked haggard, like he'd just got out of bed. A far cry from Greene's slick corporate image or the current PM's Savile Row suits.

"I think this whole tragedy serves as a damning indictment of the government's failure to support and care for our brave veterans. The attack also highlights the folly of conducting wars under false pretences halfway around the world using unethical weapons. During his tenure as Prime Minister and leader of this party, Mr. Greene famously agreed with the American term 'War on Terror', but exactly how one declares war on a tactic is beyond me. And still we continue to do business with countries which either openly or covertly support terrorists."

The segment was cut abruptly.

Claudia turned off the TV and lit a cigarette.

She was beginning to accept that Oscar had planted the bomb, but she just couldn't believe that he'd thought up the attack himself. There must have been somebody else pulling the strings and that certainly wasn't Tom. No way. She remembered the words in Oscar's diary. *4am. Mouse. Ha! Monster more like. Sends a shiver up my spine whenever we meet.* She'd assumed this was about a drug deal but, in light of all that'd happened, perhaps it was something else entirely?

She took another sip of wine and drummed her fingers on the glass. She thought about what Lady Alex had said, and about the syringe in Oscar's car. If he really had been coerced into planting the bomb, perhaps an injection to kill the pain was his only option. After he'd saved her.

Then there was the fact that the news report hadn't even named Al Fawala Stud, hadn't mentioned the Emir or Sir John Christian or Vasili Komarov.

She wanted Tom back. Wanted him out of whatever hole they'd thrown him into. She regretted opening the door that morning. Perhaps if she hadn't, they'd have been required to get a warrant to arrest him. No, who was she kidding? These days they can just get you.

She tidied away the empty bottles, lit another cigarette and paced the carpet.

Fuck it, she'd call that Wallace man and give him a piece of her mind.

He picked up, sounding tired.

"When are you going to release my boyfriend?"

"Good evening to you too, Claudia."

"And thank you so much for portraying my brother as a complete fucking lunatic. There must have been someone pulling his strings. I'd imagine they used his problems as leverage. Tell me, Inspector: is anybody actually asking *why* my brother would do such a thing and how he could possibly get his hands on depleted uranium?"

A long breath hissed out of him. "General consensus is like it says on the TV, with a possible angle of a conspiracy of disgruntled soldiers using contacts from warzones to get the DU on the black market." He yawned into the receiver.

Claudia thought she heard ice clink against a glass.

"Look, I told you I thought Oscar was murdered. Hell, you even asked me if I thought there was any foul play."

"Yes, but that was when we thought it was Murad who forced your brother to plant the bomb and then disappeared. The evidence now rules that theory out."

"How?"

Another sigh. "I suppose I can tell you. Murad's body was found with a syringe, just like the one your brother used to off himself. And the autopsy confirmed that he died of a ketamine overdose too."

"What?" She thought for a second. "Well, there you have it. Somebody must've killed them both. Oh, and I've been reading my brother's private diary. He mentions that just before the attack, he had to meet someone he refers to as '*the mouse*'."

She got out the diary and read the lines for Wallace.

"Why the bloody hell are you only telling me this now?"

"Because I thought it was just a reference to a local drug dealer."

"I'm going to need that diary."

"Tell you what, I'll scan and email you the page right now. I don't suppose I could swap it for Tom?"

"This is not a negotiation."

"Then may I at least visit him, see how he is?"

"I very much doubt it."

"Charming."

"Look … I'll call you back in the morning. Oh, and by the way, you needn't think that I'm a fan of TV news reporting either."

"Really? And do you think this attack is as neat and simple as they say, Inspector?"

"Things in today's world rarely are."

Chapter 28

The wind howled through the wreckage, throwing dust and sand around the crippled hull. He set to work making a sling for his injured arm – he daren't pull out the shrapnel in case it started a serious haemorrhage and he still had scramble to safety and wait for the distress signal to be answered.

Captain Sunderland crawled about inside the mangled Chinook, doing what had to be done. Eleven other soldiers were strewn about the wreckage. Their bodies limp, distorted. His Commanding Officer, Major General Shaw, had a piece of metal protruding from his throat. His uniform and the seats around him were a sticky burgundy mess. He paused over the CO's body. He didn't know how long it had been since the British army had lost such a high-ranking soldier. He imagined that under normal circumstances the general's death would be headline news but, considering the real reason for this ultra-classified helicopter journey, he had a feeling the story would be buried along with the general.

One by one, Tom removed rank insignia, name tags and any minor documents. As the CO's Aide-de-Camp, he was the one in possession of the pipeline plans. Reflexively, he double-checked everything was still in his bag.

He slung a weapon over his good shoulder and half-climbed, half-fell out of the helicopter. Outside, the dust stung his cheeks and filled his nose and the corners of his mouth. He made it to a recess between two boulders, crouched for cover and tried to work out how high up the mountain he was.

He cocked his head like an animal testing the air. Voices humming through the wind. Closing in. He strained his ears, filtering the sounds. Shouting, excited chattering. A deep voice barked and then silence under the whistling wind. He eased the weapon off his shoulder and slid his good hand round the grip, but the weapon was too heavy to lift without his other arm for support. He put it down and shuffled as far back into the crevice as he could. Then he saw the beard and gun-barrel appear through the dust. A dark apparition brandishing an AK 47. Captain Sunderland raised his palm and kept his head down. Submissive. There was nothing else he could do. He had no time to burn the plans or stash them under a rock.

As they led him down the mountain, he wondered how many days would pass before the torture would start. At least then he'd be able to guess how long before they'd kill him.

*   *   *

Tom woke shouting: a deep primal growl. He sat up in his cell and wiped the sweat from his brow. This small room was a palace compared to the Afghani mountains, but strangely enough he'd almost prefer to be back there than here now. The village elder had been a decent man underneath the scars of battle and religious devotion.

Here, the police looked at him like he was subhuman. Already guilty and sentenced.

It turned out the village elder was a lonely man who'd lost his family during the Russian occupation. This time around he hadn't even bothered to get upset with the soldiers. He knew they would leave sooner or later. But the local Taliban had given him orders and so he'd had to keep Tom captive after they'd finished terrifying him. In what the Army Brass would later describe as classic Stockholm Syndrome, Tom began to sympathise with the locals. They weren't the bloodthirsty savages they were made out to be. Although there were undoubtedly those kind amongst ordinary pissed-off Afghanis, for the most part Tom witnessed ordinary people struggling through their daily lives. Doing their best to cope with living in a perpetual warzone, torn between aggressive occupiers, savage local militias and hard-line religious zealots. Add poor education into the mix, and Tom had been astounded how the stress of it all didn't drive more of them crazy.

*   *   *

Tom's breakfast was delivered onto the door tray and he

picked at it. Afterwards, he was brought back to the interview room. Claudia flickered through his mind. Poor her, she didn't deserve all this shit. Hopefully Lady Alex's lawyer was working on something to get him released and back to Claud but, the trouble was, these days any perceived connection to terrorism tended to trump normal procedures and rights.

Tom took his seat and tried to practise yogic breathing in the hope that he'd be able to just ignore today's round of questioning.

*   *   *

"So," said Gibson. "I'm going to ask you again, and I really do hate sounding like a broken record: where did you guys get the DU for your bomb?"

Sunderland stared at the usual crack on the wall. "How many times do you want me to say it? *I have no fucking idea what you are talking about!*"

Gibson stared at him. If truth be told he was getting sick of interviewing Sunderland. It was now clear to Gibson that he had nothing to do with Oscar Haverford or the attack. The media, the Greene camp and *on high* wanting it to be true didn't make it so. He decided to change tack, just for a last roll of the dice.

"OK. I believe you."

"Really? Just like that?"

Gibson shrugged. "In your opinion, how would the real culprits have got their hands on the stuff?"

187

Tom narrowed his eyes, looked at the desk a moment. "Well, as you may know there was a lot of it used in the first Gulf War in '91. I mean *a lot*."

"Not the second time around or in Afghanistan?"

"Oh, it was used alright. They had to get rid of their stockpiles somehow. Just not as much as before. Anyway, it's incredibly tough. That's why it was used in tank-busting rounds. It'll slice through practically anything. So, wherever it was used, it's still just sitting there lodged in blown-up vehicles and buildings and in rock and soil. Probably in the water table too. Apparently, it's been linked to birth defects and cancers in children in Iraq."

Gibson shook his head, suddenly aware that his mouth was open a fraction.

"A nasty little surprise in the aftermath of conflict, don't you think?" Tom said.

"So, how would someone get hold of it?"

"Simplest way would be to just extract it from the target – very carefully – and sell it off in lots. Once on a tentacle of the black market it could end up anywhere in the world." He shrugged. "It's possible that terror network leaders or profiteers have teams of people whose only job is to find and extract DU and I'm sure there are people who'd think it very appropriate that some of it got recycled into a bomb in London."

Gibson scowled. "Do you think it's appropriate?"

"Of course not!" He leaned over the table, closer to Gibson. "But then again, I never thought it was appropriate to use DU ammunition in the first place."

Gibson shot a glance at the two-way mirror and got up.

"Don't go anywhere," he said.

Sunderland pulled a sarcastic grin.

*   *   *

They stared at Sunderland through the glass.

Wallace wore a pained expression. "Did we get those syringes and phones printed?"

"Yeah, was done that day. Vet's syringe had his prints on it, but Murad's syringe was clean."

"Makes sense, I suppose. And the phones?"

"Murad's was smudged to bits, but they managed to get his thumb print and another few partials which don't appear to match his. Vet's had his prints on it."

"But not the vet's prints on Murad's?"

"Doesn't seem that way. I thought that was a bit strange at first, but I suppose he used gloves. They did find a couple of used latex pairs in his car."

"Did anyone check those for DNA?"

Gibson looked blank.

"Well, fucking find out! Did you check the other partials against the database?"

"They were too blurred to get a match. Tech said they'd need more to go on."

Wallace cocked his chin at the glass. "And what about the location on *his* phone?"

"Nowhere near Newmarket – looks like his alibi checks out."

Wallace screwed up his face, breath hissed between his teeth.

"Do we let him go then?" asked Gibson.

"Damned if we do, damned if we don't. But, to be quite honest, I just don't think he had anything to do with it."

"Neither do I."

"I'm tempted to release him now just to piss the Greene camp off, but we'll get too much shit from *on high* if we do, so we might as well keep him here for the full month."

Gibson nodded.

"Oh, and I want you to call Newmarket station and find out if there are any known drug dealers or criminals in the Newmarket area with the moniker *Mouse*. Check the same on all known domestic extremists and terror suspects. Haverford had to have got that bomb from someone connected. Someone who knew what they were doing."

Chapter 29

Buzzing with caffeine and nicotine, Claudia tapped a name into the search engine. Sir John Christian threw up several pages of hits. She clicked on a link listing the country's richest people.

Apparently Christian had been the single largest donor to Adam Greene's first election success and yet he was also last year's biggest donor to the current Prime Minister's party.

Interesting. And Greene still hung out with him? It seemed money really did trump everything else.

She scrolled and clicked some more. Lady Alex was right too: according to the *Financial Times*, Christian's company CleanGas had yet to choose a successor and was now on the market, its share-price plummeting. Christian's sons were eager to sell to an American called Picklett.

Picklett. B W Picklett? Claudia frowned and clicked a link. Claudia knew the man was selling all his racehorses in Kentucky in November to concentrate on expanding his drilling company. Surely Picklett hadn't planned the attack just to buy a company for peanuts? Did Oscar even know Picklett? Did Tom? Picklett didn't have any horses in Europe and Claudia had never seen him racing over here. She gave up trying to think about it.

According to another news site, Christian's family partly wanted to sell to distance themselves from rumours that their father had not only bought his peerage but also greased wheels to ensure his fracking-licence application would be fast-tracked through the local council in Yorkshire and approved by the end of the year. Information which had all come out since Christian's death. Since the bombing and demonstrations in Durham and York, the process had stalled indefinitely, according to the journalist.

Unless someone as rich as Picklett bought CleanGas.

There was a quote from Lady Alex on an alternative-media website. *"The fight to prevent hydraulic fracturing for shale oil and gas is far from over. It is ironic that declining oil prices have made fracking less fashionable for the time being, but sadly this situation only serves to highlight the fact that providing energy is a business driven solely by profit. Concern for the planet and its inhabitants is irrelevant to those whose business is oil and gas."*

Claudia made herself another coffee. If British fracking exploration was now on hold and oil prices were down, would this help or hinder a country like Fawala to sell its gas? The Emir was well-connected politically – perhaps that was why there had been no mention of him or his farm in the news reports? Anyway, Fawalan gas was natural, wasn't it? Deep wells were drilled into massive underground fields and no bedrock was shattered in horizontal hydraulic fracturing. There was no pollution of the water table.

Tom would scold her for thinking it, but she sort of hoped the Emir would continue to make a fortune from his country's resources. That way, her job would be safe and British racing would benefit from his continued investment in horses, sponsorship and prize-money. She looked around the expensively furnished room and imagined for a brief moment how her life might be right now, if the Emir had been killed along with Seb. Without his money, Claudia would probably have to spend her time eternally scrabbling for clients in a world that was saturated with bloodstock agents and parched of decent, manageable owners. Julia would be in a mess too. She'd have to sell or at least downsize Crangate.

She typed another name into the search engine.

Vasili Komarov wasn't in the oil or gas business, so it was unlikely that he even knew Christian or Greene. Several years ago, he had inherited an electricity company from his father and had a right royal time living as an oligarch until he'd briefly landed in jail on charges of – Claudia smirked – tax evasion. Before his case ever came to trial, it had been announced he'd sold 40% of his company to a hedge fund and, lo and behold, he moved to London and bought a stud farm. Maybe Komarov was just unlucky to have been at the sale?

Last year, she'd read an article about Komarov's father, an exposé of his alleged war crimes in Afghanistan, giving proof of the scale of his profiteering when the Soviet Union fell.

Her temples began to throb. She drained her coffee and turned on the TV.

Another news channel was showing recorded footage of Adam Greene's funeral in St. Paul's Cathedral. According to the commentator, nothing had been shown live for security reasons. The ceremony was all black coats, crocodile tears, corporate speeches and handshakes. Posthumous back-patting for a fucking warmonger while Tom languished in a cell. She threw an empty cigarette box at the screen.

And, to cap it all off, the real terrorists were still out there. She wondered if they revelled in each victory, or if they simply carved another notch and moved on to planning the next atrocity.

She scrolled through her social-media feed. Suddenly it seemed nothing more than boring rubbish. Nothing more than a cosy universe of things she'd *liked* and other algorithmic offerings designed to make her smile and further retreat into her own filtered bubble. She fleetingly wondered when the trolls would begin their barrage of hate at her account.

"Fuck that." She deactivated, logged out and deleted the app.

She tossed the phone onto a chair, turned off the TV and grabbed a bottle of wine to numb her rage.

*   *   *

The following morning, she called Ed Tomlinson and Mark Gilford, then relayed the weekly report to the Emir.

When she'd finished up, he asked: "How is Hanif doing?"

"Funnily enough, I was just going to ask you about him. Bill says he's got a wonderful way with horses, but that he's a bit strange. Hardly says a word."

"He had a tough childhood. He lost his mother. I will tell you all about it someday. My father agreed to take the boy in and care for him when it became too dangerous for him to stay in his own country."

"Poor man, that's terribly sad. Where's he from?"

"Oh, just across the water from Fawala."

"Well done to your father for taking him in."

"My father was a decent man. He always meant the best and wanted to help disadvantaged people. I hope I have inherited that trait from him."

Claudia wondered if the Emir's political connections could help to get Tom released. She gritted her teeth.

"Sir, you said to ask if there was anything I needed …"

PART II

Chapter 30

Fifteen weeks later
Sunday October 4th

Claudia woke before sunrise and lay in bed scrolling through news sites on her phone – she'd not bothered with social media in months. Beside her, Tom let out intermittent snores. She used to poke him when he got too bad but in the months since his release she was so happy to have him back that she no longer cared.

The news was full of the war in Syria and refugees flooding into Europe. Just a couple of weeks ago, an attack in France had taken all the headlines and offered reliable culprits and updates of the *fear* app that seemed to be in everybody's brains. Isolationist politicians were using it as an excuse to generate further fear of Muslim refugees. There had been several huge suicide explosions in Iraq and Pakistan during the last few days, but they had barely got a mention.

All this fear and conflict made Claudia so sad.

The London bombing had long vanished from news-reporting and Claudia was trying to move on, even if she was still angry that she'd never know why Oscar had got involved and how he'd got hold of the bomb components. Wallace had told her Oscar's house had been clean when he'd informed her she was free to start packing his belongings. But she hadn't been able to face up to that so far. Instead, she'd paid the landlord four more months' rent to give her some breathing space. She'd go and stay there next week during the sales and clear it out then. Over the summer, she'd had to deal with a few reporters sniffing around offering her cash for a tell-all about Oscar's troubled life. She'd politely turned them down, but wanted to punch their faces in.

Wallace had also been decent enough to let her know that the police had drawn a blank searching for a drug dealer or extremist known as *Mouse*, or *The Mouse*, but Claudia still had trouble letting go of that. She'd discussed it with Tom a couple of times since his release, but he'd been of the opinion that if the police couldn't get a lead from it, then she should just forget about it. And yet it was the one thing that still nagged at her. At the very least, she'd like to see the dealer who'd supplied Oscar put away, and if it turned out to be more than that, well …

It had been early August when the police had finally released Oscar's body for cremation. Tom and Claudia had been the only ones who'd attended the quick ceremony. Oscar's girlfriend Sally had changed her number when news broke about his involvement in the bombing and Claudia had heard from Mark Gilford that she'd quit her job and gone to Australia to escape the Newmarket rumour-mill. Poor girl – she'd only known Oscar a few months.

Tom stirred and opened his eyes. Claudia rolled over in the bed and gripped him tightly. "I never want to lose you again." She kissed him. "Because you *were* lost to me, you know? Even though I kept badgering Wallace about you, it was as if you were on another planet."

"Feels like that when you're in there, too."

She caressed his face. "Hey, why don't you come to the stud with me today? I only have to be in for an hour or so. Julia's invited us to lunch afterwards."

"Can't we just stay here?"

"We're showing the yearlings to Ed Tomlinson and the Emir. Ed likes to look at them before the sale and he'll probably buy a couple to train for the Emir."

"Is that not insider trading or something?" he asked with a mischievous grin.

"Certainly not. The horses are either owned by Julia or clients of ours who send them to us for sales prep. It's good marketing having Ed and the Emir look at them before they ship up to Newmarket. Our clients are delighted." She poked him playfully on the chest. "Come on, it'll do you good to get out and about."

"I cycle to work five days a week."

"That doesn't count and you know it. At work you only ever see Lady Alex."

"And the odd paparazzo looking for shit."

"Well, there'll be none of *them* at Crangate this morning."
He swung his legs out of bed.

*　　*　　*

Tom leaned against the wall under the archway to the main yard. He unwrapped a mint and put the paper into one of the large recycling bins just outside the yard. Last year, he'd suggested to Seb to have them installed so all the waste from the house and stud could be separated and collected every few weeks. Seb had thought the bins ugly but Julia had won him over.

The growl of a sports car broke his reverie and he turned to see Ed Tomlinson pull up in his new Aston Martin. He slid out of the sleek beast and adjusted his tailored jacket.

"Hello, Tom," he said cheerily. "Good to see you after … Well, after so long."

Tom shook his hand. "It's alright. Nobody knows what to say to me these days." He looked Ed up and down. "Life as the Emir's trainer suits you. Claudia tells me you're training the best two-year-old filly in the country. Congratulations!"

Ed beamed. "Thanks. Secular Princess has really put me on the map. Next run, I'm hoping she'll beat America's best at the Breeders' Cup."

"*Um*, best of luck." Tom didn't really follow horse racing. "Some car you've got there."

"The Emir bought it for me after Ascot. Sort of

welcome-to-the-top and keep-up-the-good-work sort of thing." He patted his jacket down again.

"How's the fuel economy?"

Ed shrugged. "No idea. My petrol's on the Emir's account. I take it he's not here yet?"

"No."

Claudia appeared and started talking horses, so Tom wandered away down the yard, passing stables where grooms were putting finishing touches to these potential racehorses which now looked like fitness models ready to step onto the stage and pose for the judges.

In the end stable there was a slight man with rugged, deep wrinkles in his almond skin, all topped-off with a tweed cap. He held a lead rope with the lightest of touches and gently rubbed the forehead of a striking dark-brown yearling. The horse leaned into his touch and he spoke in a low, hypnotic tone which Tom found strangely familiar.

The horse noticed Tom, pricked its ears, raised its head and snorted.

The groom kept speaking soothingly.

Then it hit Tom: he recognised the language.

Racking his brains, he searched for the right words and bid the man "*Khe chare*" – good day.

The groom whipped his head round. Stared.

The man's whole body tensed. It was a reaction Tom had grown used to in the last couple of months. He wondered when people would forget and move on.

Tom cleared his throat. "*Staa num tsa dhe?*" He hoped he'd just asked the man his name.

The groom kept staring. Tom couldn't read his eyes.

"I am Hanif Ali Mengak. Where did you learn to speak my language with the soft southern accent of Kandahari?" he replied in Pashto.

Tom found once again that he could understand better than he could speak. "I … soldier, Helmand province."

Hanif bristled momentarily. Tom offered his hand. Hanif shook it with an iron grip.

Tom realised both Hanif and the horse were looking at him with the same kind of curiosity. "I … Tom Sunderland. I … " He switched to English. "I'm sorry. I'm rusty. I'll have to continue in English."

Hanif kept staring. "Most occupying soldiers never learn the language."

"I was captured. Our helicopter was downed in the mountains. I was the only survivor. The Taliban caught me and I was held in a village for a couple of years. I just learnt the words the way I heard them every day."

"That is most interesting."

"I took every chance to talk to the villagers. I mean, you see, when the Taliban had finished with me, they left me as a prisoner of the village elder. He seemed as afraid of them as I was."

"Where in Kandahar were you held?"

"I don't know, somewhere high and remote. I always wondered why they kept me alive, then one day the Taliban reappeared, blindfolded me, put me in a truck for two days and exchanged me for an Afghani prisoner. Of course, the official story was that I was rescued by Special Forces."

"Official story," Hanif let out a wheezy laugh. "What did you think of my people and my country?"

Tom sucked in a breath, screwed up his face. "When the Taliban found me, I thought they would torture me – I'd heard stories on base. Awful things –"

"There are such people in my homeland," Hanif interrupted. "They do such things as a way of releasing their anger on the occupying forces. I am sorry. Please – continue."

Tom thought he'd clam up, or have to force the words out. But they leaked easily out of him. "The Taliban tied me to a post blindfolded and shot around me every night for God knows how long. A couple of rounds ricocheted into my injured arm. I thought they'd want me to bleed to death, but they found a doctor to treat me." Suddenly Tom felt lighter. Rubbed his face. "Then they started all over again. I'd never known tiredness and despair like that. Rounds ringing in my ears. Wondering if the next would blow my brains out. I just wanted it to stop, so I started talking. I told them all about the pipeline. I thought they'd ask me the best ways to sabotage it, but they weren't interested. One of them told me to shut up. He said they'd accepted *it*, but they'd never accept *us*. That they had no choice but to allow its construction. I can't remember how long they kept shooting at me. The only thing that kept me going was the thought that they were wasting their ammunition on me and not firing at my comrades in arms. Anyway, like I said, when they left, the villagers treated me decently."

Hanif grunted, stroked the horse. "We are not a greedy

people. We only want to be left alone in our own country. But the greed of developed nations for energy knows no bounds."

"So people like me get sent out to make war." He stopped and stared at the straw. "Thing is, once we got out there and started patrolling, something struck me. Something I'd never have believed if I hadn't seen it for myself."

"And what was that?"

"I couldn't believe how jaded the people were. The way they looked at us. Like they were watching a movie they'd seen too many times before."

A tear fattened on Hanif's eye and sat there unwilling to make the descent of his cheek. He dragged the heel of his hand roughly across his eye. "That is the tragedy of my country. We have rarely been left alone. There is always somebody arriving to interfere. Alexander the Great, the British, the Soviets, now Americans and their *coalition of the willing*." He half-smiled. "I believe that is what is known as *management-speak*."

Tom winced.

"We become spectators at a festival where the main attraction is the destruction of our country. Over and over again."

Another tear. This one made it halfway down his cheek.

"That is why my father sent me away from my home. Well, that and my unwillingness to accept the Mullah's God."

Tom knitted his brow.

Hanif arched his. "You know: God, Allah, Yahweh.

206

Whatever name men choose to call the deity they create in an attempt to rationalise something they cannot understand."

Tom's eyes widened.

Hanif rubbed the horse on the forehead. "I used to ride every day as a child. I was good at buzkashi."

"That's like polo, right?"

"A bit."

"I never saw anyone play."

"Taliban banned it but my friends and I used to play anyway." He grunted. "Another reason they disliked me. Taliban started with good intentions, I suppose. Freedom fighters. They took up the fight to get rid of the Soviets, and then they became power-hungry themselves. They want to control every detail of daily life and tell us that it is God's will."

"Bit like some of our politicians," muttered Tom. "We were all told that we were fighting the good fight, destroying the terrorist threat. Yet all we've done is make it worse, but no matter because we've secured the area's resources. So much for defeating terrorists."

Hanif smiled warmly. "You tell me things I already know, but I am surprised beyond words to hear such things from the mouth of a soldier."

"Ex-soldier. I left the army and then got in trouble for throwing shit at our Prime Minister. Misguided demonstration."

"Mr. Adam Greene?"

"Yes."

Hanif's eyes sparkled. "That was you? I read about that a few months ago." He grinned, showing crooked teeth.

Tom grinned back. "I shouldn't admit it, but it was

207

hilarious at the time. You should've seen the look on his face. Photographers captured the moment but funnily enough the shots never saw the light of day."

"You must have given considerable thought and planning to the …" he paused, "you would say '*prank*'?"

"Yes, prank. Your English is excellent, by the way."

"Thank you. I was given an education in Fawala. First I was taught to read and write in Arabic, and then in English by an old-fashioned upper-class man who worked for the sheikh."

"Sheikh?"

"Emir Rahim's father. He was old-fashioned and tough, but ..."

Tom waited for him to continue.

"I have been educated, but I was still a servant. However, I carried out my tasks with loyalty, if not always with pleasure." As if on cue, another tear welled up and made its way into the first wrinkle it found on Hanif's face. "A few years ago, I received word that my village is gone. They use drones now. It has become a video game."

"I'm so sorry. I …" but Tom was lost for words. He sensed something coiled tightly around every fibre of this slight man.

They stood in silence except for the snorting of the horse.

Eventually Tom asked, "What was he like – your father?"

Hanif closed his eyes. Tom could see them darting behind their lids.

"He tried to be kind, but he was blinded by religion and

he refused to question authority. He accepted too much. He just wanted us to live quiet lives but when war comes to your country, your village, what you want becomes irrelevant. When my mother was killed by the Soviets, he accepted her death as an accident of conflict. He never showed anger towards the invaders and never took up arms against them. He just wanted to be left alone. But he knew how difficult her loss was for me and he was afraid because of my defiance of the religious men. When he became friends with the Sheik, who would visit every few months with supplies and money to help the local warlords drive out the invaders, he saw an opportunity to get me out of harm's way. He meant the best. I was his only child …" Hanif ran out of steam.

Tom felt tears of his own welling up.

Behind them, Bill's booming voice cut through the moment. "Alright, everyone. His Highness has arrived. First horse out."

Tom composed himself. "It was nice to talk to you, Hanif. Maybe I'll cycle over here one evening and we can chat over a cup of tea."

Hanif grinned. "I would like that very much."

"Or if you're ever free, call in to my office in Newbury." He pulled a card out of his pocket. "My boss would love to meet you, too."

"Thank you."

They shook hands again.

Hanif pulled his tweed cap down over his eyes and readied himself and his charge.

Tom left the stable, skirted the edge of the yard and stood under the archway. Claudia stood with the Emir and Ed as a yearling paraded past them. As the next one approached, Claudia beckoned Tom over. He shook his head, but she beckoned more insistently.

The Emir turned to face him and for a second Tom was unsure what to do. Then the Emir smiled broadly and extended a hand. Tom walked over, shook it and felt tension leave his body.

"Tom, so good to see you."

"Thank you for putting in a word for me, sir."

"Oh, I am not sure how much influence I had in the matter, but I am glad you are back with Claudia. I hope the police didn't treat you too badly."

"They were just doing their jobs, I suppose."

"Still, it is not right to keep a man locked up without charge."

Tom shrugged. "Sign of the times. I suppose if I'd never pulled that prank on Adam Greene, none of this would have happened."

The Emir's face hardened. He fixed his gaze on Tom, and for a second Tom felt cold. "It was a harmless prank. Why regret doing it? Did you not give the matter thought beforehand?"

"*Um*, well, yes."

"And I assume you felt that it was your only course of action to draw attention to your cause?"

"I did. Nobody was willing to listen to Veterans Against the War. They were branded unpatriotic."

"So there you have it." The Emir gave him a lopsided smile, looking for a second like a naughty schoolboy.

Tom almost smiled.

The Emir clapped him on the back and cocked his chin at Claudia. "You are lucky to have a woman like this with you. As am I."

She pulled an awkward smile while Ed kept his attention on the horses.

"Good afternoon, Hanif," said Ed, when the man appeared with his charge. "I can't wait to have you back next week. Secular Princess is in top form for her trip to Kentucky."

Hanif nodded politely.

"Her new lad has done OK the last few months, kept her calm and steady. But to be honest, I think she misses you."

Then the Emir spoke to Hanif in Arabic. They exchanged a few words, but Hanif never looked directly at the man.

When Ed had finished looking at the horse, Claudia watched Hanif lead the animal away. "You told me he lost his mother as a child," she said. "How awful. He's lucky your father took him in."

The Emir nodded.

"That's not the half of it," muttered Tom.

All three heads turned toward him.

"Oh, I had a chat with him while we were waiting. He's had an interesting life."

"You actually had a conversation with him?" asked Ed.

"Yes, we discussed the war in his homeland."

"War?" Ed's brow knitted. "Isn't he from Pakistan?"

"Afghanistan."

"Good lord," Ed looked at the Emir. "Is that right, sir? I always assumed …"

"That is understandable. Most of the people who come to Fawala to work are indeed from Pakistan."

*   *   *

They moved on to another stable block and an hour later they had looked at all forty yearlings. Ed dashed back to Newmarket, Tom went to the house to say hello to Julia and Claudia brought the Emir over to the office.

Inside, he sank into a plush sofa. "Claudia, Hanif asked me earlier if he could remain in Kentucky after the races and work on my stud farm there. Please tell him I have considered the matter and this will not be possible. He must return to Fawala this winter."

"I'll pass that on."

"He will be disappointed, of course, but with the political climate as it is and their jittery fear of Muslims, I do not wish to draw attention to myself by having Case apply for a work visa for him until I have concluded business negotiations with their Senate committees and other financial tribes."

The Emir's phone rang.

"Abdullah! How are the Americans treating you?" he asked in English.

Claudia closed the file on her desk and fiddled with her laptop.

"That's good news. Make sure you bring a present to the meeting. I believe he likes cigars. Good. Good." He sprawled himself on the sofa as he listened. His other phone chimed. He checked the screen and tossed the device to Claudia. "Can you take a message or tell him I'll call him tonight?"

The screen read **Case Felsom**. She answered just as Case hung up, so she tapped out a text and sent it off.

"Who cares if he's a Republican?" Rahim bellowed into the device. "I wasn't aware it made a difference anymore. They are all businessmen. Oh, those are just xenophobic chantings to appeal to the base fears of potential voters. You know this, Abdullah." He paused, listening. "After the election? That's over a year away! No. Tell Senator Daynson that I'd like to meet informally at the beginning of next month, but I don't want to be seen in Washington. Tell him I will send a plane and fly him to my Kentucky farm. Excellent. OK. Good luck and call me directly after the meeting."

He tossed the device onto the cushion and looked at Claudia. "Americans. Easy to deal with, except when they are worried about keeping their jobs or getting promotions."

"I didn't realise you did business in America."

"Not as much as I'd like to, but hopefully that will change by the end of the year. That's part of the reason I am sponsoring a race there."

Chapter 31

The next morning, Commissioner Trenton tapped his fingers on Wallace's report. He screwed up his face and glanced out the window. "I know you're not happy, but it's all done and dusted."

"You mean we're not really going to follow up on the DU? What if there's more of it being stuffed into a bomb as we speak? What about finding whoever pulled all the strings for the attack?"

Trenton raised his palms, made a shoving gesture at Wallace. "Stop. We're done here. The DU investigation has passed to the secret services. Thankfully, people wounded by the shrapnel seem to be displaying little, if any, toxicity."

"That's a stroke of luck."

"Not really. The NHS administrators have praised us

for alerting hospitals and first responders after the attack. Any survivors affected are given a good prognosis. Furthermore, we've been given a bigger budget to cover events like that horse sale, big race meetings, charity galas. Basically, anywhere there's a concentration of rich powerful people and a level of security that's not airport-tight."

"A bigger budget to cover rich arses? And yet Scotland Yard has to move to smaller, antiquated buildings?"

"Just concentrate on preventing the next attack."

"Tell me, would the budget have got a bump if the bomb had gone off in a shopping centre in Birmingham or Brixton?"

"Oh, don't start, Wallace. I know you're probably happy Greene got his arse blown off, but leave it out."

"What if preventing a terror attack wasn't about increased security in hindsight but more about how we act when we're trying to hold on to power that's slipping from our grasp?"

"Have you been drinking?"

"Not today. Next time you're having a cosy dinner with our esteemed leader, why don't you ask him the same question?"

"Wallace, you sound like a man who desperately needs a holiday."

Wallace opened his mouth, closed it.

Back in his own office, he told Gibson that he was considering taking some leave.

Gibson nodded. "When?"

He sighed. "Dunno yet."

"Do you want me to keep on at MI5 about the DU?"

215

"Leave that to me. I'm already catching shit, no point you getting dirty too."

Gibson left, closed the door behind him and Wallace tapped at his phone and put it to his ear.

Chapter 32

Abdullah's Lincoln limousine pulled up outside the Hart Senate Office building on Constitution Avenue. He and his team of four stepped out of the car and straightened their suits.

Under Rahim's instruction, Abdullah had spent the last couple of months throwing money at a K Street lobbyist, who had routed funds into Senator Rick Daynson's campaign coffers (minus commissions and fees) in order to set up this meeting. Now he needed to ensure the senator's first impression of him was as polished as an American smile.

"How is my face?" asked Abdullah.

The man closest to him inspected Abdullah's cheeks and neckline. "Not a blemish."

In preparation for this meeting, Abdullah had learned as much as he could about Daynson, West Virginia

Republican and Chairman of the Senate Committee on Energy and Natural Resources. In order to make a striking first impression, he had shaved his beard to appeal to the clean-shaven conservative and ordered his team to do the same, though they had not liked it. Abdullah had even gone so far as to apply a subtle skin-lightening cream.

They made their way up the steps and into the visitor's lobby. They announced themselves, received meeting passes and were shown towards the body-scanners and X-ray machines.

An intern arrived to escort them to the senator's tenth-floor suite.

Muted yellow wallpaper took the edge off leather furniture and a dark mahogany desk bedecked with a gold nameplate, telephone, laptop, but not a single file or sheet of paper. Two American flags hung limp from poles behind the senator's club chair. Through a slightly ajar door, Abdullah could hear secretaries and aides making calls and tapping at keyboards.

"The Senator will be with you momentarily," said the intern, extending a hand to the leather sofa and high-backed chairs.

Daynson bustled into the room and extended Abdullah a stiff grin and hearty handshake.

Abdullah thought the man's shiny expressionless face looked even more ridiculous in person. Even the immaculate cut of his suit couldn't quite hide his pigeon-chest and flabby torso.

"Rick Daynson. Please-ta meecha!"

"The pleasure is all mine, sir."

Abdullah disliked having to call Americans *sir*. Not only did they not deserve it, but they also failed to recognise Abdullah's right to be addressed with the title as a member of a Royal family. But, in the name of his country and its interests, he gritted his teeth and plastered on his widest smile.

"Allow me to introduce my team." Abdullah indicated them with his free hand as he said their names.

Daynson nodded at each man.

"Say, I heard you were at Yale with my eldest, Troy?"

Abdullah grinned. He'd made sure the lobbyist had told Daynson that. "That is correct, but I must confess we never really became acquainted."

"Hell, it's a big school," Daynson said, running his eyes over Abdullah's suit. "A man after my own style. Sheerman and Crane, right?"

Abdullah pretended to be surprised. "How observant of you! I could not resist having them make me up a few suits."

Abdullah turned to one of his team who handed him an elaborately carved humidor which he then presented to Daynson, using both hands and giving a neck bow.

"Please, allow me to give you a small token of friendship."

"Well, how d'you like that! That's mighty kind of you. I do like a good cigar." He set the box on his desk. The lid made a faint sucking sound as it opened, revealing neatly stacked Montecristos. "That's quality work right there." The senator picked one up and took a long smell.

"I hope they are satisfactory, sir."

"Terrific." Daynson replaced the cigar carefully and shut the box. "Please, gentlemen, sit."

After coffee was served, Daynson said: "OK, pitch me your deal."

Abdullah handed him a four-page document from his briefcase. Picked up his own copy and a pen. He went through the main points even though he imagined all the senator really wanted to know was how much the gas would cost, how long the deal was for and were there any extras to sweeten the deal.

Much to Abdullah's surprise, Daynson actually read the entire document.

"Your futures gas price …" He sucked air between his teeth. "And you want us locked into that for seven years? You know how the market's going, right? Oil's cheap these days. Hell, I got a buddy in the shale-gas drilling business who's selling all his racehorses so he can get back into offshore oil drilling."

"You refer to BW Picklett?"

"That's right. You know BW?"

"No, but I heard he was trying to buy British company CleanGas."

Daynson flapped a hand. "Oh, long-finger stuff."

"Perhaps we could do business with his company for offshore deep-water gas wells?"

Daynson nodded slowly. "Perhaps you could. I can make introductions. Old BW's a good man. Been in the business as long as I've been in Washington. Had several contracts to start exploring in the Arctic too, but all that's on hold for the moment."

"I thought it had been vetoed completely?"

"Nothing's ever set in stone with these things. Anyway, he'd love to help you guys out, I'm sure of it."

"Thank you very much." Abdullah nodded thoughtfully. Rahim had been right about this man.

"Anyway," said Daynson, tapping the document, "we can't go at these prices."

"Please bear in mind that Fawalan liquefied natural gas is conflict-free. It is not an energy source from a war zone."

"So what?"

Abdullah cleared his throat. "We are an ally to this country. We can deliver the product to whichever terminal you desire. With the drop in oil prices, fracking for shale gas in America is becoming prohibitively expensive, is it not? That is without getting into the environmental backlash against the procedure. Fawalan gas will give you a workable alternative. Breathing space, if you like, until your country has finalised its long-term policy."

Daynson steepled his hands, his botoxed features frozen into an eternal poker-face. "We can just keep importing oil for less than your gas. Pity your oilfields have dried up."

"You certainly could, but with an election next year and you seeking your party's nomination, I suspect moving away from foreign *oil* will be a manifest point in your speeches, given your position." He spread his hands out. "As you said, we have no oil left to sell. We are merely selling *natural* gas."

"Look, I like you, Abdullah, and I like that we can deal with your country without any ..." he paused for a moment, "ideological wrinkles, despite our differences in faith. However, I just can't do it at this time. I mean how's it going to look if I recommend the Committee signs off on this deal when I've got coal lying in the ground back home in Virginia and miners out of work?" He took a breath. "Look, bring prices down, give it a year to get the election out of the way, and we'll be able to cut a deal then. I guarantee it." His grin took just a millisecond too long to assemble itself.

Abdullah screwed his face up, hissed in a breath. "My Emir is most insistent that the deal needs to be done by the end of this year, before the election procedure dominates everyone's time. You should also know that we are also looking to upgrade several elements of our armed forces." They weren't, but Abdullah liked this last little bit of bullshit and if Jabbar got his way they might indeed buy armaments.

Daynson blinked, looked at his desk. "My hands are tied at this time, but what I can do is set up that meeting with BW."

"That would be most kind of you. I have also been instructed by His Highness the Emir to tell you that he will be in Lexington, Kentucky, at the end of the month. He will be attending the races and horse sales and visiting his stud farm. He has informed me that he would like to send his jet up here to collect you and bring you to Kentucky for an informal meeting. He may be able to offer you a better deal in such a situation. You could also bring Mr. Picklett down with you."

222

"I guess that could work. BW'll be in Kentucky anyway, at the races." He opened his laptop and fingered the mouse pad. "I'm actually scheduled to be home in West Virginia first week of November, so I guess a quick visit to Kentucky to introduce your boss to BW wouldn't be a problem at all." He tapped the humidor. "And after your generous gifts and contributions, I guess the Emir deserves the chance to meet me himself."

"Thank you very much for your time, senator."

*   *   *

At six o'clock the following morning, Abdullah stood alone in front of the US Marine Corps War Memorial, just north of Arlington cemetery. He looked up at the statue depicting the iconic image of four Marines erecting the flag on Iwo Jima.

He turned south and looked through the trees at the thousands of little white headstones and the tomb of the Unknown Soldier. Monuments were of little consolation to the dead. He wondered what would be erected to celebrate the poor brave souls who had been sent to Abdullah's part of the world to fight in the wars for energy. And, still, nobody seemed to question the logic of defending one's country by plundering another halfway around the world.

He pulled his baseball cap down, flicked his hoody up and ambled down the hill towards the Potomac river. Just another jogger cooling down. He took a deep breath and admired the panorama of Washington. From the Lincoln

223

Memorial, he followed the reflecting pool to the World War II Memorial and then to the obelisk of the Washington Monument. To its right across the tidal basin was the Jefferson Memorial. Past Washington's spike was the National Mall and then the great dome of the Capitol. He had to admit it was beautiful, even under a grey sky. A fitting seat for their empire. Not as impressive as London, but then the British had had rather a head start over the Americans, even if the British Empire was now merely financial, stripped of its physical territory.

A couple of joggers paced by and a few people walked dogs. Abdullah glanced at his watch. His lobbyist had suggested the spot would be ideal for his needs.

He had been walking a few minutes when a lithe woman with ivory skin and dark hair in a ponytail came running up the hill. She slowed as she saw him and stopped at a bench to warm-down and stretch.

Abdullah sat on the bench, pretending to scroll through his phone.

"Thank you for agreeing to meet me, senator," he said. "You look rather more athletic than your colleague."

Lynn Moorewell, senator for Oklahoma and ranking member on the Committee for Energy and Natural Resources, circled the bench, hands on hips.

"So how'd it go with Daynson?" she asked, scanning the area.

"He talked about price and told me that his hands are tied."

"He's just stalling. Everyone knows he's in bed with

224

Big Oil and that he's gunning for the Presidency."

"He offered to connect me with BW Picklett's drilling company."

"Listen, Prince Abdullah ..." She put a heel on the bench and stretched her hamstring.

Abdullah smiled – he liked to be called Prince.

"Your lobbyist needs to keep up the pressure on the other committee members but, I can tell you from where I'm standing, I need your gas and I need it now. So I have no problem recommending that we pay your price."

Abdullah put a hand up to scratch his beard, then remembered that he'd shaved it. "Forgive me if this sounds too good to be true."

"I'm gonna be honest with you: last ten years or so, we've done so much drilling – fracking – in my home state that we've basically turned it into Swiss cheese. In 2007 Oklahoma had one earthquake, last year there were more than 900 reported. Between wells and wastewater disposal into the deep bedrock, we're in a whole world of shit. Except, nobody wants to talk about it because 20 per cent of jobs in the state are related to the oil and gas industry. But I'm getting my people out there to tell folks that there's not much point in making money from a system that's poisoning and destroying the very land they live on and the water they drink." She looked at Abdullah. "Now you know what your support has been channelled into."

"You are welcome. And for what it's worth, we do agree with you. Even if we are in the business of selling gas, it is not obtained from horizontal drilling through the bedrock."

"I'll recommend to the members that we buy Fawalan gas. It'll buy us time to stop fracking, clean up our act and for me to find other means of employment in my state. Hell, the infrastructure all over the country needs an overhaul. I tell ya, whoever wins the White House this time could do the FDR thing all over again and put Americans to work repairing America." She shrugged. "But that's just my opinion."

Abdullah liked this woman, even if her tone was close to the idealism of Rahim.

"How will you deal with Daynson?"

"If he wins the party nomination, he'll have to step down from the committee. As ranking member I'll take over, as least until after the election."

Abdullah frowned, stared out at the city. "And what if he should not only win the nomination, but also the White House?"

Moorewell actually laughed. "Hey, I'm a Democrat but even if I wasn't he doesn't stand a chance." Her face became grave. "Least, I hope not."

Abdullah frowned.

She stole a quick glance at him. "I mean, who wants The Plastic Patriot in the White House, right? Lying sack of shit."

Abdullah's eyes widened.

"I mean, he shouts hateful things about foreigners, but yet he took your money and agreed to meet you."

Abdullah stood. "Thank you very much for your time, senator. I wish you luck in your affairs."

"Thank *you* very much. Oh, and tell Emir Rahim that I think he's a visionary. A real man of the people."

Abdullah pulled an executive smile. "I will do so. In fact, he is visiting Kentucky at the end of the month for the horse racing. Perhaps you would like to meet him."

She looked at her shoes. "That would be nice." She spun on her heel and bounded off, gazelle-like.

Abdullah tapped his phone and pressed it to his ear as he watched her bound away.

Chapter 33

Rahim stared at the TV. In the aftermath of yesterday's terror attack in a German train station, Senator Daynson was spouting more vitriolic nonsense about banning Muslims from entering the United States until they could be checked. Whatever checking meant.

Rahim shook his head slowly and wondered if the vain senator regretted having those Botox injections. Surely a politician needed to emote to his audience, in preference to looking stiff and shiny? Although he had to admit, the senator's hair plugs did look natural.

Rahim muted the TV, scrolled through his phone and dialled.

"Hello, Case."

"Hello, sir. I was just about to call you."

"What about?"

"I've spoken to a couple of Breeders' Cup directors. Your sponsorship funds have been received along with the advertising package and they'd like final confirmation of how you want to name the race."

"It will be called the FawGas Juvenile Fillies Stakes."

"I'll pass that on."

"Thank you. I am calling because I have just been watching footage of Senator Daynson complaining about Muslims and trying to stoke up fear."

"Oh God, I know. What can I say, sir? It's all just so embarrassing. The scary thing is, people are listening to him."

"And that is why I am calling. The groom who will accompany Secular Princess is Fawalan. I do not want him living or working with any narrow-minded, anti-Muslim types."

"Sir, I want you to know that I do not put up with any kind of discrimination on your farm, or even in my position as chairman of the Kentucky Thoroughbred Farm Managers Association. Rest assured that I'll have him living and working with decent people. In fact, I already have two guys working in the pre-training barn who fit the bill quite nicely. One's Mexican, and the other's a born-and-bred Kentucky boy. He's a little wild, but he's friendly and great with horses."

"Very good."

"Oh, and sir?"

"Yes?"

Case sighed. "While we're on the subject of discrimination,

I would like your permission to write a letter to the Governor of Kentucky on behalf of the Farm Manager's Association to point out how much you and other Muslim racehorse owners and breeders contribute to the economy of our fine State."

A pause. "I think that is an excellent idea. Oh, and please send me a copy of the letter. I hope to meet with Daynson and a friend of his during Breeders' Cup weekend to discuss a business matter."

"Really?" Case cut in, forgetting himself.

"Yes, really. During our meeting I will point out to Daynson how stupidly he is behaving."

"Good for you, sir."

Rahim could sense the grin in his voice.

Chapter 34

Hanif locked his bicycle to a railing in Newbury, walked into the outdoor clothing shop and selected a pair of synthetic-fibre hiking boots.

"I have to travel on an aeroplane with these," he said to the sales assistant. "I need to know if they will pass the metal detector without me having to remove them."

A look that could have been fear flickered across the girl's face.

"I'll ask the manager," she said, trotting off.

He walked about in the boots until she returned.

"Manager says no, they won't set off a metal detector."

"I will take them. Thank you."

He paid cash and walked across the street in the pouring rain to a large chemist where he bought travel-size toothpaste and shampoo, a new toothbrush, disposable razors and a small clear plastic bag. He also selected a travel adaptor so he could charge his phone. While he waited at the cash register, he checked the items off his list with a pencil.

He knew that Americans were very thorough and particular about baggage regulations. Although he would be arriving to the country on a cargo flight with Secular Princess and her travelling companion, he would only be taking a small bag of personal belongings and he knew it was better not to give customs and immigration any excuses.

His one bending of the rules would be a bottle of whisky. Not a fine, aged single malt like he'd bought when he'd moved in with Lee and Des, but something blended and raised in old bourbon casks. Something for American tastes.

Out on the street he stuffed his list and all his purchases into his beaten-up old backpack that had seen many years in the Fawalan desert. He pulled out the business card Tom had given him. Consulting a street map on his phone, he found that the address was just a few blocks away. Rain tipped down, and he could do with a cup of tea and a chat before he cycled back to Crangate.

Tom answered the door. "Hanif! Good to see you. You look sodden. Come in and dry off."

Hanif made his way through the terraced house that had been converted into makeshift offices. A couple of eager-looking young people in baggy woolly jumpers and baggier, woollier hairdos sat at desks doing whatever people did at a charitable environmental foundation.

"Lady Alex'll be sorry she missed you," said Tom,

leading Hanif into a bigger office with a desk, sofa and television set. "Have a seat and hang your coat on the chair. Tea, coffee?"

"I would like a tea, please. Black."

Tom left the room and reappeared with two steaming mugs.

"So, what brings you into Newbury?"

"Shopping for my trip to America." He cupped the mug with his hands. "I wanted to thank you for taking the time to talk to me last Sunday."

"Not at all. I was fascinated by your story."

Hanif thought for a moment, wanting to get the words right. "It is so rare that I get to talk to anyone about my homeland, let alone anyone who has experienced it."

"You know, despite the war and all the destruction, one of the worst things about my time there was seeing the heroin trade increase."

"I have read that opium production has more than doubled since *the liberation* of the country." He let out a wheeze of a laugh. "I dislike Taliban, as I dislike all religious extremists, but if they did one decent thing it was the control and suppression of the drug trade."

"Yeah, well, they might not even be doing that anymore."

Hanif looked at him.

"I've heard that they're encouraging it now as a way to finance their battle against what they call the puppet government. What a bloody mess."

Tom went to a wooden cabinet, produced a bottle of whisky and a glass.

"I'm assuming you don't drink, but I need a snifter if I'm going to keep talking about this."

Hanif's eyes lit up. "Actually, I like whisky."

"You are full of surprises!"

He poured two fingers-worth into each glass.

"Even when I was young," said Hanif, "I formed the opinion that my former religion's prohibition of alcohol was simply about control and rooted in an ancient realisation that people in desert climates who drank only wine when thirsty often did harm to themselves or others. So what better way to get men to stop drinking than by divine decree?" Hanif took a long deep smell, swirling the liquid in the tumbler. "This is good."

"Certainly is. Sixteen years in casks," said Tom, grinning.

They sipped in silence for a few moments.

"You know, when I was released, the most difficult thing was the debriefing," said Tom. "I mean, I had expected it to be long and thorough, but the army virtually treated me like an enemy. They seemed convinced that I'd been turned."

Hanif blinked.

"They didn't like my answers, you see. Even when I returned home and discharged, I'm sure they were keeping tabs on me. It came as quite a surprise when I was asked to that ceremony with Greene, but I suppose they needed a hero to parade in front of the cameras." Another sip. "That's when Lady Alex and I got the idea for the prank."

Hanif laughed his wheezy laugh.

Tom settled back into his chair and launched into war

stories, feeling more comfortable talking to this man than even confiding in Claudia. He didn't have to backtrack, to answer disbelieving questions. Hanif simply understood.

An hour and a third of the bottle later, Hanif had become more animated. He talked freely about his life and horses and Tom listened quietly. Then, all of a sudden, he clammed up as if his meter had just run out and shut him down. He checked his phone.

"I am sorry to take so much of your time. It was foolish of me, but I simply could not help myself."

"Foolish? Not at all." Tom regarded him curiously.

"I really should get going." He placed the glass on the desk.

Tom's phone pinged a message. "I'd love to cycle back with you but I've still got a few things to take care of. Thanks again for stopping by. It's been interesting. You'll have to join Claudia and me for dinner at home before you head off to Kentucky."

"I would like that, but I am leaving the day after tomorrow."

"Oh. I thought you were staying in Newmarket to work the sales?"

"No, Mr. Tomlinson and the Emir want the horses to travel early, so I will miss the spectacle of an English thoroughbred auction after all."

They shook hands warmly and Tom showed him out.

"Still pouring," said Tom, wrinkling his nose. "Times like this I almost wish I had a car."

*　　*　　*

As he cycled out of Newbury, Hanif realised that it was darker than he thought and his bike did not have a light. He found it difficult to focus on the road in the pouring rain and the whisky in his stomach certainly wasn't helping. He got to a T-junction, stopped, checked both ways and headed left. A sign said *Crangate Stud 3 miles.* Half a mile later, he glanced up a small road to his left, knowing that Claudia and Tom lived up there. A car shot past him, spraying water in its wake. Hanif swerved into a puddle and his front wheel jolted down into a deep pothole, stopping his bike suddenly. He got off, stepped around the flooded pothole and pulled the bike towards him.

Then he noticed the flat front tyre.

He let out a few Pashto obscenities and started walking, pushing the wounded bike beside him. Just ahead, headlights came into view. Hanif stepped into the verge to make sure the car didn't splash him. But instead of driving past, it screeched to a halt and the window slid down.

"Hanif! Are you alright?" asked Claudia.

"I have a puncture."

She got out, wrapping her jacket around her. "I'll give you a lift back. Stick the bike in the boot." She opened the hatchback. Rain soaked into her hair.

"That is very kind."

He picked up his bike and they both manoeuvred it into the small car's boot, but the rear wheel stuck out so they couldn't shut the hatch.

"Never mind," she said. "Not far to go."

He swung his backpack off and stuffed it under the bike.

Hanif liked Claudia, but all of a sudden he was starting to regret having talked to her boyfriend, even if it had been therapeutic. He shrugged. Perhaps he shouldn't overthink and worry – after all, the man was damaged goods.

He glanced at her. She took her eyes off the road and smiled politely.

Her brother, too, had been a nice, damaged guy. It was just a pity that one could never trust an addict. Hanif sighed.

He was looking forward to this trip to America. He was tired of functioning on anger but, at the same time, it kept him focused and he had to admit that it was all he had left.

Claudia pulled up near the yard archway. They got out and Claudia raised the boot hatch fully. She grabbed a strap of Hanif's backpack and tugged. It stubbornly refused to budge. Her hair soaked, rain dripped down her neck. She gave the bag a yank and it came free with a ripping sound. Shopping bags and small items spilled out of the torn bag. A chemist's bag and a pair of new boots fell onto the wet gravel.

"Oh bugger! I'm so sorry, Hanif," she said, picking things up. "That bag looks like it's been everywhere with you."

Hanif inspected the torn backpack.

"I'll buy you a new one first thing tomorrow, so you'll have it for your trip."

"Please, that is really not necessary. It is not the first time I have had to stitch a repair. There is no need to buy me something new."

They gathered his things and pulled the bike out together.

"See you in the morning, Hanif."

"Thank you very much."

Hanif parked his bike behind the bins and watched her drive away.

Chapter 35

The following night, Claudia sat in her office hunched over Kentucky sales catalogues. She yawned. Her stomach growled. She made herself a coffee and returned to the desk, her eyes settling on the framed photograph of Oscar. She gave it a sad smile and then had to blink back the tears.

Out in the little kitchenette off reception, she heard a snapping sound. She investigated and found a mouse caught in the trap she'd asked Bill to set. She really didn't want to touch it, but blood was seeping from its nose. Charming. She gingerly wrapped the device in a piece of kitchen towel, carried the little package outside, pulled back the lever and deposited the dead rodent under the hedgerow. She left the trap on the windowsill, washed her hands and returned to her desk. When she looked at

Oscar's smiling image, she thought again of the note he'd written in his diary. If only *that* mouse had been caught in a trap …

She heard the door opening. "Hello?" she called.

Tom appeared, brandishing a cooler bag. "Meals on wheels. I gave up waiting, made us a picnic instead." He produced sandwiches and poured soup from a thermos into mugs.

"Oh, you're a star. I'm tired and famished, but at least I squashed that bloody mouse that was nibbling and shitting on the biscuits."

"Yeah, I saw the trap on the window. It, *er* …" He frowned.

"What?"

He blinked, shook his head. "Never mind. It's gone."

She sipped the hot tomato soup and thought of Oscar. It had been his favourite.

Tom pulled up a chair and leaned his elbows on the desk. "What time are you off to Newmarket?"

"Crack of dawn, I'm afraid. I've got to beat the lorries there." She rubbed her forehead. "And I still have to pack."

"Are you giving Hanif a lift up?"

"No, he'll go up on a lorry, then he'll go to Ed's yard and pick up Secular Princess." She smiled. "I'm glad he got on with you. It's funny though, when I picked him up the other night, he never mentioned he'd had a drink with you."

"Probably embarrassed. He was a bit squiffy after the whisky." He sipped his soup. "There's so many people in

240

Hanif's position: displaced, unable to return. I mean, look at all the refugees on the news."

"I'm tired of the news. Sick of policemen and politics too." She glanced at Oscar's photo again. "When I'm up in Newmarket, I'll empty his house, meet the landlord and close out the rent. Oh, and I'll stay up there until we leave for Kentucky. The Emir'll want to fly out of Stansted, so it just makes sense."

*　*　*

Up in his flat, Hanif wiped down the kitchen sink, threw the cloth and the empty bleach bottle into the bin bag. He ran his gloved hands under the tap and glanced out the window across the yard. Down through the archway, he could just make out the light from the office window.

He placed another pair of gloves in the bathroom with another bleach-soaked cloth. He'd use them to finish off in the morning after his shower.

He peeled off his gloves, tossed them in a bin bag, went over to the table and stared at the spare device and receiver. Pondered taking them with him, but there might be questions at the airport he could do without. So he opened the receiver, took out the battery, dropped all the bits into the bag and knotted it. He could just dump it outside, but the bins had been emptied today, and he knew from watching the collections all summer that it would be at least two weeks before the truck returned. Bill was always complaining about it to the local council.

No, he'd take the bag with him on the horse lorry and dump it somewhere along the way. However, there was no chance he'd be able to retrieve the other device. Not that it mattered anymore.

Chapter 36

At 4.45 the following morning, the tack room buzzed with chatter and excitement. After three months working nearly every day on the stud, all the grooms were looking forward to the work-hard, play-hard atmosphere of a yearling sale.

Bill entered and silence descended. He announced that five lorries would arrive shortly to transport all twenty-nine yearlings to Newmarket.

Under Bill's instruction, they filled large wooden boxes with everything needed to billet the horses, show them to clients and get them through the auction ring.

"Right," said Bill. "Leave all your travel bags and stuff out at the loading ramp then go and get your horses ready. Hanif, you can help me move all this lot out to the ramp."

When the others had left, Bill stuck out a hand.

"It's been a pleasure, Hanif," said Bill. "You're a great worker."

"Thank you very much. I have found my time here to be most interesting."

Bill nodded curtly. "Alright then, let's get on with it."

Twenty minutes later, a lorry arrived and backed up to the loading ramp just as the sky was turning blue.

Hanif dashed off to get a horse.

"Morning, Bill," said the driver, climbing down from his cab.

"Morning, Chas. Right, seeing as you're here first, you'll take the gear."

The hydraulic ramp descended with a whirr and Bill and Chas worked with efficiency born out of experience and minutes later everything was loaded apart from the grooms' luggage.

Chas flapped a hand at him. "You get the horses coming, I'll stuff these in."

Bill spun on his heel and darted under the archway.

Chas snatched up the holdalls and chucked them two at a time on top of the stacked feed bags. Beside the last bag, he noticed a knotted bin bag which seemed to smell of bleach. Frowning, he pulled the knot open and inspected the contents. "What the bloody hell?" he muttered. "Mine's not a rubbish truck." He went to the large wheelie bins by the wall, opened the one marked *Recyclables Only*, and tossed the bag in.

A second later Bill appeared ahead of grooms leading

horses. They loaded up and closed the ramp.

"Chas, this is Hanif," said Bill. "He's the only groom travelling with you. When you get up there, Claudia'll meet you at the ramp and oversee the unloading."

"Gotcha."

Bill handed Hanif a large thick envelope. "Here's all their passports and paperwork." He turned to Chas. "Hanif stays on the truck with you. He's going to America with Secular Princess."

"Right you are, Bill ... Hanif, you'll have time to kill before we collect her. The flight's not till this afternoon."

"Oh, I am good at killing time," he said cheerily, as he climbed into the truck.

Chapter 37

The soldiers went house-to-house, room-to-room. They opened goat pens and shooed the animals out, which pissed off their owners.

A stone flew out of nowhere and hit a soldier's leg.

Dust swirled. Soldiers shouted. Despite their training, they too were a hair's breadth from blind panic.

An old man shouted back and advanced on a soldier. There was a shot.

For a second everything seemed to freeze. The whole scene looked paralysed. Until the old man dropped to his knees.

Then someone else threw a stone and everything became a storm of lead, screams and dust. His mother had sent him inside, told him to hide under the table. He came out when the gunfire stopped and ran into the next room to find her and for a second thought she was praying.

Hanif woke with a start on the tiny bench. His watch told him he'd only had an hour's shut-eye. Strange he kept dreaming about that day after all these years, because it wasn't her death that had really affected him: mountain life was harsh and people died young. No, it was the rudeness of war that shocked him.

Hanif had barely slept since he'd discovered back in Newmarket that his bag of rubbish was missing. He'd questioned the driver, who'd said he had "chucked it". After weighing up the options and possible outcomes, he'd decided that the chances of the bag ending up with the police were remote. But still, he would've preferred to dispose of it himself. Thinking back, he should've been more thorough back in June as well, but there was little point in worrying about any of that now.

He stood, stretched and rubbed Secular Princess's forehead. The truck slowed and pulled off the interstate highway. The filly and her travelling companion had handled the journey well enough, even though they'd sweated profusely and guzzled their way through six 40-litre containers of water during the eight-hour flight from Stansted to Chicago. Another seven hours later and here they were, finally on the outskirts of Lexington, Kentucky.

Hanif looked out the windows. Rolling acres of lush bluegrass stretched out on both sides of the road. Tall trees, colonial mansions and miles of white railings. After a few miles, the truck pulled off the road and stopped at a huge wrought-iron gate. Set into the cut stone wall flanking it was a blue-and-gold sign reading Al Fawala Stud USA.

247

Hanif patted the filly and spoke in soothing tones in his native tongue. "This will be our home until big day."

He knew he too was under pressure: he had just two weeks to get everything organised.

The truck eased through the 900-acre property before hissing to a halt at a barn.

When the ramp was let down, Hanif eased his charge out of the truck. A tall plump man with a flawless smile greeted the arrivals.

"Hanif! How're y'all doing? Case Felsom." He stuck out a meaty hand. "How'd the star filly travel?"

"Both the horses and I travelled well, thank you very much. Please inform His Highness that we have arrived."

"Don't you worry." Felsom laughed. "OK, normally this thirty-stall barn is full of yearlings in pre-training, but the Emir ordered it emptied out so Secular Princess and her workmate could have the place to themselves."

Felsom cocked a thumb at two wiry young guys standing behind him. "Hanif, this is Garth and Eduardo. They'll be helping you out."

Both looked early twenties and wore Al Fawala USA caps.

"S'up dude? I'm Garth." He flicked the peak of his cap with a finger.

"How'you doin,' man? You can call me Eddie."

"It's nice to meet you both."

Secular Princess yanked on the lead, stretching her mouth down to the grass.

"Garth, you get the other horse," said Case. "Eddie,

you show Hanif to the stables."

Hanif lead his charge to the barn. Garth appeared with the other filly and put her in a stall beside Secular Princess. The dividing wall was mostly wire grill. The fillies snorted contentedly and sniffed each other through the bars.

"This is excellent!" said Hanif. "I told her trainer some months ago that Secular Princess doesn't like their style of stables with full brick walls. She likes to sniff and touch horses and people. It keeps her calm."

Later on, the three of them sat in the tack room. Garth emptied coffee grounds into a percolator and Eddie rolled a cigarette while Hanif unpacked the tack box.

"You from Fawala?" asked Garth.

"I am."

"We had some of 'em here four-five years ago when y'all first bought the farm, but they kept getting shit from assholes. You know, people afraid of Muslims." Garth looked at him with squinty eyes. "Hell, don't get me wrong – I don't give a shit where you come from or what God y'all worship. Hell, your king pays my wages."

Hanif was pleasantly surprised Garth held such a point of view.

"Emir," said Eddie. "He's a fuckin' Emir."

"Whatever. Coffee?"

They all took cups.

"You smoke, Hanif?" asked Eddie.

His accent appeared to be Central American, as did his appearance. Very promising. It also seemed that Eddie and Garth might actually be friends, not just colleagues.

"No, thank you, I do not, but …" He rummaged in the bottom of the large aluminium travelling case and produced a cylindrical package. Unwrapped it carefully and triumphantly placed the bottle on the table.

"Holy shit, you smugglin' devil!" beamed Garth. "And I thought you guys' God kicked your ass for drinking alcohol?"

Hanif decided to assume that Garth and Eddie were at least partly religious. "If God had not wanted us to drink, then he would not have given people the power to create such wonderful things, would he?"

"*Ha!* Reckon you've hit the nail on the goddamn head." Garth beamed.

Eddie grinned and lit his smoke.

"I thought we could put a drop into our coffees."

"We ain't supposed to drink at work but, hell, no-one's going to catch us," said Garth. "Hell, techincally, we're supposed to be in quarantine here. Felsom said the only people authorised to go near these horses before the races are us three and your trainer when he arrives."

"Hey, how come you don't have an assistant trainer or a vet travelling with you?" asked Eddie.

"There was a vet on the plane, but Ed Tomlinson doesn't have an assistant yet. He himself was assistant to Mr. Craddock, but got promoted after Craddock's tragic death."

"Yeah, that bomb attack was all over the news. Is it really true there was depleted uranium in the bomb?" asked Eddie.

"I believe so." Hanif splashed whisky into each cup. "Ed requested directly from the Emir that I take responsibility for the horses until race day. I have a full work schedule that he wrote out for me. Which one of you will ride the other horse?"

"Hell, either of us could," said Garth. "We both been here breaking yearlings and pre-training for three years now."

Hanif smirked: only the young talk about three years being a long time.

As if reading his thoughts, Eddie asked, "How old are you, Hanif?"

"I do not exactly know. According to my passport I am forty, but that is a nearest guess which we made when I applied for the document."

Garth's eyes stood out. "Who doesn't know their own age? What about your birth certificate?"

"I was born in a mountain village. Not every birth was registered. I am sure my mother knew my date of birth, I am sure I used to as well, but after her death such details became unimportant to my father and me."

Garth's mouth was hung open.

Eddie looked thoughtful. "If you don't mind me asking, how'd your mom die?"

"In a war."

"Shit, I'm sorry, man. Was she a soldier?"

"No. I believe the modern term is collateral damage. My father used to say that she was simply unlucky and that it was the will of Allah."

Eddie closed his eyes. "May she rest in peace."

A softness flickered across Hanif's face. "Thank you, Eddie."

"I lost my brother in Iraq," said Eddie. "He was a soldier an' all, but it still hurts and my mother's been depressed ever since."

"And I am sorry for *your* family."

Eddie stared at the floor for what seemed like an age. He looked as if anger was simmering behind his eyes.

Garth broke the silence. "*Yo*, Hanif, after work you want to let off some steam American-style?"

"Cut it out, Garth," snapped Eddie. "I know what you're going to say and he don't want to do that."

Hanif shrugged. "Whatever it is, I would like to experience something new." He smiled at Garth.

"Well, count me out," said Eddie.

"Aw, c'mon, man! We'll grab burgers after and take him to Pure Gold."

Eddie broke into a grin, nodding slightly. "I guess we could do that."

"Cool! OK, let's get these horses walked, fed and watered."

Hanif's eyes darted from one to the other. "What is Pure Gold?"

They both laughed.

"Patience, man," said Garth. "You'll find out."

*   *   *

Hanif showered, threw on clean clothes and went to the sitting room. Eddie and Garth were shouting expletives at the TV. Onscreen a man was shouting in dramatic half-sentences about immigrants. Mexicans were being singled out for particular abuse. Until he started on Muslims. Hanif recognised the man spouting fear from the lectern instantly. The man critics and satirical news programs had dubbed The Plastic Patriot.

"Garth, turn that asshole off, man."

"Who is that man?" asked Hanif.

"He's a fucking asshole talking trash about people like me and my dead brother. He wasn't complaining about Hispanic people when they wanted soldiers to fight in Iraq back in the day."

Hanif supressed a smile.

"Amen to that!" said Garth. "Hell, scary thing is, I reckon he's going to end up in the White House."

"You cannot be serious," said Hanif. "The election is a year from now. How can anybody predict the result?"

"Bet your bottom dollar I can. Hell, I've got friends think he's going to be our saviour." Garth clicked the remote. "You ask me, he's just another asshole full of shit looking out for his own kind." He jumped to his feet. "Fuck it, let's hit it!"

They walked to the barn, checked the horses and waited for the evening shift watchman. A large pick-up truck rumbled over the hill and pulled up beside the barn. The driver waved at them.

"That's us good to go," said Garth, sliding into his

Toyota SUV. "I'll meet you guys there."

Eddie cleared magazines and old soda bottles off the bench seat of his pick-up. Hanif noticed it had double-wide rear wheels and looked like it could pull a trailer containing a dozen horses.

"This is yours?" he asked.

"Yeah, sorry about the mess in the cab. I don't usually have passengers."

Hanif ticked off another positive attribute. "Where are we going?"

"You'll see."

They headed east through an endless sea of rolling pastures and post-and-rail fencing. Everything was massive and immaculate. In one paddock a huge tractor pulled a wide grass cutter while gardeners riding lawnmowers cut acres of grass verges.

On the other side of the town of Paris, they took a road several miles into a forest and swung into a parking lot just as the sun was dipping to the trees.

When Eddie cut the rumbling engine, a rattle of gunfire outside made Hanif flinch.

"Relax, man. Nobody's shooting *at us* but that's why we had to go so far out of horse country." He gestured to a wooden building. "The range is behind that."

"Where is Garth?"

"He'll be here any minute. We're not allowed to keep guns on the farm, so he keeps his at his parents' house."

"That surprises me. I thought Americans had the right to have guns anywhere."

"So they say." Eddie cut him a sideways glance. "Couple years ago, some guys living on the farm threw an end-of-season party … Guns, alcohol and egos – never a good combination."

Eddie led the way into the building. An elderly man behind a counter greeted him with a smile. "How can I help y'all?"

"Oh, we're just waiting."

Hanif strolled about looking at racks of camouflage gear. He noticed all the clothing had been manufactured in a disruptive pattern markedly different to standard military uniforms. Next, he came to a selection of targets: from basic paper to life-size foam replicas of people. Curiously, few resembled animals.

He approached the glass-fronted display case full of handguns and the elderly man shuffled over.

"There's some mighty fine pieces there. You looking for anything in particular? We got a twenty-per-cent discount on all handguns and ten-per-cent off anything back here."

The man threw an arm wide at the racks of shotguns and assault-style rifles on the wall behind him.

"Somebody could equip an army with everything in this shop," Hanif muttered, almost to himself.

"*Ha!* My pops always used to say that you can't have too much protection. We can do same-day purchase with a Kentucky driver's licence and proof of address. Course, we'll have to check that you're not a felon, but no doubt that's just a formality."

Hanif chuckled, raised his palms. "Thank you, but no. I am just looking. Admiring, really."

"That's not an American accent. Where you from?"

Hanif gave the man a warm smile. "I am visiting this great country. I have flown from England with a filly called Secular Princess which will run at the Breeders' Cup."

The man's face lit up. "That so?" He leaned over the display case. "She goin' win?"

"I am sure she will give an unforgettable performance."

The man looked puzzled. "Well, good luck to you and God bless."

Hanif wanted to burst out laughing.

"Garth's here, man!" called Eddie.

Hanif thanked the man and they made for the door.

"Oh, by the way!" the man called after them. "If you've got a green card, I can get a purchase approved in about three days."

"Ignore him," whispered Eddie, ushering Hanif through the door. "He's always trying to sell shit."

"Is it really so easy to buy guns here?"

"Easy? Shit, Hanif, that's the *hard way*."

A few metres away, Garth had opened the rear door of his SUV and was pulling two hard cases out of the vehicle.

Eddie cocked his chin at him and whispered. "He has buddies who can get all kinds of stuff, no questions asked."

Hanif made his eyes bulge.

"I'm telling you, man. Hand grenades, sticks of TNT, all kinds of shit. Hey, I was at a barn party on his dad's farm once and they blew a massive tree stump nearly a hundred feet into the air." He shook his head slowly. "Crazy sons-of-bitches."

Hanif flicked his eyes from Eddie to Garth.

Garth picked up the cases and spit a wad on the ground. "Y'all ready to kick some ass?" he said to Hanif.

"No, thank you."

"Aw, man, don't tell me you're like this guy." He nodded at Eddie.

"Hey, man, fuck you! I don't get my kicks shooting things. My brother was into all that, thought it'd be cool to join up and serve and now he's in a fucking box."

"Chill out, dude. I's just messing with you." Garth put down a case and offered Eddie a hand. "Cool?"

"Cool."

They slapped palms and pounded fists.

Hanif found the exchange to be fascinating. He was sure he had just found his man. Now he simply had to convince him. "You know, I think I will give it a try," he said.

Garth cackled. "Well, hoo-fuckin-haa for you!"

Dusk was closing in as Garth found an unoccupied shooting station and opened the cases on a table.

There were ten stations arranged a bit like a driving range at a golf club. Three other men popped off rounds from handguns. Hanif winced at the rattling sounds. Unpleasant memories flickered in his mind.

Garth handed out three pairs of ear defenders. Then he pulled an AR-15 assault rifle out of the case. The AR was basically the standard military-issue weapon, but restricted to fire on semi-automatic. Garth handled the gun as if it was delicate or sacred. He removed seven full clips from the case and snapped one into place. "She's ready," he said to nobody in particular, turning his attention to the second case which contained an ordinary-looking hunting rifle and a pair of .50 calibre pistols: they looked powerful enough to disable a car with one shot.

Hanif whistled. He'd never seen such guns in the hands of a private citizen before. By comparison, the ornate antique weapons in Rahim's father's collection seemed quaint. Hanif recalled that his English tutor had used exactly that term when they had been shown the collection one day. Hanif had been given many shooting lessons back then, but he had never enjoyed using guns.

He looked further up the line. Beyond the ten stations there was an open area for rifle shooters which seemed to be at least the length of two football fields. The targets set into the banked earth at the edge of the woods were barely visible. Two men were lying prone and shooting like soldiers.

Garth turned his hat backwards and made the thumbs-up sign.

"But how can you shoot in near-darkness without night-vision equipment?" shouted Hanif.

Garth checked his watch, held up a finger. A moment later massive floodlights clanged into life and bathed the whole range in a stark white light.

Hanif's mouth dropped open. He remembered how much energy was used in Fawala creating a desert paradise for the rich but he had never seen a shooting range lit like a football stadium.

258

He watched Garth send a target down the range and open fire, changing magazines every few seconds. After he'd emptied three clips, he reeled in the target and inspected his handiwork. Hanif had to smile when he saw the shredded remains of the cardboard silhouette of a man.

Garth clipped a new target in place and send it back the range. Then he changed clips, cocked the lever and offered the weapon to Hanif. "Your turn, man."

Hanif took the semi-automatic assault rifle, checked the safety was on and gauged its weight. He pressed it to his shoulder and leaned over, placing his elbow on the table.

He took a few breaths, clicked the safety and squeezed off ten rounds in as many seconds. He put the safety back on and placed the gun carefully on the table.

"That is quite a nice weapon, but I would not find it suitable for hunting."

Garth laughed. "Shit, no! You open up on duck or deer with that thing, y'all have nothing left to eat. Truth be known, all this is for is lettin' off steam or killin'." He reeled in the target and let out a whistle. "Awesome, dude! Where'd you learn to shoot like that?"

Eddie glanced at Hanif and the target. Two close groupings: five shots in the head, five centre-chest.

"I used to shoot with old rifles. However, they were elegant weapons and easier to control. I find that thing quite difficult to aim."

Garth replaced the target. "Who gives a fuck about aim, when I got seven 10-round clips on the table!" This time, he tried leaning over the table and resting his elbow.

Hanif watched him with interest as he emptied the rest of the clips and destroyed as many cardboard men.

Later, they stopped at what Garth called a *mom-and-pop* diner. The décor reminded Hanif of a dated TV show he'd seen during his time in Newmarket. All pine furniture and red-checked tablecloths, it was certainly different to the neon palace he'd eaten in on the journey down from Chicago airport.

Eddie saw him looking. "These places are dying out fast, man. Big chains and corporate power's killing them."

"Yeah," said Garth, devouring fries. "My uncle used to have a place just like this over in Frankfort. Now it's a Starbucks."

Eddie swore. "Meanwhile our state senator does shit about it and that fucking Daynson asshole keeps on about great American workers, but all he does is sell out and talk trash about guys like me and my brother. Seems to forget that it's people like us that get sent off to fight when guys like him need troops for their bullshit wars."

Hanif didn't respond, but inside he was smiling.

At the next booth, two young men in oily shirts and John Deere caps stopped eating.

Garth stopped eating too. "Easy man. Shit, I know Daynson's a slimy sonofabitch, hell, they all are. But don't forget your brother died a hero defending his country."

"Bull-fucking-shit he did." Eddie took another long swallow of beer. "And even if that was true, then how come Daynson gets to talk trash about Mexican people?"

"Cos he's an *asshole*."

"So, how come people's listening to him? Come on, man, you saw the news."

Garth shrugged and ordered three more beers.

Hanif flicked his eyes from one to the other. This got better and better. He just wished he had more time.

The John Deere caps paid their bill and slipped out, cutting furtive glances at Eddie and Hanif.

"We going to Pure Gold or what?" said Garth, when they all tossed dollars on the table to pay the bill.

"You bet."

As they finished their drinks they asked Hanif to guess what kind of an establishment Pure Gold was. He got it right second time. They chuckled and stepped out into the dimly lit car park.

"See y'all there," said Garth, hopping into his SUV.

Eddie and Hanif were about to get into his pickup, when the two John Deere hats appeared from the shadows.

One slammed his hand on the bonnet. The other spat at Eddie's feet and fondled a baseball bat.

"Fuck you, José. I heard you in there. Y'all got some fuckin' balls coming here, taking a job and talking shit about our leaders an' our country."

Eddie opened his mouth to speak, closed it again and opened the pickup's door instead.

The baseball bat slammed into the bonnet.

"Hey, man! What the fuck?" said Eddie.

"You ain't going anywhere." He cocked a finger at Hanif. "You neither, sand jockey."

"Careful man," said the other hat. "Maybe he'll blow himself up on us."

Hanif slowly rounded the front of the pickup, all the

while flicking his eyes from one hat to the other.

"You got one of them bomb vests on, little fucker?"

"Of course not," he replied. "I am not a stupid suicide bomber."

Across the car park, Garth's SUV rumbled into life and he swung the vehicle so its lights bathed the scene.

The hats cocked their heads, using their peaks to shade their eyes.

Garth got out, leaving the engine running. "S'up, fellas? We don't want no trouble."

"Who's fuckin' side are you on?"

Garth raised his palms. "Easy, guys, we're all on the same side."

"These two ain't."

"Man, I've had enough of this shit," said Eddie. "I was born in this country and my brother died in its uniform, you ignorant motherfucker."

Eyes bulged. The bat swung. Eddie ducked. His wing-mirror shattered.

Hanif darted to the closest guy and shot a fist into the man's throat. Not hard enough to collapse his windpipe, but enough to leave him stunned and gasping. He followed that up with a swift kick to the man's groin, keeling him over.

His friend froze, hands still gripping the bat. Hanif glanced at Garth, who seemed paralysed too. Eddie recovered and delivered a punch into the guy's stomach. He dropped his bat and doubled over. Hanif darted, light-footed, and kicked him in the groin from behind, toppling him over.

Garth's mouth hung agape. "Hot damn! My man! You kick some fuckin' ass!"

Hanif shrugged.

The hats groaned on the ground.

"I think we must leave now," said Hanif.

"And don't bother getting up till we're gone, assholes," said Garth.

"We should go home," said Eddie. "I've had enough for one night."

*   *   *

The following morning when Case Felsom turned up at the barn, he was pleased to find Eddie, Garth and Hanif getting on well and giggling like kids with a secret.

"You make friends easily, Hanif," said Case.

"I try to get on with people, whenever it is possible."

"Amen to that."

"I wonder if I might be able to borrow a car or pick-up truck. I would like to do some sightseeing during the afternoons.

"Why sure. No problem at all. You got a licence?"

"Of course."

"Come to the office this afternoon so they can photocopy it for the insurance company then we'll find you a vehicle. I can arrange for you to visit some studs if you like?"

"Thank you very much."

"By the way," he said. "Ed Tomlinson called me this

263

morning. He says he tried to call you, wants a report on the horses."

"I rarely carry a phone at work, but I will attend to it now."

*   *   *

Case got through on his second attempt. "Sir, I'm just checking in. All's going well. The horses and Hanif have settled in well. He's asked for a jeep to do some sightseeing."

"Really? What does he want to see?"

"Local sights, stud farms. You want me to send someone to accompany him?"

"Do you think he requires a babysitter?"

"Not at all, he's a real capable guy. Oh, one more thing, sir. Your cousin Abdullah called me this morning – he would like to spend a few days here in your house."

"That is fine. I am sure he could do with a break from Washington."

Chapter 38

The strip club was flashier than Hanif had expected. When they'd pulled up outside, Hanif noticed that it was the only building in the area which had its entrance and parking lot at the rear – out of sight of the road. Inside, despite the dimmed lighting he could see the place was clean and well-maintained. Garth ordered three beers and parted with as much money as they'd spent on dinner. Hanif had imagined that they would bring him to a cheaper strip club, the kind he had been advised to frequent, searching for the kind of people who could get him what he wanted. He hoped that a place like this would still prove useful.

They sat round the stage and watched a succession of toned women display their dexterity and pretty much everything else. Eddie and Garth beckoned each of them over and folded banknotes into their G-strings, buying themselves a little more attention on the meter.

"If you wanna tip them, only use singles," said Eddie, winking. "Don't waste anything bigger, they can't even tell in this light, anyway."

Hanif laughed. A moment later, he realised he should follow their lead. Still, he supposed it was cheaper and probably healthier for everyone concerned than opium, cocaine, prostitution or slavery.

An hour or so later Hanif was beginning to be bored with the place, if not the beauty of the girls. A group of guys came in and leaned on the bar. Garth jumped up and went over. There was a lot of whooping, high-fiving and laughing.

"Those are the guys I was telling you about," Eddie whispered to Hanif. "One of 'em's a crystal-meth dealer." He downed his beer. "We should go."

Garth returned. "Where you guys going? Let's take a table with my buddies."

"Nah, man, I'm beat."

"C'mon, man. Yo, Hanif, you gotta meet Warren and the guys. Wait till I tell 'em how you can shoot."

Hanif glanced at Eddie, shrugged and followed Garth to join the group of six guys.

Eddie tapped Garth on the shoulder. "I'll catch a cab, see you guys in the morning." He looked at all the faces. "Have fun, guys. I'm beat."

"Sure thing, man."

Garth introduced Hanif to everybody, explaining that they had all gone to high school together up in Montgomery County.

Warren was of slight build, with narrow darting eyes, while the others looked like they'd played high-school football before becoming professional drinkers. Whenever Warren spoke, the others deferred to him. Even Garth.

After Garth had regaled them all with Hanif's abilities with an AR-15, Warren shook Hanif's hand.

"Good shootin', man. So where you from?"

"A small country called Fawala."

Warren frowned.

"Garth and I have the same boss. I am here with a horse running in the Breeders' Cup."

"Your horse gonna win?"

"She will give an unforgettable performance."

"What's her name?"

"Secular Princess."

"Might have to get me some of that action with a bookie."

Hanif grinned and sipped his beer.

"I thought you Muslims didn't drink."

"Oh, I am not religious."

"You don't believe in God?"

"I did not say that." He paused a beat. "But I do not believe that God is a man in heaven controlling us with a grand plan."

Warren's eyes narrowed more.

"You know what God is?" Hanif continued. "God is energy. God is everything in the universe." He waved an arm. "Therefore, we are all allowed to consume stimulants and admire beautiful women."

A lopsided grin broke Warren's stare.

"However, that does not mean either should be abused."

A wheezy laugh escaped Warren's mouth. "Man, I like your style. Hell, I reckon you even make more sense than some preacher who prob'ly fucks kids on the sly." He looked Hanif up and down. "Say, y'all want a proper buzz?"

Hanif looked at him quizzically.

Warren leaned in. "Tina."

Hanif looked nonplussed, even though he knew what Warren meant.

"Nah, never mind."

"No, wait. I am sorry – it's just that in England people called it speed or whizz or things like that."

"That a fact?" Warren grinned. "You want a sniff? First one's on the house."

Hanif's crooked teeth gleamed under the ultraviolet light.

Warren got up and Hanif followed him into the toilets under the watchful eye of a waitress.

The two skinny men shut themselves into a stall. Under the light, Hanif noticed Warren's face looked as lined and craggy as his own and he had a scabby wound at his hairline. He thought briefly of farmers in his homeland who had taken a liking to their crop.

Warren produced a tiny Ziploc bag from his boot and

emptied a few pale crystals onto the cistern. He crushed them with the blade of a flick knife, formed them into two lines, hoovered one into a nostril and offered Hanif the rolled-up banknote.

Hanif took a breath and did what had to be done. It hit him immediately. The world rushed around him, seemed to lift him up by his heart. His senses were light, fine-tuned and razor-sharp. He almost felt like he'd have to hold on to the toilet to stop himself soaring into the air. Leaving the stall, he staggered, reached for a wash basin and turned on the tap. Splashed water on his face. He could hear insects scuttling in the drain. Then there was a background noise drowning his thoughts and cutting into his brain like a chainsaw. When he looked in the mirror, he realised it was Warren's wheezy laugh.

"Hot damn, man. You gone!"

Hanif mustered all his will to focus. "Congratulations, Warren. Your tina is really something."

Warren kept wheezing. "Best in the State. OK, get a grip. We gotta straighten up some, to go out there."

Hanif splashed more water on his face and gulped some from the tap. He wiped his mouth and turned to face Warren. "I am only going to be here until the Breeders' Cup, but if I wanted to purchase some of your fine product and some," he paused for effect, "other things, so that I may have some real American fun, would you know where I could find such things?"

Warren stared at the floor, but Hanif could see the wheels turning. "What kind of things?"

"Things that I would usually need to be a resident to purchase through regular channels."

Warren's eyes narrowed.

"Of course, I would be willing to pay for the privilege of by-passing those regular channels and when I leave you could even have the items back."

A big smile. "That a fact? What did you have in mind?"

"Let me make a list."

Warren shrugged and made his way to his seat. Hanif went to the bar and ordered another round. In the mirror he saw Warren whisper into Garth's ear. Garth's eyes darted to Hanif, but his look remained affable. He started nodding his head, then he pounded knuckles with Warren.

A waitress brought the beers to the table and everyone clinked bottles with Hanif as he took a place beside Warren.

A couple of the guys got up and went to the stage while another disappeared with a girl for a private dance.

Warren said, "Whatever you want, man. Garth says you're cool but, most important, he says you got a way with horses. Says that filly you ride's a fuckin' screwball, but you get her sweet. Says you got hands like silk, even when she pulls like a train."

Hanif shrugged. "I do what I can." He pulled a napkin from the tray of a passing waitress, a pen from his jacket and scribbled quickly.

Warren squinted to read the list of items.

"What you want all this for?"

"Like I said, I want to have some real American fun.

But I only have a temporary visa, so I could not buy such things."

"Fuckin' government. Think they can control everyone. Yep, I can get you them things. It goin' cost you though."

Just then a fight broke out between two of Warren's associates.

Hanif watched bouncers swoop down and eject them in a hail of fists and cursing. There seemed to be so much anger amongst the working classes. He simply needed to channel it.

Chapter 39

They sprawled themselves on armchairs and stared at the TV as darkness fell outside. Garth channel-surfed in an attempt to find something interesting to watch between commercials. Eventually they settled on two men brawling in a cage. When the fight ended in a bloody mess after two rounds, Eddie grabbed the remote and found a music channel playing oldies. Bruce Springsteen's "Born in the USA" came on. Hanif's face lit up and he tapped his foot to the tune. "Please turn this up."

Eddie fingered the remote and music flooded the room.

> *Born down in a dead man's town,*
> *The first kick I took was when I hit the ground,*
> *End up like a dog that's been beat too much,*

Till you spend half your life just covering up.
Born in the U.S.A.,
I was born in the U.S.A.

Got in a little hometown jam,
So they put a rifle in my hand,
Sent me off to a foreign land,
To go and kill the yellow man

A later verse made Hanif supress a grin.

I had a brother at Khe Sahn
Fighting off the Viet Cong
They're still there, he's all gone.

When the song had finished, Hanif shot a glance at Eddie. Was that a tear in his eye?

"You like The Boss?" asked Garth.

"Oh yes, I very much like this whole album. It is still relevant today."

"How'd you mean?"

"Well, he shows us the small-town heroism of ordinary people just trying to get along in a system which is rigged against them."

Eddie and Garth stared at him.

"But this song is the best on the album – how a country fails the people who serve it."

Eddie nodded thoughtfully and changed channels.

On a news channel, there was more coverage of Senator

Daynson's latest rantings. This time he was promising jobs to coalminers in his home state.

"You ever noticed he's always saying different shit to people, depending on where he is?" said Eddie.

"Don't they all do that?" said Garth. "Still, it makes good TV."

"Running for political office is not supposed to be a gameshow," said Hanif. "A couple of months ago, I saw TV news footage of this man speaking to a group of servicemen and women. He told them he considered them to be America's greatest heroes."

"Damn straight. They are," said Garth.

"Man, fuck that," said Eddie. "Like the song said, my brother was born in the USA, and it's motherfuckers like Daynson who sent him and all the others off to fight their bullshit wars and they think it'll all be OK if they just call everyone a hero once in a while."

Garth sighed. "Well, I'm off home to see my folks. See y'all in the morning."

When the noise of Garth's SUV had faded, Hanif got beers from the fridge.

"You really miss your brother, don't you?" he said, offering Eddie the ice-cold bottle.

"I wouldn't even mind if he'd died for something worthwhile. You know, like if some army had invaded us and he actually had to defend the country, but like what …"

They both stared at The Plastic Patriot on TV.

Hanif's mind whirred. "I know a man in England who served in Afghanistan. He was held prisoner there for two years. When he was released, he found an opportunity to throw a condom full of shit at the British Prime Minister." He spoke without removing his eyes from the TV.

"No fucking way!"

"I assure you it is true."

"I bet *he* got into some shit for that."

"Not really. Adam Greene – the Prime Minister – wanted to appear merciful to a soldier suffering from PTSD, so he got off with a fine and probation."

"Shit, if you did that to the US President, they'd go fucking nuts at you."

Hanif pointed his bottle at the TV. "But *this* man is not the President. He is just a trash-talking senator."

Eddie watched Daynson's face as the crowd chanted.

"Mr. Felsom fuckin' hates this guy too. Says he insults ordinary hardworking people; insults people from my part of the world and he even insults the memories of men and women who served and died."

Hanif thought that despite the short timeframe, this might turn out easier than he'd expected. Almost as easy as the drug-addled English vet.

Chapter 40

Hanif thanked the stallion manager, walked out of the palatial barn and drove out the avenue. Over the last few afternoons, he had visited the most famous Kentucky stallion farms, revelling in the history of the area and the magnificent horses they produced.

Normally he drove straight back to tend to his charges with the others, but today was a little different. He drove north of Lexington until he found the Walmart. He parked and checked his watch.

Ten minutes later a blue Ford slid to a halt beside the white pickup and Warren's narrow eyes stared out at Hanif. There were two bulky guys in the back seat. One of them got out cradling a holdall. He opened the pick-up's passenger door and placed the bag in the footwell. Hanif could tell it was heavy. The guy opened the zip to display the contents.

Hanif nodded. "Thank you very much." He pulled a fat envelope from the glovebox and handed it over. "This is 4,000 dollars. You may keep the change."

The guy was about to slam the door when he pulled a small baggie from the waistband of his jeans. "Almost forgot," he grunted, tossing it onto Hanif's lap.

Hanif fondled the pale-yellow crystals through the plastic. When he looked up, the Toyota had already gone.

On his way back to Lexington, he stopped at a hardware megastore and bought something that would serve the purpose, even if it wasn't exactly the same texture. He stowed his purchase in the holdall and fondled the small bag of crystal meth again. Perhaps he'd share some with Garth this evening. He double-checked the holdall's contents and pushed it under the seat. He would have to wait until Eddie and Garth were in bed before he got things ready, but he didn't care. He was glad everything had fallen into place.

Before he drove off, he pulled out his phone and sent a text. Maybe the last one he would ever send.

Chapter 41

Claudia devoured a cigarette as she watched the removal truck pull away from Oscar's cottage. The landlord would be here in a few minutes to take the keys back and just like that it would be as if Oscar had never lived here at all.

Last week had been a nightmare. As soon as she'd arrived at the sales, a few people had thrown accusatory glances in her direction and Claudia just knew the rumour mill was still doing overtime. She'd been trying to forget that her brother had been a global news item for a couple of weeks during the summer. Although the media cycled quickly on, the horse business clearly hadn't forgotten that she'd escaped the bomb her brother had set and then got a promotion because of Seb's demise. Horse people loved gossip like that, even if they'd never admit it publicly.

Her only consolation had been the Emir's good mood and his instructions for her to buy him an unlimited number of horses. But she'd only been looking at horses for an hour when two vendors had refused to show her their yearlings, telling her that they'd lost loved ones in "*your brother's terror attack*".

Devastated, she'd fled to her car and driven straight to Oscar's house. She'd called the Emir to apologise and offer her resignation once more, but he'd been so supportive and kind. "Not to worry, Claudia," he'd said. "Forget about Newmarket. I am not short of horses and you'll be able to work without prejudice in Kentucky."

So she'd hidden in Oscar's house and spent the week packing up his life.

She took a final drag on her smoke, opened the door of her car and stuffed the butt into the ashtray. Fuck the gossipers. She still had Tom, her job and the Emir's support and that would do her. Hell, in a year it would all be forgotten. Maybe sooner if Secular Princess won in Kentucky tomorrow.

In the house, six boxes of small items sat next to her suitcase. She hadn't wanted to give these to the removal men; she'd leave them in her car while she was away and go through it all when she returned.

She carried two boxes to the car, flicked open the hatchback and began collapsing the seats. When she folded the backrest, she found a piece of cardboard stuck under it. Picking it up, she saw it had neatly written lines of Arabic script on it. She frowned for a moment, then remembered the evening she'd ripped Hanif's backpack open when she'd picked him up in the rain on his way back from his shopping trip. She folded it and went back to the house. In the kitchen she went to the bin to dump the cardboard.

Then, as her hand hovered over the bin she saw the back of the card.

She unfolded it and stared at the lettering. Her mind raced for a moment, before she realised she was probably just adding one and one and getting three.

Still, she fished her phone out of her back pocket. It rang in her hand as she scrolled, making her jump.

"Hi," said Ed. "Can you let the Emir know I won't be joining you on the jet. Too much to do. I'm booked on a commercial flight later this afternoon."

It took her a moment to focus and process his words.

"Can you hear me, Claudia?"

"Loud and clear. Sorry, I was miles away. You're cutting it fine to get to the races. He won't be very pleased."

"Can't be helped. I don't have an assistant, so I'm dividing tasks between my head lad, travelling head lad and secretary. I only have one connection, so I should make it with a few hours to spare. See you there."

"Yeah." Claudia heard a car crunch to a halt on the gravel.

"Oh and Claud? Just between us," he continued. "I just spoke to Hanif. He says the filly's in cracking form, thinks she'll give her best performance ever and, to be honest, so do I."

A voice outside called her name.

"OK, look, I have to dash, Ed." She hung up and hurried to the front door.

The elderly landlord appeared in the doorway.

She stuffed her phone and the card into her pocket. "Thanks for coming this early, I'm in a rush for the airport."

"No problem."

She locked the house and handed over the keys.

"I'm terribly sorry how it ended up for your brother," he said. "Sometimes you just never know, do you?"

Claudia knew the man meant well, but he was just like everyone else: only too happy to believe that a drug-addled lunatic had turned on his country.

She forced a tight smile. "Thank you."

She hopped into her car, desperate to get away from this place.

*   *   *

Twenty minutes later she stopped at the entrance to the private travel area of Stansted airport. The three buildings were situated far from prying eyes at the other side of the runway to the commercial terminal. Administered by private-jet leasing companies, they offered a bespoke service and were never short of clients.

Stansted was now the UK hub for smaller or older private jets needing to refuel after a transatlantic crossing. Companies based themselves here to take advantage of better rates and taxes and low traffic volume compared to other London area airports.

"I'm a passenger heading for the Fawair terminal," she said.

The gateman waved her through to the car park.

Inside, the terminal was all white leather, walnut panelling and gleaming chrome. A uniformed representative greeted her with a polished smile beneath heavy make-up. Claudia handed over her passport.

"I'm a passenger on the Emir of Fawala's jet." She checked her watch. "He'll be arriving at any minute."

"Yes, madam. His convoy is en-route, they will proceed directly airside. When they arrive, a car will take you to the plane. Now, if you'd just like to step through security."

A porter placed her case on the conveyer belt and passed it through the X-ray machine. Claudia pulled her phone out of her pocket and placed it in her handbag.

"Excuse me," said the porter. "You dropped this."

Claudia looked at the piece of card in his hand. Good God, in her rush to get here she'd forgotten about that.

She took it and went through to the lounge. Chucked her bag on a chair and dialled Tom but the call wouldn't go through. Her phone seemed confused. It appeared to freeze the way smartphones sometimes do. Then it started ringing: Tom.

"Wow, that's real telepathy," she blurted. "I was just trying to call you."

"Claud, thank God! I've remembered was bugging me the other night in your office. When you told me you'd caught the mouse in the cupboard. It's Hanif's name."

"What?"

"*Mouse.* Hanif Ali Mengak. Well, Mengak isn't a name at all. Given that he's such a small, shy little guy, I'd say it was probably just a nickname that stuck and when he moved to Fawala he kept it."

"You're saying his name means '*mouse*'?"

"Yes – *mengak* is a Pashto word for mouse. I learned it because there were a lot of mice in the village grain stores. My guards were always complaining about them."

She looked at the card in her hand. Suddenly it didn't seem as if she was getting three from one-plus-one.

"Tom, remember last week when I gave Hanif a lift back to Crangate, when his bike punctured?"

"Yes."

"And I told you I ripped his bag yanking it out of the car."

"Yes."

"Well, I've just found a scrap of card in my car with things written on it in Arabic. It could be a shopping list – Hanif bought stuff for his trip that day."

"So?"

"It's written on the back of a ketamine box. Oscar and Murad both died of ketamine overdoses."

Neither of them could speak.

Claudia pressed the phone to her ear. Sweat dripped down the screen.

"Miss Haverford," the steward returned her passport, "His Highness has arrived. Your transfer car is waiting."

"You'll have to call Wallace," said Tom.

"I'm at the airport. The Emir's already on board."

283

"Jesus Christ, Claudia. We've just discovered that someone who works for him might be a bloody terrorist mastermind. I don't think he'll mind waiting."

"You're absolutely right," she said, picking up her bag and walking robotically out to the car. Her mind raced. "I'll tell the Emir and we'll take it from there. Here's a thought: Hanif might have left evidence in his flat. Go to Crangate and check."

"Honestly, we should leave that to Wallace. I don't want to get hauled in again for disturbing evidence at a scene."

She hadn't thought of that. She wasn't much of an amateur sleuth.

"OK, but give me a few minutes to break it to the Emir. He deserves to find out first. I'll call you back from the plane."

She stopped at the foot of the steps and chewed her lip. How do you tell someone like the Emir that they have a lunatic working for them? Bizarrely, she found herself thinking of Secular Princess and having to get the groom who'd filled in for Hanif to fly out with Ed to look after her. Case Felsom should be alerted too. She rubbed her forehead. She'd rather hand all this over to Wallace and the Emir. Let them deal with it.

Claudia stepped into the serene interior, her shoes silent on the carpet. She managed a smile for the stewardess and a nod at the entourage seated around a long table. She dumped her handbag on the sofa she usually sprawled out on and made her way back to the

Emir's private suite, which took up the aft section of the Boeing Business Jet.

Her palms clammed up as she knocked on the door.

The Emir sat at his desk, staring out the window at the handler loading Claudia's bag. He turned on his beaming smile. "Good morning, Claudia. How *are* you?"

"I need to tell you something."

He gestured with an open palm. "Please sit down and buckle up."

There was a whirring sound as the cargo doors were closed and secured.

Claudia didn't sit. "Sir, we have to delay take-off. I'm afraid I have some shocking news." Then the words tumbled out of her. "I found a reference to someone called *Mouse*, in my brother's diary, and it kept niggling me. Then we discovered that Oscar and Murad both died of ketamine overdoses. And this morning I found a shopping list Hanif had written, at least I think it's a shopping list – it's in Arabic. But, anyway, it was written on the back of a ketamine box and I thought, that's weird. Then Tom called me to say he remembered that Hanif's surname, Mengak, means *mouse* in Pashto." She took a breath. "He's the missing link, sir. The man the police seem to have given up looking for. The man who made the bomb …" She dried up.

The Emir stared for a second. Then he burst out laughing, slapping his thigh.

Claudia's jaw dropped open.

He composed himself. "I am sorry, Claudia. I can see you are very serious. It's just that your theory is ridiculous.

Hanif? An Islamic terrorist? No, no. It simply cannot be."

Her brow knitted. "But …"

"Claudia. As you know, I don't have much time for religion and its manipulations, but Hanif," he sucked air between his teeth, "Hanif hates religion." He raised a palm. "Now, I know that hatred is a strong and often violent emotion, but even so."

She looked at the desk, reached for a pen. "May I?"

"Please."

She sat, grabbed the pen, tore a sheet of paper from a pad and scribbled notes as the Emir watched her intently. It became clear. Claudia exhaled in relief that she was finally able to confront the Mouse issue and solve Oscar's death.

"OK. Right, sir. Tom's been talking to Hanif quite a lot lately. He told him all about growing up in Afghanistan, his mother's death and then his father exiling him to Fawala with your father to keep him safe."

The Emir nodded thoughtfully. "Hanif's dislike of religion – even as a child – was the primary reason he was, as you say, exiled to Fawala."

"So, isn't it possible that – given his life history – he has his own murderous agenda, that he wants revenge?"

"Against religion? But there were no religious people at the sale in London. OK, I know Adam Greene had what he called his faith charity, but that hardly makes him a religious leader."

"No, sir, I don't think religion has anything to do with it. I think he organised the London attack for vengeance against the nations that have invaded his homeland over the years. It's like this." She tapped her pen on the paper. "In the days of the Raj, the British Empire occupied what is now Afghanistan. And we know that Komarov's father was a big deal during the Soviet occupation. Likewise, we know about Adam Greene's involvement in the latest war there, not to mention Iraq. Hanif must have blackmailed Oscar into planting the bomb in your mare. He probably threatened expose his drug addiction ... though that might not have been enough ..."

The Emir blinked. Shook his head. "That is quite a theory. Except that Seb told me some time ago that your brother's condition was an open secret in Newmarket."

"It seems that Oscar and I were the only ones who hadn't a clue about that," she said icily. She felt the blood fall from her cheeks. "What if Hanif threatened to do something to me if Oscar didn't comply?" She rubbed her temples. "But he knew that I'd have been at the sale ... so, Hanif must have told him that I wouldn't be killed in the blast, no matter what. Oscar must have believed it too, or he'd never have agreed to do it. But how could Hanif convince him of that?" She ran out of steam and pulled cigarettes out of her bag. "Do you mind if I smoke?"

He shook his head and she lit up and sucked hungrily on the little white stick.

"Then Hanif killed Oscar and Murad to cover his tracks." She looked the Emir in the eye. Her stomach churned as something else occurred to her. "He would have known you'd die in the blast, too."

The Emir's eyes widened.

"Oh God!" she said. "What if *you* were his primary target and all the others were just a bonus?"

"No, no, Claudia. That is impossible. Why would Hanif want to kill me?"

"Sir, I know you're trying to change Fawalan society. I also know that your older brother Jabbar was passed over for you …"

The Emir wagged a finger. "Be careful, Claudia. Do not disrespect my family."

"I'm not, sir. But maybe somebody is using Hanif to get you out of the way?" She felt the plane shudder and glanced out the window. "We're moving! Why are we moving? We have to stay here and call Chief Inspector Wallace!"

The Emir showed her his palms. "Please, give me a moment." He looked at his desk, eyes darting. "Hanif is now on my stud farm in Kentucky. How exactly do you suppose Wallace will be able to convince the FBI to arrest him? Really, what have you just told me? That your brother wrote about someone called *Mouse*? That Hanif wrote a shopping list on an old medicine box? And, most ridiculous of all, that Hanif was trying to kill me, the son of the man who gave him a better life? Let's face it, Claudia, the evidence is circumstantial." He gave her a sceptical look. "I understand how much you lost in that awful incident and what a strain it must be on you, but we have to look at this logically. Please, go back to your seat and calm yourself."

"I still want the Kentucky police to interview Hanif."

The Emir's jaw stiffened. "Claudia, Hanif was unfairly harassed at Ascot some months ago. Why? Because he has dark skin and black hair and was reaching inside a bulky jacket to use a handkerchief on a warm day."

"But –"

"I know that was not the fault of your policemen, but they still detained, checked and questioned him. And let's not forget they cleared him."

She finished her cigarette. He was right, the evidence was circumstantial. She'd have to call Tom and hope that he found something in the flat at Crangate.

The Emir gave her a look that seemed fatherly, despite him being about the same age as her. "Claudia, get some rest. I will make a personal call to Inspector Wallace during the flight and we will discuss the best way to proceed."

"Thank you, sir." She let out a long sigh and walked to the door. "Oh, I nearly forgot. Ed called me. He won't make the flight, he's booked commercial this afternoon."

"He's not on board? That does not leave him much time to get to the races."

"He said not to worry – he'll be there to saddle your runner."

The Emir nodded. "Oh, by the way, does Hanif know that you suspect him?"

"*Um*, no. How would he?"

Chapter 42

Tom burst through the door and yelled, "*Anyone here?*"

Julia Manton came out of Claudia's office. "Do you mind not barging in?"

"Claudia sent me to get the keys to Hanif's old flat."

Julia folded her arms. "What on earth for?"

"We think Hanif might've been doing something dodgy up there."

"What do you mean, *dodgy*?"

Tom fought the urge to bark an order at Julia. "We're not sure, that's why we need to see the flat."

Julia brushed past him to the unoccupied desk in reception, yanked open a drawer and searched for the correct bunch. Tom held out his hand.

She gave it a sideways glance. "Not bloody likely. It's

my place, you know."

Inside, the flat was immaculate and smelled of bleach.

"How nice," said Julia. "I wish all the seasonal workers would leave their accommodation like this.

Tom crouched down by the kitchen sink and worktop so light reflected off them. Smooth and spotless, not even a smudge.

"This place was cleaned like a Sandhurst Cadet's room before an inspection," he muttered.

If Hanif was that disciplined it didn't bode well for finding a clue. He wandered over to the window – it too was spotless, and looked down at the yard. Through the archway he could see a County Council refuse truck reversing towards the wheelie bins.

"Julia, how often do the bins get emptied?"

"Supposed to be every two weeks, but you know the bloody council."

Tom was already bounding down the stairs and across the yard.

"*Stop! Stop!*" he roared at the man working the hydraulics.

The man hit a red button. "What's up with you then?"

"Have you emptied any of them yet?" he asked breathlessly.

"Yeah, general waste's gone into the front compressor."

"*Shit*. Can you lower that one, please, I might as well check the recycling."

"Dump the family silver, did you?"

"Something like that."

The bin whirred its way to the ground. Flipping it open, Tom dived in and began taking out all the clear plastic bags. After about four or five sacks of newspapers, cartons and old sales catalogues, he came to a black bag for general waste.

"Tom, what's going on?" said Julia who had followed him outside.

Ignoring her, he opened the knot of the bag and looked inside. It smelled of bleach and contained cleaning wipes, several pairs of latex gloves and a small black device. He carefully picked up the small black device with his index finger and thumb and inspected it. Lady Alex had a couple of listening devices she used when she wanted to secretly record meetings and interviews with captains of industry. Those receivers looked similar to this.

"What is it?" Julia asked.

"Wait – I must call Claudia."

He tried several times but no joy. Surely she hadn't taken off?

His mind raced. He knew he'd have to bite the bullet and call Wallace now. Suddenly, he was glad that Wallace had given him a business card when he'd released him.

He pulled out his wallet.

"Here," said the bin man, "are you gonna clean all that up again, or am I just going to drive off?"

Tom looked at him without really seeing him. "I'm keeping this." He indicated the black bag. "The rest you can take, thanks."

*　　*　　*

After he'd talked to Wallace, Tom and Julia went back to the office and he explained it all to her.

"Good God, I need to sit down," she mumbled. "Whisky?"

"Love one."

They sat and stared at their drinks in a kind of shocked limbo. Eventually, Tom broke the silence.

"Hanif must've been the one who forced Oscar to do what he did. But why would he agree to it? Exposure of his weakness? Turns out half of Newmarket knew about him." He shook his head. "There had to have been more to it. I suspect Hanif threatened to kill Claudia if Oscar didn't comply."

"But Claudia was at the sale. Meaning Hanif had to have had a plan to ensure her safety."

"Or at least convince Oscar that he had … Holy shit! What if at the last minute Hanif told Oscar that he'd have get Claudia away from the sale himself without alerting the police, or she'd die anyway?"

They stared at each other, open-mouthed. Incredulous.

"Tom, if that's true … My God, it's cruel!"

"She doesn't like to think about that call anymore. It makes her mind boil. You know, you asking her to take over Seb's business and the Emir agreeing to put her in charge of his European racing and breeding affairs have been all that's kept her going."

Julia raised an eyebrow.

"It's true," said Tom. "I know she likes to be all-soldiering-on kind-of-thing, but I tell you, if she pauses to think too much, I'm worried she'll have a breakdown. She'd given up smoking years ago, but she's been back at forty-a-day ever since Oscar's death and now it looks like she's somewhere over the Atlantic with nothing else to do *but* think and smoke." He fiddled with his watch. "Still, at least she's safe with the Emir and his team."

*　　*　　*

An hour later a grey Ford pulled up. Wallace looked strained. He eyed Tom up and down before slowly extending a hand.

Tom shook it. He imagined it was as close to a peace offering as he would ever get. Gibson simply nodded at him.

He led them in to the kitchen where Julia greeted them and pointed to the bin bag on the floor.

They snapped on latex gloves. Wallace knelt over the bin bag while Gibson spread a sheet of plastic on the floor and prepared several evidence bags.

Gibson called out the list as Wallace tapped at his iPad. "Three pairs of latex gloves. Two empty bottles of bleach-based cleaning spray. About forty-odd used cleaning wipes. A damp towel. Two used disposable razors. One used toothbrush. A small black device which may be a receiver for a listening device, two AA-sized batteries for said device. What the bloody hell was he listening to?"

Tom wondered too.

Gibson continued. "A couple of rotten tomatoes and the end of a loaf of bread."

"Keep the bin bag. We'll print that, too." Wallace flicked

glances between Tom and Julia. "Thanks for bringing this to our attention."

"So, are you going to contact the Americans and have Hanif detained?" asked Tom.

"I'll have to wait for the results back on this lot, but if we can match DNA on the gloves or the toothbrush to anything found on Murad Kazemi or in Oscar Haverford's car, then we're in business."

"*What?* Hanif's at large in America for crying out loud! Don't tell me you can't just round him up?" He stared at Wallace. "Like you did to me."

Wallace's face darkened. "We had a file on you. Hanif, on the other hand, was checked, cleared and printed when he entered the country with a temporary work visa on a biometric passport. Now he's entered America in the same fashion."

"And?"

"If the system had thrown up any kind of flag, he would've been detained in Chicago airport."

Tom snorted.

"After what you've been through, I'd have thought you'd think twice about demanding arrests on based on nicknames and circumstantial evidence," said Wallace. "Anyway, if what you tell me is true, what's his motive?"

"He wants to strike at countries which have dominated his. He doesn't care who he kills, merely that he gets revenge." Tom hesitated a beat, a pained look on his face. "I know all about wanting revenge, because I once felt that angry with my country. I just knew it was wrong to kill to express my frustration. But some people don't think it through, or don't want to. Or don't care."

Wallace tapped away at his iPad. "Possible, I'll give you that. Oh, by the way, where's this famous bit of ketamine box?"

Tom's shoulders dropped. "Claudia has it."

"And she's on a plane to America?"

Tom shrugged despondently.

*   *   *

Wallace shook his head, walked around the yard and dialled Trenton.

"Chief Inspector Wallace," said Commissioner Trenton. "I thought you were supposed to be on leave."

"Something came up. We may have a new lead on the Orangery bombing."

He told Trenton about Hanif the Mouse and the bagged evidence.

Trenton sucked air through his teeth. "And you said this guy works for the Emir of Fawala and he's the same guy that Greene's men accosted in the parade ring at Ascot races?"

"That's correct."

"If memory serves me, that was a false alarm. He checked out clean."

"On the surface of it all, he *is* clean."

Through the phone, Wallace could almost hear the wheels turning.

"OK. But I will not make a hoo-haa over this guy without evidence tying him to the scene of either murder. Understand? I don't want the Emir of Fawala crying harassment or the PM'll have my guts for garters. You get the evidence and I'll inform the PM and let the Americans know."

Wallace grunted. "Stuff'll be in the lab in an hour or so."

"Good."

"In the meantime, Commissioner, I should at least warn the Americans. Who do I call over there?"

"You don't. I just told you not to do a thing without evidence."

"Alright. But I need the lab to fast-track all this. I'm going to be dragging everyone I can back to put in the hours this week end. If it takes at least sixty-odd man hours to process DNA then I want people working round the clock. There will be a considerable overtime bill."

"Will a few hours really make *that* much of a difference?"

"What if he's planning another attack? I've just been told he's escorting a horse to a big race meeting. For all we know it could be stuffed with explosives too. It's the same MO for God's sake!"

"I suggest you get evidence connecting him to the last attack before you start jumping to conclusions, Chief Inspector Wallace."

"Is it really such a jump to think that a successful terrorist who slipped the net once is going to strike again in America?"

The line went dead.

"*Wanker*," he said to his phone.

He barked at Gibson and climbed into the car. If all this checked out, he didn't even want to think about how Hanif could've got his hands on depleted uranium. He made another call.

Chapter 43

Claudia was lying on the sofa as the plane moved above the clouds. She just couldn't work out how to think or what to do. She wasn't cut out to deal with Islamic terrorists. She just wanted to do her job, buy racehorses and bring the Emir success with his horses.

She stared at the dazzling blueness outside and became vaguely aware of laughter in the background as the entourage indulged in their usual backgammon tournament. Crystal decanters rattled in the drinks rack. She rummaged in her bag for a cigarette, opened the table ashtray, reached for a glass and for the first time felt she could understand the despair and disillusionment which drove Oscar to drugs and Tom to his prank. She gulped down whisky. Maybe she wasn't stronger than Oscar after all.

*   *   *

Rahim reached for one of his phones.

Chief Inspector Wallace picked up on the second ring.

"I have just been told a most bizarre theory by Claudia Haverford. I felt it was my duty to inform you, even if I do consider it to be ridiculous."

"Is she with you now?"

"She is resting in the main cabin. We are flying to America."

"I thought you couldn't use phones on planes?"

"It is only forbidden on commercial airliners."

"Right. So, tell me Miss Haverford's theory."

Rahim recounted Claudia's words as close to verbatim as he could.

"Sir," Wallace said quickly, "I understand you once offered your resources to my commissioner to help with our investigation."

"Of course. Anything at all. What can I do?"

"We have discovered new evidence at our end, possibly more than circumstantial, which will be processed as soon as possible."

"Concrete evidence?"

"I can't divulge that at this time, sir, and it could be nothing at all. In the meantime, I need you to carry on as normal. Do not do anything to alert Hanif Ali Mengak. Can you quietly find out from your farm manager if Hanif has been in contact with any vets who might have examined Secular Princess in the last few days and, most importantly of all, find out if there is a vet check scheduled for the morning of the race."

"Oh Inspector, now you are the one being ridiculous."

"Nevertheless, I need that information as soon as possible, because the DNA results might not be in by then."

"DNA results?"

"Rest assured, sir. I will inform you as soon as I know."

"And what about the local authorities? Who will contact them?"

"You leave all that to me. I'll be in touch with you on this line the moment I know how this is going to play out. Thank you for your cooperation."

The line went dead.

Rahim rubbed his temples. He was starting to feel like a character in a Hollywood movie. He wondered if the British police would drop the ball again.

*   *   *

Wallace ended the hands-free call and kept his eyes on the road. They were almost at the M25 London ring road.

Gibson was scrolling through his phone. "Secular Princess is due to run at the Breeders' Cup tomorrow. Estimated attendance figures, 50,000. Jesus Christ."

"Forget about 50,000. If this really is about Hanif orchestrating another attack using a horse as cover, then he's not trying to kill thousands –"

"You hope."

Wallace scowled. "Find out what dignitaries are going to be at the races that day."

"Dignitaries?"

"Yeah. You know, rich powerful people. People like Adam Greene, Sir John Christian, or Vasili Komarov."

Gibson blinked.

"Well, you've got fuck all else to do while we wait for the lab to process that lot." He cocked his thumb at the back seat.

"You think he's our man?"

"It's a distinct possibility. You know I was never happy with the version of events that I was forced to accept: that the vet was behind it all. Real question is though – is Hanif a lone nutter or just a cog in a wheel?"

"Who knows with these religious loonies?"

"Whatever this is about, it's not religion."

Up ahead red lights blared as cars slowed to a crawl. Wallace swore, flicked on the unmarked car's hidden blue lights and pulled onto the hard shoulder, but he only got another mile before he was stopped by an overturned truck blocking the entire motorway. He checked his mirror and considered reversing, but it was 20 miles back to the previous exit.

Chapter 44

The plane hit the tarmac at Lexington Bluegrass late evening local time. Claudia woke with a pounding head and an empty whisky decanter in the rack. A smiling stewardess offered her painkillers and water just as the Emir came out of his cabin. He took a seat beside her. "I decided it was best to let you sleep. During the journey I spoke to Inspector Wallace. He informs me that he is processing new evidence and that we are to do nothing to alert Hanif that we suspect him."

"But –"

He raised a palm. "I know how you feel. But if he is innocent, then *I* do not wish to cause him any further inconvenience, and if he is guilty and we make a premature move, he will surely disappear. You do see that, don't you?"

She managed to nod.

"The police are doing their jobs and the Americans will be informed."

"Just to be extra cautious, do we scratch Secular Princess from the race and keep Hanif on the farm?"

"What did I just say? Apart from following Inspector Wallace's instructions, I am not going to deprive Secular Princess or any of my people of the pleasure of a victory. Have you forgotten I am sponsoring the race?"

"No. But –"

"The filly will run no matter if Hanif is her groom or not. If he is arrested at the last second it will be inconvenient, but there are people who could take his place. I am sure one of the men helping him look after her now could easily fill in for him."

Another nod, then a frown. "Will you be presenting the prize?"

"Actually no. They prefer that an American celebrity performs that task. Anyway, I expect to win, so I can hardly present the prize to myself, can I? However, due to the delicate situation with Hanif, I have decided not to stay on my house at the farm. We will stay at the Hyatt Regency in downtown Lexington. I usually have a floor reserved there when I visit Kentucky, just as a contingency because I often prefer hotels to my own houses."

"So, we won't have to go to the farm?"

"No, Claudia. Under the circumstances, it is best if we do not."

"We should warn Case and the staff."

"I am afraid that we can do nothing to alert them either." A sadness flickered in his eyes.

As they disembarked, Claudia counted 75 private aircraft lined up by the hangar and let out a whistle. Lexington, like London, was no stranger to gatherings of wealthy influential people who indulged in horse racing and breeding, but 75 jets at a small airport? It was unheard of.

They slid into waiting cars and the Emir's phone rang.

"Abdullah!" he answered in English. "Where are you, my cousin? I believe you enjoyed a few days' rest at the farm. Are you still here for the races? And why not? Oh. Well, that's OK then. Call me as soon as you know."

*　　*　　*

Claudia got to her room and decided to call Wallace herself only to discover her phone had died. Swearing, she plugged it in and showerd.

Afterwards, she pulled her robe tight round her and picked up the device. It rang in her hand.

"Thank God," she said to Wallace. "I was just about to call you."

"I've been trying you for ages. How come I could call Emir Rahim on his plane, but I couldn't get you?"

"Apparently my phone had died."

"And you didn't charge it on the plane?"

"I, well, I passed out on the flight."

He told her about their findings at Crangate and about Tom's statement.

305

"Oh, that's brilliant! When will you have the results?"

"Forty-eight hours, best case."

"That's no bloody good. He's supposed to be leading up a filly at the races tomorrow afternoon! I thought these things could be processed in a few hours."

"This isn't *CSI Miami*. It's the middle of Friday night here and we've had to draft in people to keep the lab open all weekend."

Maybe it was stress or just her nerves, but Claudia found that comical. "Keystone Cops," she muttered.

"Don't get me started on overtime allowances and bureaucratic bull –" he caught himself. "I need evidence."

"Well, you didn't need it for Tom!"

"Mind your tongue, Claudia. Things are never as straightforward as they seem."

"*Hmm.*"

"I'll be in touch."

"Oh, by the way. Earlier, the Emir got a call from his cousin Abdullah. He's been staying at the farm, but apparently he's left now."

"Interesting."

She could hear his fingers tapping his iPad.

Next, she called Tom and he told her exactly what they'd found in the rubbish.

"A listening-device receiver?" she said. "Meaning he planted a bug somewhere at Crangate?"

"It gets better: after Wallace left, I tore your office apart. He'd put the device in the cup Secular Princess won, between its base and plinth."

"Why on earth?"

"I suppose he could never have planted it in our home, so that was the next best guess to keep tabs on you. See if you were suspecting him – I don't know."

"And here I am in Kentucky about to attend a race meeting with him tomorrow."

"Just pretend you're sick and don't go to the races."

"That's not a bad idea."

"After all, you and the Emir have narrowly escaped one bombing – what are the odds you'll survive if he tries it again?"

She dashed to the bathroom and vomited.

Chapter 45

The following morning Claudia paced her room chain-smoking in her bathrobe after a sleepless night. She knew it was pointless trying to tell the Emir not to attend the races and she had no idea how to tell him *she* wasn't going.

Was Hanif really going to try something? It would mean his death if he did, and if there was one thing she knew about supposed jihadis: the leaders and planners never carried out attacks themselves. They were always safe and far away when the bomb went off. Just like Hanif had been for the Orangery bombing. So was he really going to lead Secular Princess into the parade ring?

Perhaps she should just ring in a bomb threat? But, if she did that, Hanif would probably disappear like the Emir said and she'd end up in a cell facing charges, just like Tom had.

She glanced at the catalogues in her case. She'd much rather be at the sales complex looking at horses and putting all this out of her mind. At least she hoped she'd be able to work here without a backlash like the one last week in Newmarket.

She thought of Oscar probably going through worse than this before the sale in London, knowing he'd planted a bomb that might kill her. No wonder he'd wanted to get high using the most available thing. And if he'd been out-of-it on ketamine, it wouldn't have been too difficult for Hanif to give him the fatal injection.

Suddenly, she knew she had to go to the races. Keep an eye on Hanif and not let him get too close to the Emir. How would she manage that? Well, she didn't really know that either. She almost laughed at the absurdity of it all. Still, if she was there she might be able to figure something out before it was too late. There were bound to be policemen around. She wasn't just going to curl up into a ball and leave it all to the Keystone Cops. Something was better than nothing, or at least, it was better than going crazy in a hotel room.

Chapter 46

They sat in the back of an enormous blacked-out SUV and swept out of the Hyatt Regency's underground car park. Lexington city streets gave way to iconic white railings and lush pastures. As they approached the Keeneland complex, the Emir's vehicles were ushered into the line for the Clubhouse entrance and valet parking lot. They turned into the long avenue which swept through rolling parkland and then gave way to the tree-lined car parks of the racetrack and sales complex.

The Emir flicked through a sale catalogue. "I could not sleep last night," he said to Claudia. "So, I decided to look through these."

That was unlike him, thought Claudia. He usually never opened a catalogue until he was about to make a purchase, preferring to leave the selection process to her and Seb. Was he, like her, trying to keep his mind off the possibilities? After all, he should've been standing with Seb when the bomb went off.

There was a chiming sound and he pulled out his phones.

"Abdullah! Tell me." He listened for a minute. "Excellent. Thank you." He ended the call with a look of relief. "Senator Daynson and his friend do not want to be seen with us at the races. Too many eyes, I suspect. But they have agreed to lunch in the Panoramic Restaurant tomorrow when the place will be all but empty. I'm sure Daynson doesn't really want to come here at all, but I did send him my plane and another large cheque towards his campaign."

"I'd forgotten you're meeting Daynson – good luck!"

He cut her a sideways glance.

Out of the corner of her eye she saw an advertising banner announcing the dispersal of BW Picklett's breeding stock at the sale. Picklett would surely have a runner today.

They got out at the Clubhouse entrance and Claudia was relieved to see airport-style metal-detectors at every entrance.

They were shown up to their table on the top floor and Claudia gulped down a glass of champagne while she flicked through the race card. She didn't plan on moving from her chair and a TV screen until they had to go to watch Secular Princess being saddled up.

Her phone chimed with a text from Ed. He'd made it in early that morning and was out at the farm checking the horses. He used several racehorse and trophy emojis in his message. She hoped it would all be that straightforward.

311

Chapter 47

Darkness closed in above the Saturday evening glow of London. MI5 chief, Lauren Condicote was still at her desk when an email came in on her encrypted line. The subject matter read: **Out of Courtesy.** Although she recognised the sender, she'd never received correspondence from him before.

She clicked and waited for the video attachment to decrypt.

One of her desk phones rang: the green line used only by other senior Security Service members.

"Hello, Lauren," said Sir Christopher Medley, head of the Secret Intelligence Service, MI6. "While you're waiting for it to tee-up I thought I'd give you a call."

"How kind. I've become quite used to getting ambushed

at Downing Street with things that your end neglected to inform me of."

Medley ignored the dig. "It's about the London attack, and I do recall that you took some shit from the PM over the DU in the bomb, so out of courtesy I wanted to keep you in the loop. You can even take it to the PM yourself."

She gave the receiver a sideways glance.

"Look, I know our branches were rather," he paused, "at loggerheads during the Greene years."

Lauren wondered what his angle was. "Go on."

"In the spirit of putting all that behind us, call this an olive branch. One of our men in Iraq found the man in the footage I've just sent you. He's a war-wreckage scavenger, dismantles and sells-off discarded tanks and such."

"Yes, I do know what those people do."

"Well, it seems that he also realised the value of depleted uranium. He'd been extracting it from old Iraqi army vehicles."

"How the bloody hell did he manage that?"

"The old-fashioned way: manpower and elbow grease. Anyway, he's dying now from continued exposure, so my man offered him treatment in return for information."

She clicked the icon onscreen.

The footage was dark. Lauren could almost feel the heat and sweat in the room. There was a thin man on a bed, his skin pallid and greasy. A voice behind the camera asked a question in crisp English. A stout man wearing a taqiya cap and sitting on a stool beside the thin man's bed, repeated the question in Arabic.

The bedridden man spoke in a weak voice with shallow breaths, dragging out his words.

The stout man translated for the camera as he spoke.

"Last time I sell uranium, was night. Client want to meet in sea. He send me GPS number. I hire small fishing boat and go out with no moon. I wait for two hours. In distance, I see ship like island of light. I think it may be freighter or oil tanker. Then inflatable comes out of darkness. One small man on it. He throw me packet of money and gold. I hand him lead container and he speeds off to big ship."

The sick man stopped, exhausted.

The man behind the camera asked, "Is that all?"

The stout man repeated the question.

A cough, then the man on the bed spoke again.

The stout man translated: "I stay where I am and watch the man go. Then I realise ship is not tanker. It is floating palace so big I cannot believe it. I go closer, gunshots spray water beside me. I turn my boat and speed away. I am lucky bullets miss me."

"Whose ship was it?" asked the Englishman.

The stout man listened and then translated. "People call it '*big ship from tiny place*'. Fawala. That is all I know. Please, take me to your hospital. I need to get better."

The man behind the camera tossed a stack of dollars onto the bed.

"That was not our agreement," the sick man said. "I need medicine."

The crisp English voice spoke again. "Tell him he's

314

dying from chronic uranium toxicity. Too late to stop it. The money is for his family."

The footage ended.

"Illuminating," said Lauren.

"We believe the floating palace to be that of Jabbar Bin Faisal Al Bahar."

"You're sure? There must be dozens of super-yachts in the Persian Gulf."

"This one is the biggest in the world. It's a very distinctive vessel."

"So it's not exactly the logical choice for a covert weapons deal."

"Oh come on, Lauren. You know how arrogant these guys are. Plus, it was dark and they sent the launch a couple of miles from the ship. Furthermore, we established that it was out of port that night but was back before first light. Unusual for a pleasure cruise, don't you think?"

Now she understood Medley's eagerness to let her to take the info to Downing Street. "The PM won't like that, not after he so proudly announced the gas deal with Fawala."

"Luckily that's not our problem. We don't set policy."

"That DU ended up in a bomb on British soil and you're saying it's not our problem?"

"What's done is done," he said.

"*You* take it to the PM during his Sunday breakfast then."

"No, no, I feel that honour should be yours. Goodnight, Lauren." He hung up.

Buck passed.

Lauren slammed the receiver down. *"Fucking arsehole!"*

She swivelled her chair to the bulletproof window and studied London. She knew this would get buried, but she also knew people who deserved access to the information. People like her, who worked hard and had to kowtow to useless politicians.

She made a call on her private mobile.

Chapter 48

The entourage formed a perimeter around the Emir and Claudia as they left the elevator and pushed through the seething crowd towards the paddock and saddling-up enclosure.

Claudia had always liked Keeneland racetrack. It had a slightly European feel to it and was one of the few tracks in America where spectators could get a proper view of the horses before they raced. Today was different though, this small track had to accommodate a crowd five times its normal capacity. Most people had dressed up for the occasion, suits and dresses. But there were also groups of T-shirted student-types clutching plastic beer cups and waving betting slips. Some people had even come in fancy-dress colours to support their favourite horses. The air buzzed with hope and money.

She tried to call Wallace again, hoping for news, progress, anything to calm her nerves. Four attempts and she couldn't get through. Same when she tried Tom. She looked around: other racegoers were having similar problems. It seemed the phone network boosters were as overloaded as the facilities. She settled for a group text demanding *news?* Rahim watched her send it and put a reassuring hand on her shoulder.

She admired his calm demeanour despite the knowledge that an employee had tried to kill him. Then again, she'd read enough about Middle-Eastern politics to know that every ruling family had its jealousies and in-fighting. Then there was the fact that he was younger than Jabbar and yet he'd been chosen by their father to succeed him as Emir. Death threats were probably never far from someone like Rahim bin Faisal Al Bahar. What must *that* be like?

Their group entered the grassy paddock and dodged through throngs of connections all vying for a place to watch their horses as they arrived from the track stables, or in Secular Princess's case, directly from the Emir's farm.

There were sixteen runners competing for the two-million-dollar purse in the FawGas Breeders' Cup Juvenile Fillies. A couple of fillies trained right here at Keeneland arrived to shouts and whoops from the crowd and were led around in circles.

A moment later Secular Princess appeared at the paddock gates. A vet stopped her and ran a scanner along her neck until the device beeped and displayed the microchip number. When the sunlight hit her coat she looked every inch the athlete. Rippling muscle, relaxed gait, light steps. Like a conditioned reflex, Claudia found herself in full horse-assessment mode when the filly approached. Only when she caught sight of the groom did she snap out of it.

The man she believed had killed her brother grinned broadly at her and the Emir.

Try as she might she could not return the expression. Hanif's eyes searched her as he passed. Did he suspect? Did he know? He was wearing an Al Fawala Stud USA jacket over neatly ironed trousers and his usual tweed cap. A few steps later he disappeared into the crowd and all Claudia could do was follow the horse's grey ears above people's heads. Secular Princess came around again and she thought Hanif looked relaxed and happy. Was that how terrorists or murderers acted just before they committed their crimes?

A tap on her arm broke her thoughts: Ed looked gaunt and stressed, a saddle and number cloth under one arm.

"Can I have one of those?"

She offered him the cigarette box.

Ed took a long slow drag, held it in for a moment. "I thought the Ascot stress was bad enough, but this is on another level."

"I know exactly what you mean." She checked that the Emir was talking to his men, before edging closer to Ed. "You came from the farm with the horses. Does Hanif seem OK to you?"

"What do you mean?"

319

"And the filly? Is everything OK?"

"Funny, the Emir just asked me if she'd had a visit by the vet." He took another drag. "She hasn't, by the way, but Hanif says she's in-season. Never bothered her before but you know fillies sometimes resent running when they're ovulating."

Secular Princess passed them again and this time Claudia couldn't even look at the man leading her.

"Next time round, Hanif, we'll saddle up in our stall," said Ed.

Each runner's name was displayed above their assigned saddling stalls, like boxers in their corners. Ed went to his stall and Claudia noticed two cops crossing the paddock, forcing the crowd to part. They were escorting a rock star and his model girlfriend over to the TV cameras. As the crowd closed behind them, she caught a glimpse of oil-and-gas driller BW Picklett waiting for his filly to enter her saddling stall – right next to Secular Princess.

Secular Princess suddenly stopped walking, spread her hind legs and urinated on the grass. A few ladies in sandals and bare legs retreated from the pungent puddle. When she'd finished, she stood there a moment longer, appearing to strain and causing a traffic jam of horses as she made them all come to a halt behind her.

Claudia frowned. It was rare for a horse to need to urinate just before a race. Usually adrenalin and nerves made them clench up and concentrate on the crowds.

It dawned on her: Secular Princess looked like she was in-season and looking like she was straining to eject something from her uterus. Claudia knew that the only chance to get something inside a young filly like Secular Princess was to do it when she was in-season and her cervix, vagina and uterus were as relaxed as they could be for a filly.

Claudia grabbed the Emir's shoulder. "I know what Hanif's up to," she blurted.

"What on earth are you talking about?"

"I think there's a bomb inside Secular Princess. Ed just told me that she's in heat. Hanif could've done it himself without a vet if he'd watched Oscar put the bomb in the mare."

The Emir looked sceptical.

"Please, sir, we have to stop this now. There's nothing to lose by getting the cops to check Hanif for a detonator or a phone, we could even check the filly too. There are vets present here."

The Emir put an arm on her shoulder. "My poor Claudia, I do not wish to cause a scene or panic the crowd, but if it will allay your fears, we shall go to Hanif right now."

The Emir barked at his men. They cleared a path through the crowd, everyone arrived at the stall and the Emir spoke to Hanif in English.

"You will slowly open your jacket and empty your pockets."

Hanif looked startled. Then wounded. He hesitated, then keeping one hand on the lead rein he unzipped his jacket and opened it wide. His shirt stuck to his skinny torso. No vest or device was strapped to him.

The Emir nodded and Hanif reached into his trousers.

Ed glanced at him as he placed the tiny saddle on the horse's back. "Hanif, both hands on the reins while I do the girth." Ed reached under the horse's belly and pulled the girth up to meet the strap on the saddle.

Hanif ignored Ed and obeyed his Emir. He handed over a phone, his passport and a handkerchief.

Claudia let out a breath, her shoulders dropped a few inches. She had a brief feeling of déjà vu, like the parade ring in Ascot when Greene's goons had grabbed Hanif. Then her mind spun as she realised the London bomb had been set off remotely. When Ed tightened the girth, she edged past him to the horse's rear, gently rubbed her on the flank and lifted her tail with her other hand.

The filly whinnied and kicked back, slamming her hoof into the padded wall.

"Claudia, what the hell are you doing?" asked Ed.

"Just checking." She peered round the horse's rump at her vagina, but all she saw were stitches closing the top half. It was common for trainers to do this to fillies who tended to suck air into the vagina when they ran – the stitching procedure caused the horse no discomfort and often made their lives more comfortable until they retired to the breeding shed.

Claudia could tell that these sutures hadn't been done recently. Nothing could've been inserted into her. She didn't understand.

"She's stitched," was all she could say.

"Of course she is," said Ed, peering at the filly's genitalia. "So what?"

"I thought. I …"

"Claudia, are you satisfied, now?" said the Emir.

Hanif looked from face to face. "What is it? What is going on?"

"A misunderstanding," said the Emir. "Please take the filly out before she gets excited."

Hanif gathered his lead rein and set off, glancing back at Claudia.

The blood drained from her face. "I–I don't know what to say, I …" She'd been so sure. What was going on? She was tempted to run off and find those two cops, cause a massive scene and have the races called off … and thus complete her ostracism and probably end her career.

"Claudia, it's OK," said the Emir. "You have been through so much in the past few months that I do not expect an apology. Come, let us enjoy the race."

The entourage looked at her as if she was weak-minded. The Emir seemed to pick up on this and barked at them. A few people were staring at their group, but most were just too engrossed in their own horses and pre-race nerves.

Jockeys appeared, mounted and the horses left the paddock, went through the tunnel and onto the track.

Claudia watched Hanif release Secular Princess and wondered if she'd been wrong about him. She wondered if having closure on her brother's death had clouded her judgement and made her cling onto her mouse theory for dear life. But then how did that explain the listening device? No. Hanif had killed Oscar and there was something going on here, even if it wasn't another bomb inside a horse. She wanted to scream.

Out on the track, Secular Princess missed the break and got dirt kicked in her face for the entire 1 and 1/16th miles of the race. She finished third.

The Emir was bitterly disappointed. He ordered his men to get the cars round and they went back to the hotel while the rock star presented the trophy to BW Picklett.

Claudia got to her room, took the phone off the hook, turned off her mobile and collapsed onto the bed. She fell asleep, wishing everything would just go away.

Chapter 49

Tom was glued to the TV before and after the race. He was incredulous that he'd seen Hanif release the filly onto the track as if he wasn't a wanted criminal, disappointed she hadn't won for Claudia and the Emir, but also frustrated he couldn't reach Claudia to find out what had happened.

He felt almost as caged as when he'd been in a London cell. It was just gone ten p.m. but he didn't care. He called Wallace.

"I'm assuming you know what time it is? I did tell you that I would inform you as soon as I knew anything."

"What the bloody hell's going on? I've just watched our man lead his fucking horse back from its race like it's a normal day."

"I'll thank you not to waste police time with angry

phone calls, Mr. Sunderland."

"Why can't you just arrest bad guys and stop harassing people like me?"

"Will that be all, or are you looking for another night in jail?"

Tom slammed the phone down. For the first time in his life, he wished he'd never pulled that prank on Greene. Surely there were better ways to make a point than making yourself look like a lunatic? He found it ironic that Greene could bomb two countries and be hailed as a peacemaker, yet one prank branded him a lunatic.

When Tom had talked to Hanif, he'd seemed smart, so perhaps he'd worked that out too and abandoned his cause?

Chapter 50

Wallace didn't sleep that night either. He got up in the darkness and went to Scotland Yard. Lauren Condicote's phone call had left him conflicted. He needed to inform Trenton and get the Americans involved but he should really wait until Lauren had presented it to the Prime Minister. As it stood he hadn't even seen the video, but he did trust Lauren and he knew she also cared little for politicians.

Fuck it, he was tired of doing nothing. He called Trenton at home.

"This better be about the DNA results."

"No, it's not." Without revealing who'd informed him, he told his commissioner about the DU smuggler. "The Prime Minister is being briefed as we speak," he added.

"Bloody hell. That'll make things awkward."

Awkward? He wished Trenton would think more like a policeman and less like a politician. "Sir, I need you to contact the Americans on this. Right away."

"I'll have to liaise with the Prime Minister."

"Jesus, what if he's taken DU into America?"

"Is Jabbar Al Bahar *in* America?"

"How the hell would I know that? Anyway, he'll be as far away from Hanif Ali Mengak as possible."

"I'll talk to the PM. Wait for your DNA results and we'll take it from there. Not a word to anyone until I call you back." He ended the call.

Wallace swore so loudly the glass door to his office rattled.

*   *   *

When Claudia woke, she was still in her clothes and daylight shone through the crack in the curtains. For a second she felt calm, rested. Then it hit her all over again. She turned on her phone and called Tom.

"Thank God," he said. "I was out of my mind with worry. I even got the hotel to call your room. What the hell happened?"

"Basically nothing. I looked a right fool in front of everyone."

She mumbled the day's events to him.

He was as bewildered and frustrated as she had been.

"I haven't heard from Wallace," she asked. "Have you?"

"I called him during the night. Probably not my smartest decision. Look, I did some thinking: do you reckon Hanif's had second thoughts? Given up his cause? Maybe London was enough for him?"

"I don't give a shit if he's found Jesus. He has to pay for what he did to Oscar and Murad and all those people at the sale and, yes, even Greene. I want to see him behind bars for the rest of his miserable life. I swear, I thought *I* was going to explode having to look at him yesterday. I know it's wrong, but I wish Greene's goons had done him in that day at Ascot."

"*I* wish that you were back here and that I'd never thrown that shit at Greene all those years ago."

"What would that change?"

"It would've made my – our lives easier."

"Would it have saved Oscar from Hanif?"

"I don't know, Claud."

She sighed. "Sorry, I'm just so angry."

"It's OK. I get it, I really do."

"Right, I need to clean up and get to work, keep my mind occupied. I'll call you later."

"Love you."

She tried Wallace. Forced herself to sound calm and polite when she left a voicemail asking about his progress.

*　　*　　*

Claudia watched the eight-month-old foal being walked in front of her. She made her notes, thanked the consignor and made for the next barn, crossing the show area quickly, dodging between the horses on display and the people assessing them. She kept her head down, but she could feel the gossip surrounding her.

Earlier, one consignor had looked at her as if she was the dangerous one: literally a ticking timebomb. At least they hadn't been hostile and they'd still shown her the horses, of course. Just in case she might buy one for the Emir of Fawala.

And the worst of it was the real culprit was not only free, but here in Kentucky right now, under everyone's noses and fuck all was being done about it. She lit a cigarette and leaned against a tree, rustling fallen leaves with her foot. She'd almost like to drag a few cops out to Al Fawala Stud USA.

She moved on and looked at a few more horses before returning to the sale auditorium for a coffee. Her mind frazzled, she sat outside in the brisk sunshine and considered quitting the horse business … to do, to do … Well, she really couldn't imagine herself doing anything else.

She found a quiet corner, took deep breaths and cleared her mind. After ten minutes, she felt less angry and ready to look at horses again. It was almost lunchtime, but she knew consignors were on-duty all day and she didn't feel hungry anyway.

She crossed the internal roadway which connected the sale grounds, the racetrack grandstands, the groom's kitchen and went to the back entrance to the complex. She pulled the spring-loaded gate open and let herself into the next row of barns. Turning back, she held the gate for an elderly man behind her.

"Thank you, ma'am," he said.

She noticed a white pick-up truck rumbling up the road as she eased the gate closed so it wouldn't snap shut. Then, as the truck passed, she jumped and let go.

The passenger in the pick-up wore a baseball cap pulled low, but she couldn't mistake his craggy features. He looked tiny in the huge American vehicle, his head just above window level. He seemed to be talking to the driver.

Her heart pounding, she watched the truck head up to the back of the grandstand and paddock enclosure. It swung into a parking spot beside men removing tables and chairs from a marquee that had been erected by the paddock to cater for yesterday's huge racing crowd.

Hanif and the other man got out and walked towards an opening in the marquee. They wore bulky blue-and-gold Al Fawala Stud USA jackets and appeared to be walking gingerly. What the hell were they doing?

"*Oh my God.*" She remembered that the Emir was probably due to arrive for his lunch meeting with Daynson and Picklett in the Panoramic Restaurant. Three birds with one stone and Hanif even had an accomplice.

When they disappeared into the marquee, Claudia yanked open the gate, dropped her catalogue and sprinted for the marquee.

She burst through the marquee, bounded down some steps and landed in the paddock. The back of the grandstand was in front of her and up on the third floor she could see the bay windows of the Panoramic dining room. She ran across the paddock, looking around for security guards, but couldn't see any. On sale days, Lexington Police usually stationed a car at the entrance to the sale auditorium, but that was back where she'd come from and by then it might be too late.

Chapter 51

They stepped into the elevator and Eddie hit the button for the top floor.

"I'm nervous," he said.

"I am too. It is only natural. Close your eyes and take a few deep breaths. It will all be over in a few moments. Remember, your family already have the money."

"What happens when we've done it?"

"I presume bodyguards will restrain us until the police arrive."

"They'll definitely call the police, then?"

"Somebody will."

The doors slid open and they stepped into the corridor.

"Eddie, you deal with the politician. After all, he is the only one you have a problem with. Leave the others at the table to me. Understood?"

Eddie was white with fear.

Hanif hoped Eddie wasn't going to mess it up. He'd considered doing this alone, but getting access to the restaurant would be easier for a man of his appearance with Eddie by his side. Half the workers in the horse industry in Kentucky seemed to be of Mexican heritage, but he knew his skin was several shades darker than Eddie's, so to some people he would just fit the profile of a *Muslim terrorist*. So he needed Eddie beside him.

"Smile. Relax. We must both look friendly," he said, already beaming.

Eddie forced a grin as they approached the hostess, who stood behind a lectern at the restaurant's entrance.

"Can I help y'all?" asked the bouncy-haired brunette, eyeing them up and down.

"Yes," said Hanif. "We work for His Highness the Emir of Fawala. He is lunching here today with two other gentlemen. He summoned us."

"*Erm*, OK," she said, checking her list. "Are you members of the dining party?"

"No, madam." His eyes sparkled. "We are simply employees who have been ordered to present ourselves."

"*Hmm* ..." She glanced at the logos on their jackets and caps and looked at Eddie . "Have I seen you around Keeneland before?"

"I'm sure you have, ma'am. I've been working around Lexington for years."

She smiled. "OK. I'll take you to their table."

334

Hanif looked past her and caught sight of his quarry. "There is no need. I can see His Highness from here."

"Oh. Well, I guess that's alright then." She gestured with her hand and they entered the restaurant.

There were about thirty tables, but only half a dozen were occupied. Hanif knew that Rahim would not be bringing his team up here and that Sheikh Abdullah would not attend the meeting either. He scanned faces. The other diners looked like genuine horse people, apart from two men with military haircuts and loose-fitting suits seated away in a corner eating sandwiches. Private security. Hanif had been told that at this stage of the presidential race Daynson would not yet have been assigned a Secret Service detail.

The next few seconds would be crucial. He had to get the guards down and the people screaming and hiding.

Nobody turned a head as Hanif and Eddie approached the square table. Hanif supposed that grooms were usually invisible to the kind of people who could afford to eat up here.

Rahim was seated between the plump, suited men. He spoke in a low voice but his hand gestures were full of passion. Daynson's face was stiff and Picklett smiled a little too eagerly.

Eddie gently brought the bulging condom out of his jacket, cupping it with both hands. When they got to the table, he raised it above his head.

The three men stopped talking and leaned back as if they expected waiters bearing plates. There was a moment of stunned silence. Rahim opened his mouth to speak, but

Picklett beat him to it.

"Who let you guys in here? What the hell you got there?"

Eddie brought his hands down on Daynson's head like a slam-dunking basketballer. Oil exploded over his carefully coiffed hair and polished forehead, dripping down his collar onto his suit and splashing into his water glass. He clawed at his face.

Eddie burst out laughing, probably more from nerves that amusement.

"Hey, what the hell?" roared Picklett, getting to his feet.

Rahim just sat there, his features frozen. Other diners gasped. The two men at the corner table sprang to their feet, darted for Daynson.

Hanif whipped his hands from his pockets. Raised his left. Jammed the pistol into Eddie's temple and fired.

*   *   *

Claudia climbed the stairs to the top floor and arrived just in time to see the Hanif and the other man walking past the hostess, who was pointing down the restaurant.

"No! No!" she roared.

The hostess whipped her head round and frowned.

"Stop those men!"

The woman glanced back inside as Claudia reached the doorway.

Then there was a bang. Shouting, screaming, the clatter of cutlery and crockery.

Claudia threw herself to the floor behind the lectern.

The hostess just stood there until Claudia pulled her down by the hem of her skirt.

*   *   *

Hanif lined both guns up at Daynson's guards. Fired at their groins – below the body armour he assumed they wore. They fell as their right hands reached under their jackets.

Another shot with his left blew the back of Daynson's head onto the bay window. Picklett tried to run. Rahim dived for the ground, hands over his head.

Hanif raised his right hand at Picklett and two rounds hit the man's back, sending him down hard.

Hanif let off another round at Rahim, hitting him where he lay.

He scanned the scene. Whimpering people cowered under tables. He laughed. American bravery: the stuff of blockbuster movies.

Then he calmly walked to the two fallen guards and finished them with head shots.

*   *   *

"Go and find the police," Claudia had whispered to the hostess as the first shots rang out. "*Now! Take off your heels and run!*"

The woman had made for the elevator. Claudia somehow had remained rooted to the spot – more than that, she just had to see for herself.

On her elbows and knees, she had peeked out from behind the lectern in time to see Hanif fire at a man on the ground who could've been the Emir. Then he'd walked over to two other fallen men and fired at their faces.

Looking around the room, he shouted *"Allah hu akbar!"*

To Claudia, the words felt like an afterthought: the Emir had told her that Hanif hated religion. She stared as he dropped to his knees beside the body of the man he'd arrived with.

Another shot rang out. Claudia gasped. What the hell?

Hanif sprang to his feet and whipped round. Claudia shot backwards, pressing herself against the lectern. Should she try and make a run for it? Hanif fired off several more shots, they were getting louder, closer to her position. He was leaving.

She held her breath. Run or stay? Yesterday she'd been so angry she imagined herself dragging Hanif in front of a cop but now she was scared and a sitting target. She got into a sprinter's crouch just as Hanif appeared. Staring right at her, he aimed the gun.

Her heart thumped. If this was it, she had to ask him. There was nothing to lose. "Are you going to kill me like you did my brother?" she managed in a surprisingly calm voice.

He hesitated. Something flickered in his eyes, but the gun never faltered.

He threw a glance into the room, sensing movement. Fired a quick shot into the restaurant and put the gun back in her face.

"Your brother was a nice man," he said. "He loved animals and you. Hated politicians and war. And admired

Tom. But he did not understand for a second what his country had done to mine and of course, sadly, you can never really trust an addict. I am sorry that he had to die, I do not like collateral damage, but it is acceptable in modern warfare. At least, that's what they say."

Outside, a siren blared.

"And so, I must keep killing Americans until they rain bullets down on me." He lowered the gun. "But you will stay here. Go back to your fractured soldier and take care of him. You remind me of my mother. You like to take care of things, don't you?"

Perhaps it was because the gun wasn't stuck in her face anymore, but Claudia fleetingly thought that she'd hardly been able to take care of herself since Oscar's death.

"I thought Soviet soldiers killed your mother. Why take it out on Americans or British?"

"Because they all took part in the killing of my country at some time. Oh, I know there were other nations involved, but they took the lead."

"But you had Fawala. You were given a nice life."

"I was never more than an educated servant to Rahim's father. I respect Rahim, he has a noble vision, but it will never happen."

"So you shot him too?"

Hanif opened his mouth, hesitated, closed it again. Then he ran off down the corridor, both hands gripping his pistol.

Claudia heard him descend the stairs. She ran into the restaurant. People were emerging from under tables, sobbing and wailing. She saw Rahim face down on the carpet, a hole in the shoulder of his jacket and a dark stain spreading around it. She dropped to her knees and rolled him over. He opened his eyes.

"Thank God!" she gasped. "You're still alive."

Looking up, she saw a waiter shouting into a phone while looking out the floor-length windows down to the parade paddock and entrance gates. "He's going for gate two," said the waiter.

Claudia stood and saw a police car screech to a halt, blocking the turnstiles, but Hanif vaulted over the hedge into the paddock, sprinted across to the marquee and disappeared into it. The cops below hadn't seen his manoeuvre. The waiter was waving and pointing.

"*Shit.*" Claudia knew he'd be able to exit the back of tent directly to his truck. "*Get this man an ambulance!*" she yelled at the waiter, darting out of the room.

She flung herself down the stairs and burst out the back of the grandstand, shouting at the police, waving her arms. She hopped the low hedge and ran across the paddock as Hanif had done.

The policemen burst through the turnstiles and hauled themselves after her. She grabbed the glass-fronted marquee's door and ripped it open. Found herself inside before she'd even considered that Hanif might be in there aiming his pistol at the door. But the cavernous space was completely empty. The flap at the end was still taped open, she ran towards it. She could see Hanif was already in the driver's seat, looking straight at her with the window open. A gun barrel rested on the door frame.

Behind her, a cop shouted: "Ma'am. Put your hands where I can see 'em!"

But she was already doing just that.

Without taking his eyes off her, Hanif started the engine. The vehicle eased forward.

Claudia turned to the cop. "He's out there, armed." She pointed, keeping her hands in the air.

The cop looked past her. There was a thud-crack sound and something whizzed past Claudia's ear. Another crack and something slammed into her shoulder. Spinning from the force, she fell to the ground. Another crack. One cop fell beside her gurgling, his throat gushing blood. Behind him, his partner opened fire on the truck as it turned.

Seven, eight, nine shots from his pistol.

The truck's rear window shattered, its engine roared as it sped up, but instead of heading to the exit road, it turned sharply, hit the railing and tipped down the steep grass verge to the sunken sales pavilion. The truck rolled, throwing up grass and turf. An assault rifle was flung from the vehicle, clattering against the wall of the pavilion. The truck hit the glass divider between the auditorium and the pre-sale walking area for horses.

Glass shards flew through the air. There was screaming, whinnying, scuffling and skidding as the horses in the area knocked their grooms over and bolted.

Claudia gripped her shoulder. Blood seeped through her fingers. God it hurt, but she couldn't stay here. "*Help me up!*" she called to the other cop, but he was already hauling his bulk down the verge. "*Shit.*" Claudia pulled herself up and into a wobbly run. She had to tell the cop to capture Hanif alive. People had to know who was behind him. Jabbar? Abdullah? Both of them?

Blood seeping from the cuff of her jacket, she lurched and stumbled down the verge towards Hanif's vehicle. The cop's pistol was cocked at the wrecked pick-up as he breathlessly blurted into his radio.

Claudia saw a hand appear from the wreckage, then another. Hanif slowly dragged himself clear.

"Sir, don't move. Get your hands where I can see 'em."

Hanif started to laugh as he lay there, gripping his side. The cop edged towards him. Claudia could see the cop's pistol shaking.

When the cop got close enough, Hanif looked at him, wheezing, coughing. "Even as you plan to shoot me, you call me 'sir'? Are you a drone?"

The cop sneered. "*Fuck you, asshole!*"

Claudia took a step closer. "Please, officer, don't shoot him. He has to be interviewed. Tried. Sentenced."

"Ma'am, stand back!"

"Please don't kill him," she pleaded. Her shoulder was agony. "*We need to find out who he was working for!*"

"Ma'am, get back!"

Hanif pulled a mocking smile at the cop. "I suppose you expect me to chant '*Allah hu akbar*'?"

"Whatever. You're going straight to hell, asshole." He took a step closer.

Hanif coughed, blood trickled from his mouth. "You

fool. What if there is no hell?"

The cop fired. Three, four times.

Claudia jumped with each shot. *"No! No!"* Her ears jangled. She watched Hanif's chest explode in a red mess like special-effect squibs in a movie.

The cop lowered his gun and turned to her. "Ma'am, it's OK. The threat is neutralised."

"What did you do that for?" she roared.

"Ma'am. You need to calm down."

"Why did you fucking shoot him?"

The cop looked at her strangely. "He was a Muslim terrorist scumbag, he deserved to die."

"He deserved to be put on trial for his crimes. He murdered my brother!"

"In that case, ma'am, you should be thanking me."

"But now we'll never find out who he was working for!"

"You heard him – he thought he was working for Allah."

Claudia blew out a breath and shook her head. She wanted to slap the cop. Instead, she pointed at Hanif's corpse. "He got off easy. What a waste."

The cop just kept looking at her like she was as crazy as the terrorist.

Sirens wailed and several other cops and sales-company security guards arrived. Everyone shouting and waving guns.

Claudia's shoulder throbbed. She staggered backwards, wobbled. Somebody caught her. "Ma'am, are you OK?" was all she heard. The rest was a blur until she found herself on a stretcher in an ambulance. A female paramedic shone a light in her eyes while another cut off her jacket and dressed her wound.

Her phone seemed to be ringing. The paramedic pulled it from her pocket and placed it on the stretcher.

A man in a dark suit appeared at the door of the ambulance. He flashed an ID.

"Sir, not now! She has to go to hospital," said a paramedic.

Claudia asked if anyone had found her sale catalogue. She must have dropped it somewhere, but it had all her notes in it. She needed it.

The paramedic closed the ambulance door.

*   *   *

When she woke, she couldn't move in the bed. Her whole body ached. A nurse came and said she'd get her surgeon. When he arrived, he smiled kindly and said the bullet had passed through her shoulder, but nicked her shoulder blade. They'd operated late last night to remove bone fragments and set her collarbone. She'd been lucky.

She felt lucky for the first time in a long time. Even more so when she searched her mind for who'd shot her. Hanif? Or the policeman? If Hanif had wanted her dead, he'd surely have shot her outside the restaurant … So, had she been shot in so-called friendly fire? She realised the surgeon was looking at her strangely.

"Are you OK, ma'am?"

"Never mind." She shook her head.

"And the Emir of Fawala?"

"He was equally lucky. The bullet glanced off his scapula, and passed out through his arm, chipping his humerus but miraculously missing the artery. We operated on him last night too. He's recovering in a room down the corridor. The whole floor is under police protection. Try to rest."

They gave her an injection and she drifted off.

Later on, she remembered sitting up in bed telling a grey man in a dark suit the events of the last few days. Over and over again. Words tumbled out of her but she felt disconnected, as if she was on autopilot allowing all the stress of the last few months to gush out of her.

Another doctor examined her and told her shock was perfectly normal in these circumstances. All she really wanted was a drink and a cigarette.

At some point she asked the grey man, "How are you going to find out who Hanif was working for? It's not as if you can question a dead man."

"More and more, we see these kind of lone wolf attacks. They don't work for anyone except their twisted God. They find radical stuff on the internet that feeds their anger and that's all they need."

"*No!*" she yelled, sending a sharp pain down her arm. "Hanif wasn't a lone wolf. He knew too much about the Emir's movements. He bugged my office in England and I've told you that he said he was a middle-man. He knew he'd get the blame. That was part of the plan."

The agent narrowed his eyes. "You seem to know a lot

about the terrorist's plan. Tell me everything again."

"Oh, for fuck's sake!" She rolled her eyes.

"Ma'am. There's no need for that kind of language."

She went through it all again, wondering how Tom had put up with *his* interrogations.

*   *   *

The following morning, she woke feeling groggy and sore. A nurse brought in an FBI agent who said he was one of a team watching her room and Rahim's.

"Feel free to use electronic devices, ma'am," he said. "But I have orders not to allow you to leave the room until you have been cleared by your doctor and my superiors."

She nodded and thanked him, not really wanting to go anywhere anyway. When he left, she sat up in bed. Her clothes and handbag were in a heap on a chair. She eased herself out of bed, shuffled over and pulled her phone out of her jacket: dead. She rummaged for her charge cord, plugged it into a socket and flicked on the TV.

A Presidential press conference filled the screen.

"Our thoughts and prayers are with the families of Senator Daynson and Mr. Picklett. Senator Daynson was a man who selflessly served his country in Washington for the past twenty-two years. He was a patriot, one of the men who led the way in the war on terror after 9/11 and a man who always had the national interest at heart. BW Picklett was a great captain of industry, a shining tribute to the enduring qualities of the American Dream. From humble beginnings he created a

successful company and even showed his compassion and love of animals with a successful stable of racehorses. It is tragic beyond words that they were gunned down in such a cowardly way. Our prayers also go out to the families and loved ones of the security detail of Senator Daynson, who gave their lives trying to save their senator."

He paused for effect, allowing the cameras to soak up the emotion on his face. Then he cleared his throat.

"I am happy to report that another victim of the attack, His Highness, Emir Rahim of Fawala – also a lover of racehorses and an investor and job creator in America – is recovering from his wounds and will be released from hospital very soon. The terrorist Mengak was that new breed of lunatic who requires no specific affiliation or nationality, just a murderous agenda of hatred for us, our freedoms and way of life and even for the secular-leaning leader of his own country. That's the kind of lunacy we're dealing with here folks: Mengak tried to kill his own head of state. Individuals like this will take any opportunity and use any means necessary to get into this country and weaponise themselves. However, that said, law enforcement agencies are currently searching this man's online presence, including social-media profiles, and we are not ruling out links to the remnants of ISIS or even Al Qaeda. It is believed that Mengak's accomplice, a young American of Mexican heritage who lost a loved one in Iraq, may have procured their weapons and helped Mengak gain access to the restaurant. It is unclear if this young man committed suicide at the scene or was shot by Mengak. Police are also investigating the death of another young man, found apparently overdosed on crystal-meth at Mengak's

place of work.

Working with law enforcement counterparts in Britain, we now believe that Mengak may well have been the mastermind behind last summer's attack in London, recruiting a troubled veterinarian to help him that time. It is as yet unclear how Mengak became affiliated with the violent environmental extremism of Nature's Wrath, which claimed responsibility for the London attack. This time, however, Mengak was unable to escape justice.

Rest assured that extra security measures are being devised and put in place to ensure against further attacks of this nature. God bless you all and God bless America."

Claudia wondered what the security measures would be.

* * *

A while later, her phone buzzed and shuffled on the bedside locker.

The Emir sounded chipper, all things considered. "Claudia! I believe we are at opposite ends of a corridor crawling with policemen. How are you?"

"Stiff and sore. Never been shot before. More importantly, how are *you*?"

"I have been patched up and they expect me to regain full use of my arm in a matter of weeks. I am lucky, according to my surgeon."

"That's what mine told me, too ... You know, I can't help wondering who shot me – Hanif or the police."

Silence on the line. Then, "It sounds like you were

caught in the crossfire. Don't worry about the details, be thankful you are alive."

"Yes, I suppose you're right."

"Forgive me calling you, but they won't let me leave my room. I reminded them that I hold diplomatic status, but they insist it's for my safety. Anyway, I want to offer you my sincere apologies. You were right about Hanif. I should have listened to you and not that Wallace man. I would like to make it up to you by inviting you to accompany me to Fawala when they let us leave this place. You deserve a holiday – so does Tom."

She hesitated.

"Oh, come on. We've all been through a lot."

"You know what? I'd love that. I need a break."

"Then it is settled."

A week later, her surgeon said she could be discharged but recommended she should follow a course of therapy for post-traumatic-stress disorder. She actually laughed at that.

Chapter 52

Trenton pulled up a chair as the Prime Minister inspected the cover sheet of the DNA report.

After the failure to prevent an attack on US soil, Trenton had reluctantly agreed with Wallace's opinion of politicians and deeply regretted behaving like a junior minister and not the Commissioner of the Metropolitan Police. Trouble was, he'd been in the PM's pocket for so long now he couldn't see a way to go against the man without getting shafted.

"The Americans killed him and that's end of that. I don't see the point of making a song and dance about it," said the Prime Minister.

"We do need to act on this, Prime Minister. I am aware of information gathered by our security services, which link this Mengak and the smuggling of depleted uranium to Crown Prince Jabbar Bin Faisal Al Bahar of Fawala."

"Who told you that?"

Trenton pursed his lips.

"Yes, well, *that* is a delicate political matter for the security services, not the Metropolitan Police. It is certainly not something which needs to be discussed by bobbies on their tea breaks."

"And the next time Eton-educated Jabbar Al Bahar sets foot on British soil?"

"He will hold diplomatic status as a visiting royal and member of a foreign government. Surely you don't think I can permit you to haul him in for questioning when his country is supplying us with gas?"

"And the issue of depleted uranium being smuggled into this city?"

"That will be dealt with by MI6 at the source. They will see that it never happens again. Measures are being put in place."

Trenton wondered if he should start drafting a letter of resignation.

Chapter 53

Claudia knocked and put her head around the cabin door.

"They said you were already on board. How're you feeling, sir?"

"Claudia!" With his one good arm, the Emir took a glass from the rack and gingerly poured champagne. "Drink?"

She hesitated. "Take it. Celebrate. You helped apprehend Hanif. You are a hero." He grinned.

"I don't feel like a hero. Do you realise just how lucky we are? Cats have fewer lives."

They glanced at each other's slings.

"Fawalans are tough and you British have your stiff upper lip! We are survivors, Claudia." He reached into his pocket, extricated his phones and placed them on the table.

He took a gulp of champagne and screwed his eyes shut.

"Perhaps you need to take more painkillers?"

"No, no. I am not in physical pain, at least nothing serious. I am actually still in shock over the death of Hanif."

She blinked.

He drained his glass and refilled it. "He was a good man underneath everything. Loyal."

"Loyal? Sir, he tried to kill you – twice. You really *must* be in shock."

"I am sorry that he was killed, no matter what he did."

Breath hissed between her teeth. "I am too. I can't believe that cop shot him. So much for due process. So much for justice for Oscar and Murad and all the other victims."

"You can always rely on the Americans to shoot first and ask questions later."

The pilot announced take-off. They sat in silence until the plane levelled out.

"If Daynson had a Secret Service detail with him, Hanif would surely have failed," Claudia remarked.

"More than likely … The closer a man gets to the White House, the more protected he becomes. Daynson, however, was still one of at least a dozen men in his party who hoped to win the nomination. At this stage, the Secret Service cannot protect them all. He had private security of course, but decided to bring only two up to the restaurant, just as I failed to bring my team with me."

"It still puzzles me. How would Hanif have known you wouldn't?"

He shrugged. "In six months or so, the nomination

process will be complete, then everybody will turn their attention to the Presidential elections. Soon after that, nobody will even remember Daynson or how he was killed. He has already been replaced at the head of the Senate Energy Committee."

Claudia felt uneasy. She shivered.

The Emir topped up their glasses. "And now," he continued, "Senator Lynn Moorewell will become Chairman of the Energy Committee. Abdullah tells me she is a nice woman. Like me, she has the concerns of people in her home State at heart. And she is not afraid to make tough decisions to achieve her goals."

Claudia stared.

"In every cloud there is a silver lining. Isn't that the saying? This tragedy means that I have been able to secure the future of Fawala, despite us having bigger, more powerful rivals in the Gulf area. And as a result of *that*, your job and my racing ambitions are also secure."

Silver linings indeed.

The Emir chuckled. "Thanks to my negotiating tools and, let's face it – a little bit of luck."

"Luck?"

"In life, as with horses, Claudia, one always needs luck. You of all people should understand that."

Just then, one of the handsets on his desk rang. He snapped it up and answered with a broad grin. "Abdullah! Yes, we are finally on our way home. Claudia Haverford is accompanying me to Fawala for a well-earned break. When did you get back?"

On the desk, his other phone shuffled and buzzed. He went to pick it up, forgetting his arm was in a sling. "Claudia, would you please show me the screen?"

She offered it to him.

"It is Mark Gilford. I told him not to call me directly. Please answer."

She put the device to her ear and spoke in a low voice as the Emir continued bellowing at Abdullah in English.

"Mark, hi. What's up?"

"How's the Emir?"

"Like I said yesterday, we're both healing well."

"Yes, it's just I sent him a message but got no reply. I just wanted to wish him all the best."

"He's on the other line. I'll pass it on. I'm sure he'll call you back if he wants to speak to you."

"Oh, OK. Have a safe trip back."

Claudia hung up and was about to put the device down when she saw Mark's message notification still unread. She knew the Emir wouldn't ever read it, so she swiped and deleted it along with several commercials. Amazing, she thought, how junk texts even got onto the phone of a man like him. At the end of the list was a message from an unsaved number. But she recognised the Kentucky area code and the message preview showed the message was written in Arabic. She glanced up at the Emir. He was giggling like a schoolboy and swivelling in his chair as he spoke, now having switched to Arabic.

She tapped the screen and saw a lengthy message. Something niggled at her. Who did the Emir know in

Kentucky who spoke Arabic? Abdullah was in America, but he was on the other line … So … Hanif flashed across her mind. She forwarded the message to her own phone and to Wallace's, then deleted the evidence from Rahim's sent message folder. She glanced at the Emir again, still swivelling his chair. His Arabic was peppered with English words and phrases, his tone jovial. She put the phone down, gulped her drink and stood.

The Emir stopped swivelling his chair. "Where are you going?"

"Bathroom. And painkillers in my bag." She forced a smile.

She walked through the main cabin. The entourage were busy rolling dice and moving backgammon pieces at lightning speed.

She locked the bathroom door, opened the message and copied and pasted onto Google Translate. The slightly garbled English translation made the blood drain from her face.

She more than got the gist and in that instant she realised that terrorism wasn't necessarily about injustice or war. That might be the pretext or even the motivation for the foot soldier but, to those who planned it, it could simply be a business tool.

Anger welled up inside her once more, just as it had when she'd seen Hanif in the parade ring at the Breeder's Cup.

Now she wondered who to call first.

Chapter 54

Rahim had ended his call and was fiddling with the other device. He looked up as Claudia returned and sat opposite him. His gaze bored into her but his smile remained fixed in place. "You deleted messages from my phone?"

"Only Mark's and a few ads. Tidied up your inbox a bit."

He tossed the phone on the desk and turned on the TV.

The leader of a neighbouring Gulf state was being interviewed on a news channel. He seemed to be having a dig at Fawala for producing a terrorist. Rahim smiled. He knew how much money *that* sheikh had invested in American markets.

"When governments and leaders fail to address instability and persistent serious challenges, they create an ideal environment for hateful ideologies to incubate – and for terrorist

organisations to fill the vacuum."

Rahim flicked a glance at Claudia. She was riveted to the screen.

"This man knows that I am a secularist in a struggle against religion and social inequality, yet still he makes statements like this. He should be more worried about his own country, where he gives little concern to living standards for migrant workers and the poor."

Claudia cut him a sideways glance. "Tom once told me that *any* country where there is great inequality of income and living standards coupled with anger at the system will always produce a supply of lost souls embittered by life and willing to work for anyone with a plan."

"That is correct, Claudia, and that has been part of my reasoning for wanting to change Fawala, but you need not think that the concept applies only to countries like mine."

She nodded in agreement. "Tom said that it applies equally to places like the UK, America, France and so on. But I never really gave it much thought until this whole Hanif thing. I never understood how someone with even a semi-comfortable life could consider killing as a solution."

"You mean that you sympathise with Hanif?"

"Not at all. But I'm beginning to understand that it can be difficult to remain calm and rational when world leaders use violence as a business tool."

Rahim smiled. "Welcome to geopolitics." He inspected Claudia's face.

She fidgeted. Looked at her watch. She averted her gaze to the TV.

He swivelled in his chair, his mind whirring. *It is far better to commit one act on foreign soil to prevent many from happening in the homeland.* He was sure he'd read that somewhere.

He stared at Claudia again. Perhaps she had reached tipping point?

Chapter 55

Wallace paced the carpet in Trenton's office. "Jabbar Al Bahar hasn't set foot in Britain for two years. He prefers to holiday in Paris."

"And?" asked Trenton.

"After the Kentucky thing, I couldn't bring myself to just sit on my hands while you dealt with the PM, so I decided to send a forensics team to the Marriot Park Lane Hotel."

Trenton raised a brow.

"After that, I had them drive up to Newmarket to find out from trainer Ed Tomlinson where Hanif Ali Mengak stayed. Apparently, the room was still unoccupied: supposedly Hanif was to return to the UK with that racehorse after the race."

"So, he could've been used to plan another attack here?"

Wallace shrugged. "Anyway, Hanif's old room lit up like a Christmas tree for DU, phosphorus and thermite plasma."

"Christ. How come his flatmates didn't suspect anything?"

"They're partial to the old *wacky-baccy*. We found an ounce in the freezer and took them in for questioning. They think they met Murad with Hanif once, but I wouldn't call them credible witnesses."

"What about the hotel?"

"Took fucking ages, they had to check the whole floor." He paused. "Only one room showed up anything: slight traces of DU in the second bathroom in the George III suite. The suite was reserved for the summer right up to a few weeks ago for the use of only one man: Emir Rahim of Fawala."

"You mean Jabbar?"

"No. Like I said, Jabbar hasn't been to the UK for years. His brother stayed in that suite on-and-off all summer."

"Christ. Under our fucking noses." Trenton buried his head in his hands.

Wallace stared, deadpan. "Brilliant, isn't it?"

"No wonder he was so keen to offer assistance with the investigation."

Wallace snorted. "I even asked him not to do anything to alert Hanif that we were on to him. Can you believe it? What a fucking idiot I am."

"If the PM forbade us to arrest Jabbar, you can forget

361

about going anywhere near Emir Rahim."

"What if we could just interview him, get him to admit to something – anything? Present that to the PM? Surely, *that* would make a difference?"

"And how do you expect to make that happen?"

"I have a friend in MI5."

Trenton smirked. "How *is* the grieving widow?"

Wallace knew his boss didn't care for Lauren. "She's as pissed off with Whitehall as we are."

"At least we have something in common."

"Look, Rahim's been released from hospital. He's just boarded his private plane with his team and Oscar Haverford's sister Claudia – Thomas Sunderland's girlfriend. She called me from the plane and forwarded an Arabic message she found on one of Rahim's devices. Lauren had it properly translated. Read this." He handed his phone to Trenton.

Trenton frowned and read: *I had thought that I would not have enough time to get organised. Happily, I was wrong. Over the last two weeks, I found this society strange. I observed a kind of everyday heroism in the struggles of the working classes here. Most still have an unshakable zeal for their famous dream, but a growing number are becoming disillusioned and unhappy. These are the unwitting people that have helped me to ready myself with a little bit of false charm and paper money. There was not enough time to ensure that my subject could be convinced or coerced to operate alone. So, as we suspected, I will have to be hands-on. You are kind to have set me up with that bank account and the means to live in hiding after this operation, but I think we both know I will not escape American bullets. Goodbye and good luck. May the energy of the universe stay with you and Fawala.*

Trenton pursed his lips. "We'll still need more than this for the PM or the courts. Where's the plane headed?"

"Back to Fawala, but here's the thing: it has a refuelling stop scheduled at Stansted in a few hours. Apparently, it's an older model Boeing BBJ. Can't go from Stateside to the Middle East without a pit-stop and good old Stansted is the cheapest stopover point in Europe."

"Get up there. Now."

"MI5 are on it, but I have been invited to join them." Wallace would owe Lauren a favour after this.

"You mean this is already in action?"

Wallace grinned. So did Trenton.

Chapter 56

Claudia watched the Emir pick up his other phone again. He scrolled through the trash folder. Then he opened sent messages, saw the folder was empty.

Her stomach flipped.

Frowning, he went back to his inbox and read Hanif's message again. He almost welled up. He was about to toss the phone onto the table when he saw the tiny icon on the preview denoting the message had been forwarded. He tapped on the icon and saw Claudia's number followed by another British number.

"You forwarded this message to yourself? And to who else? Your boyfriend? That Wallace man?"

Claudia's eyes bulged. She felt her fists clench. She wanted to scream and hurt this man she'd served so faithfully, so blindly. But here she was 30,000 feet up in the air with him. In his plane. She lit a cigarette.

The Emir poured more champagne. "Please, drink."

She looked the glass on the table next to the phones. "You once told me that you owed it to your father to look after Hanif."

He nodded.

"So you sent him to his death in Kentucky?"

"We gave him every chance to escape." He shrugged. "But it was inevitable that he would die. As I said, Americans love to shoot first and ask questions later." He blew out a breath. "Hanif and I shared a common bond: a dislike of religion and western powers. That made him valuable to me." He sipped his drink. Smiled. "In a similar way that you or Abdullah, or the pilot of this plane are valuable to me."

"Is Abdullah your right-hand man, or just another middle-man?"

"Abdullah doesn't have a clue. He likes to play at being a statesman and will go anywhere I tell him as long as he gets to live like a prince."

"I used to think you were a visionary. A peaceful, considerate man. But what you and Hanif have done: murdering innocents for your own agenda. You're just the same as ISIS or Al Qaeda."

"ISIS?" he flapped a hand. "No, no. They were religious lunatics who believed in a Caliphate and 7th Century rules, but they were too stupid to understand nobody wants to live in a society with ancient levels of boredom.

As for Bin Laden, he was a spoiled brat who wanted to inflict his naughtiness on the world using his own money and that of his financiers. Do you know why Bin Laden was not put on trial?"

Claudia stared.

"Because he'd have told the world who financed him and Taliban. Who trained them, encouraged them and gave them the means to industrialise their lunacy."

She felt as if Rahim was trying to get away from his own atrocities. "In the London bomb, you used depleted uranium."

"Yes."

"Why?"

"It seemed fitting to give a little back. After all, so much of it was left behind in other people's countries. But," he paused, "I do regret collateral damage ... That is part of the reason I wanted to be present at the sale. So that I could at least witness the carnage and use my men as first responders. It affected me, you know. I was determined the second necessary act should be cleaner. Tidier."

"I need to know how you persuaded Oscar to insert the bomb in the mare."

"Hanif got to know Oscar through Murad. I believe they discussed his war experiences and his hatred of Adam Greene. You know, at first he refused to insert the bomb in the mare and threatened to go to the police. Hanif told him that he if he didn't cooperate, he would have *you* disappeared into the sex trade in a country where religious appearances prevent men from having normal, unserious relationships with women before marriage."

Her mouth fell open. Not from his words, but from his matter-of-fact, business-like tone.

"Naturally, he believed Hanif. He also believed that the bomb was small enough to merely kill the horse and spray bystanders with blood and body parts." He chuckled. "I suppose at the last moment under the influence of drugs he became convinced that you would die in the explosion, but I would never have allowed that. You would have stood with me. You know, I wanted to save Seb … But his arrogance was his downfall."

"*His* arrogance?" She laughed.

The Emir gave her a hard stare. "Has it occurred to you that Adam Greene may have got what he deserved in London?"

She looked away.

"Of course it has. You're a little bit glad he's dead, aren't you? After what he did – sending men like Tom and Oscar off to fight for his agenda."

Her eyes darted about.

"Likewise, surely you can see that Daynson's death might actually be a good thing for America and maybe even the world? He was xenophobic, racist and pro-oil and coal."

"And you're pro-gas! What's the difference? Guys like you, Greene and Daynson are just businessmen who'd do or say anything to close the deal."

"Of course. You are a smart woman – surely you can see the irony that Greene's agenda, and mine, are actually subsidising modern life. We make it all possible. Without people like us, energy would be a luxury product, not a daily disposable."

"That's like something Tom would say."

"And yet your government makes no effort to explain this to its citizens. *No government does*. Because it is a truth that would lose them elections."

"So we should just go around killing them and blowing innocent people up? You think that's a reasonable way to behave?" Her chest heaved. Breaths became tight and shallow. Her fists were clenched so tightly, her knuckles were red.

The Emir grinned at her. "It feels good to vent your anger, doesn't it?"

She narrowed her eyes, then widened them. Unclenched her fists.

"You remind me of Hanif," he said.

"Hanif was a cold-blooded murderer. I am nothing like him."

"And yet you wanted to kill him in the parade ring at the races, didn't you?"

She looked away again.

"If a catalyst for your anger had been provided, who knows what you might have been capable of?"

He watched her face turn red.

A phone rang. Inspecting the screen, the Emir said, "We will have plenty of time to finish this discussion in the company of Tom, during your Fawalan holiday."

Chapter 57

In MI5 Operations Centre, Lauren Condicote stared at the real-time flight path on the screen. "How long till they're in our airspace?"

"Ten minutes, ma'am."

"How many on the manifest?"

"The Emir, ten Fawalan citizens, one British citizen – a Claudia Haverford – and three crew."

"Crew nationalities?"

"Pilots are Turkish and Irish. Steward is a Somali woman."

"Make and model of the plane?"

"Older model Boeing Business Jet. Basically a short-haul 737 set up as a private aircraft."

"Do we know if this one has any counter-measure deployment capabilities or weapons facilities, either inflight or on the ground?"

"Not according to the customised design specifications, ma'am. However, there's no way of knowing if they have an armoury on board."

She inserted her earpiece and made a call.

Chapter 58

The wheels hit the tarmac at Stansted and the jet taxied to a halt near the Fawair terminal. A fuel truck pulled up beside the wing and two men hopped out and began connecting pipes.

Claudia sat in the main cabin and stared out the window, tapping her feet on the carpet. There was no sign of Wallace or any police outside. What the hell was going on?

She asked the stewardess to let her out for some fresh air. The tall Somali picked up her handset and called the flight deck.

"Captain says he has not put in for clearance for anyone to disembark. As soon as we are refuelled, we will take off."

A bead of sweat formed at Claudia's hairline. "Can't I just step out for a minute?"

The stewardess shook her head.

Claudia looked at the door. She wondered if she would be able to get it open and jump to the ground without an air-stair. Not a hope with one arm in a sling and she'd probably break a leg hitting the tarmac. Maybe she could deploy the fire slide?

She gazed out the window again, hoping to see a squad car and uniforms, but there was only a fuel truck. Had Wallace had managed to stop Tom boarding his commercial flight for Fawala? Should she chance calling Wallace? She found herself glancing about the cabin, looking for hidden cameras or microphones, even though she knew such things were bound to be almost microscopic.

Just then, the intercom crackled and the captain spoke. "Refuelling has been delayed due to a bowser jam. Safety protocol demands that everybody disembarks while this is rectified. Estimated wheels-up in forty minutes."

Out on the tarmac, Claudia saw a maintenance vehicle approaching along with an air-stair, a limousine and a minibus.

*   *   *

Rahim's face darkened as he listened to the pilot's message. Surely the British Secret Intelligence Service had found the uranium smuggler and got him to talk about

Jabbar's yacht? Maybe they had failed to pass on the information, or maybe the man had died before they found him? Anyway, Rahim assured himself they could never have any actual proof to connect *him* to the attacks. Still, if they really insisted on having someone's head on a plate, he'd offer them Abdullah. The poor fool wouldn't know what hit him.

He looked out the window at the approaching vehicles. They had probably engineered this little charade just to extract Claudia.

He checked his diplomatic passport, opened his desk drawer and picked out a small black device. Pressed a button, checked the tiny screen, clipped it to his breast pocket and covered it with his sling. He eased himself to his feet, went into the main cabin, shot a look at Claudia and barked at his men. They bounded down the steps to the tarmac.

The captain appeared from the cockpit. "Sorry for the delay, Your Highness," he said in his cheery Irish lilt. "Fuel bowser jams are not uncommon with these older models."

"It has never happened before," snapped Rahim.

"Oh indeed it has, sir, but fortunately you've never been on board."

Rahim eyed Claudia as she managed to pull her case out of a locker. "Sir, I've been thinking," she said. "I really have a lot to do back at Crangate. Manton Bloodstock and Crangate Stud do have other clients to take care of and other horses to sell. I really should put work first and postpone my Fawala trip till Christmas."

"I agree," Rahim knitted his brow, feigned thought. "But what about Tom? He has already boarded his flight, has he not?"

She checked her watch. "I might just catch him," she said, pulling out her phone.

Rahim swept past her and down the stairs, thinking once more that she wouldn't make a poker player.

A moment later, she joined him in the limo while the entourage and crew piled into the minibus.

Chapter 59

The car glided to a halt at the terminal. Claudia and the Emir were ushered towards the lounge by two men. Claudia noticed there were no waiting passengers and nobody manning the check-in desk, but four more men blocked the exit doors.

"Well, I'll be off then, sir," she said. "I'll call you in a few days when I've had a chance to get your horse report compiled."

"Thank you for everything, Claudia. And good luck."

She gave him a quick double-take then swivelled her suitcase on its wheels. "I won't be reboarding. I'm going straight to my car," she said to one of the men.

Surprised flickered across the man's face, but he moved aside and the others parted to let her out of the terminal.

Outside, she looked about for Wallace. The door of an unmarked white van slid open and he and Gibson stepped out.

"Tom?" she asked. "Did you get Tom off that plane? I tried to call him, but I couldn't get through."

"He's in custody at Heathrow. Don't worry, you're both safe now," said Wallace, making for the terminal.

She let out a long breath. Thought she'd cry with relief, but her emotions and face remained dry. She was still too angry.

Gibson took her case and led her towards a squad car and a uniformed officer. "Stay here."

"I'm not going anywhere near that building," she said, lighting a cigarette.

Gibson spun on his heel and followed Wallace inside.

*   *   *

Rahim plonked himself in a chair and pretended to check his phones, even though he knew they couldn't work.

The lounge doors slid open and six men swept in and sat in pairs, two near the door, two behind Rahim and two in front of him.

A moment later, Wallace and his partner entered and sat opposite Rahim. Wallace placed his iPad on the low table between them.

Rahim grinned. "Good morning, Chief Inspector. What brings you up here?"

Wallace pulled several sheets of paper from his jacket pocket and slid them across the table.

Rahim craned his neck and read the top sheet.

"What has this got to do with me?"

"We found evidence that depleted uranium had been in the bathroom of your suite at the Park Lane Marriot."

"As you know, I could walk out of this building right now and board my plane. But in the interests of helping you with your investigation and because my employees carried out these attacks, I am willing to hear you out." He opened his palms. "Please, how can I help you?"

Wallace clenched his jaw and tapped his phone, bringing up the message Claudia had forwarded to him. He offered the device to Rahim.

Rahim leaned forward and read the message, careful not to touch the phone. He shrugged and sat back. "How interesting. What is the origin of the message?"

"It was forwarded to me from one of your phones."

"Certainly not from a phone registered to me. Any decent lawyer will tell you that in itself the message is proof of nothing. Perhaps it was indeed written by Hanif as a sort of confessional or suicide note, but perhaps it was not. You know, Claudia has suffered so much these past few months, I fear it is beginning to affect her mental state. She is so determined to believe that Hanif was doing my bidding when he carried out the attack, that she could well have composed that message herself. I strongly recommend that you provide her with psychological counselling. Or preferably, you could just leave both her and me alone to get on with our lives."

"Think you're untouchable, don't you?" Wallace tapped

the papers. "I've got DU traces in *your* hotel suite, you arrogant prick."

Rahim rolled his eyes. "And I have a team of lawyers who could destroy that evidence in a court of law – if it ever made it to trial." He flashed his teeth.

"Let's see how far your money and connections get you when I slap the cuffs on you."

"Do you realise I purchased the building you work out of? My money is more important to your city than *your* offices." Rahim worked hard to stifle a laugh. "I also have tens of millions being played with by your bankers, propping up the Stock Exchange. And let's not forget that your country needs my gas."

Rahim could see Wallace was boiling with anger.

"So, as you can see, even putting my diplomatic status aside. Your government would *never* let you arrest or prosecute me."

Wallace leaned over the table. "You're not getting it. You ordered an attack on British soil."

"No, no! You are mistaken. That attack was carried out by a deluded young lunatic assisted by a drug-addicted British vet. Regrettably the young man worked on my stud farm and the mastermind worked at my training stable, so I will screen my workers more carefully in future. You forget that I was an intended victim."

"Lucky man, aren't you?"

"I have always thought so. Anyway, those men killed but a handful of people. It's not as if they declared war on countries or carpet-bombed cities."

"You killed innocent people. You've got blood on your hands."

"Tell me, Chief Inspector: is there a modern leader who does not?"

Rahim saw doubt flicker in Wallace's eyes. He gave Wallace his hard stare.

"Innocent people die in *'just'* wars every day," he went on. "Your politicians with their safe, clinical euphemisms make it sound so clean and efficient. But it is not."

Wallace tapped his phone, but the call wouldn't go through. He scowled.

Rahim raised a brow. "Is there a problem?"

*   *   *

Wallace left the lounge, marched through the terminal and out the front door to the white van.

"What the fuck's going on?" he barked at the tech. "My phone won't work in there."

"I can't record a bloody thing either. He has to be wearing a signal-disrupter."

Wallace swore, threw his phone at the wall and marched back to the lounge.

"Let him go," he said.

Gibson's jaw fell open.

Rahim stood and extended a hand. Wallace glared. The other men all looked at Wallace as Rahim left through the airside door.

"Sorry, lads," said Wallace. "Thanks for your time. The

fucking microphone got nothing but shite. He blocked every signal around him." Wallace kicked a litter bin. "Fuck it, we'd never have been allowed to charge him anyway. At least we got Claudia and Tom back."

Deflated, they all went over to the maintenance building and informed staff and passengers they were free to return to their places. Wallace thanked the MI5 men and went to the squad car.

Claudia jumped out. "Is he cuffed and captured?"

Wallace blew out a breath. "Got a spare cigarette?"

The air filled with a roar as the Fawalan Royal jet leaped into the sky behind the Fawair terminal. Claudia's mouth dropped open.

*   *   *

The plane levelled out. Rahim clapped his hands together. The British police might know, but they couldn't touch him.

He put on the TV and channel-hopped. An image of Hanif was displayed on a news review. Rahim closed his eyes a moment. He was sad to have lost a good man, but there was no shortage of disaffected angry people from areas of conflict or the suburbs of the West's great cities. Still, he preferred people he could trust completely. He wondered how long before Claudia would be angry enough to kill a politician. He'd let the dust settle and then insist that she and Tom spend their Christmas break on a Fawalan beach.

Chapter 60

"I can assure you that the mission would be accomplished with minimal losses," said the general. "A shock-and-awe aerial bombing campaign would soften the target before the deployment of a small ground force backed up by drone cover."

"Thank you, General. That will be all."

The old soldier left the room. The Prime Minister turned to Sir Christopher Medley, Chief of the Secret Intelligence Service, MI6.

"I want to keep Fawala conflict-free. Look at the shambles my predecessor left in Afghanistan and Iraq, and Syria's a complete mess."

"Nevertheless, Prime Minister, you do have all the justification you need for an invasion."

The Prime Minister sucked air between his teeth, shook his head. "If we come clean about London now – five months later – we'll look inept. And, on top of it all, I've got an election next year. No, I'm not going before parliament to propose another war. No fucking way." He tapped the file on his desk. "I'm inclined to think we should just present Emir Rahim with what evidence we have on him and use it as leverage to renegotiate the gas prices and get him to commit to an arms deal. How does that grab you, Christopher?"

"It's certainly workable, Prime Minister." He made a face. "However, I would like to remind you of another motivation for removing Rahim from power."

The Prime Minister raised a brow.

"Unlike most of his ilk, Rahim is putting his people's interests first. He might actually manage to educate and secularise them."

"Meaning what? That he'll use his gas revenue wisely? Re-invest in his people and not in shiny bits of British-made military kit?"

"That's exactly what our men on the ground are telling me."

The Prime Minister drummed his fingers on the desk. "Find out from those men on the ground if we can establish a back-channel conduit with his brother?"

"He would jump at the chance to seize power."

"Then let's help him do just that. As long as he never forgets who put him there."

"I have people who can make sure of that."

"Good, then there's definitely no need for another war." He stood and extended a hand. "That will be all, thank you, Christopher."

When the man had left, the Prime Minister picked up his desk phone. "Get me a secure line to Sir Bernard Trenton," he said and hung up.

A few minutes later the call came through.

"Good evening, Bernard. I'll come straight to the point. Find a way to make sure that bloody Wallace keeps his mouth shut about this whole Emir Rahim mess. Furthermore, he seems to have had a direct line to Lauren Condicote. Make sure Wallace understands that her successor will not be in the business of passing notes or classified information to mid-ranking members of the police force." He hung up without waiting for a response.

Chapter 61

One Month Later

Claudia sighed as she scrolled through newsfeed on her phone. Economic woes, energy sources and climate change. What a mess! She read a short piece about Lauren Condicote's resignation as head of MI5 citing that **'the stress of her husband's death last year had left her unable to perform her duties as she would have liked'.**

She tossed the phone away and turned on the TV news.

There was a picture of Rahim behind the newsreader's head.

"His Highness died of a heart attack. He was 39. His brother Jabbar Bin Faisal Al Bahar succeeded him to the throne. In his first press conference, Emir Jabbar promptly announced a five-billion-dollar arms deal with Britain and America as part of his nation's efforts to eradicate terrorism."

Jabbar was shown being interviewed.

"My brother's death at such a young age is a tragedy, such is the mystery of Allah's will. Rahim was a great leader and his country will miss him. In many ways he was a visionary, but he overlooked the reality that in today's market energy is cheap, so as a gesture of good faith, I will renegotiate our gas contracts to reflect the changing times. This will put Fawala on course to become the world's largest exporter of LNG and dry natural gas. We will also upgrade the equipment for our police and armed forces, and remain vigilant against the threat of terrorism. We will take every conceivable measure to ensure that people such as the terrorist Mengak never again gain citizenship of our nation."

Claudia hadn't wanted Hanif or Rahim to die, she'd wanted a televised trial and an admission that they'd killed her brother along with Murad, Daynson, Picklett and all those other innocent people – but she supposed she'd have to make do with their deaths.

Next up was a report on the aftermath of yesterday's terror attack in France. She wondered if that one was also just a business tool or perhaps revenge for a drone strike? Fucking arseholes.

She threw her glass at the TV and slammed her fists into the armrest.

*   *   *

Tom ran into the room, saw the cracked screen and examined Claudia.

He knew that look.

"Talk to me, Claudia. Let it all out," he said, gripping her hand.

She looked away, her eyes liquid with rage.

"If not to me, then to a professional. Please. Don't let it all fester inside. That was my mistake."

The End

Printed in Great Britain
by Amazon

41567003R00229